PRAISE FOR *THE LIE: A MEMOIR OF TWO MARRIAGES, CATFISHING & COMING OUT*

"At once brutal and beautiful, William Dameron's memoir unearths layers of secrets and decades of deception in startling, vivid prose. *The Lie* could not be more honest."

—Augusten Burroughs, *New York Times* bestselling author of *Running with Scissors*

"William Dameron's memoir is an unflinchingly honest and brave work that explores the secrets and lies of his lifetime as a married, closeted Southern man. But like all good books, it's really about so much more. I dare anyone who reads it to not think of their own struggles to admit who we truly are at heart. In a way, *The Lie* is a coming-of-age story that reminds us it's never too late to become our true selves."

—Ann Hood, *New York Times* bestselling author of *The Book That Matters Most: A Novel*

"In his first memoir, William Dameron shares a little-understood experience in queer life: that of the closeted parent. Writing with uncommon grace and compassion, Dameron does more than describe the burdens of carrying "the lie"; he shows us how to live honestly and what it means to be human. This book is a beautiful and necessary read."

—Alysia Abbott, author of *Fairyland: A Memoir of My Father*

"Honest, wise, lyrical, funny—if memoirs (or love stories) come better than this one, I haven't read them."

—Andrew Tobias, *New York Times* bestselling author of *The Best Little Boy in the World*

"What does it mean to live in the closet? We use the term almost unthinkingly, forgetting what a dark and sealed-off place it really is. In *The Lie*, William Dameron digs deep to explore a life shrouded in shame and secrets. In vivid, clear prose, he bravely and candidly shares his story. I found myself rooting for him to save himself, while also understanding the impact this salvation would have on his wife and daughters. This memoir overflows with insights into the nature of marriage, family, and desire. In the end, it's a story of how to live responsibly, love truly, and find a place in your heart for forgiveness."

—K. M. Soehnlein, Lambda Literary Award–winning author of
The World of Normal Boys

"You certainly should be excited about *The Lie*. This wise and generous memoir answers questions in living an examined life. Dameron has written his own confession as Saint Augustine did and has managed to make the telling of one man's moral struggle include everybody. The writing is clear and true and evocative with a momentum that doesn't frustrate or disappoint. The people are fully realized. It is a book that will help readers feel less lonely as they stumble toward their light."

—Gail Godwin, three-time National Book Award finalist and
New York Times bestselling author of *A Mother and Two Daughters*

"When his identity is stolen online, William Dameron is confronted with the most obvious metaphor—after all, he himself had been putting forth a false identity. This is a book about that crucible moment, that lifelong lie—a memoir of a life held back and held in, of his steroid abuse and self-loathing, a memoir about faces stolen and revealed and about how a gay man who is a husband and father comes to terms with a later life awakening. In achingly beautiful and searingly honest prose, Dameron comes face-to-face with the fact that he dearly loves aspects of this falsified life. In the wake of this experience, Dameron drills down deep into a life he thought was authentic and true to find layers of self-deceits and cover-ups, in order to let both pain and beauty, eroticism and happiness come rushing in."

—Elizabeth Cohen, author of *The Family on Beartown Road:*
A Memoir of Love and Courage

The
LIE

The
LIE

*A Memoir of Two
Marriages, Catfishing
& Coming Out*

WILLIAM DAMERON

Portions of this book were previously published in altered forms:

"After 264 Haircuts, a Marriage Ends" in the *New York Times*, Modern Love,
February 10, 2017

"My Face Is Catfish Bait" on Salon.com, August 28, 2016

"Splintered Light on Clear Creek" in *Saranac Review*, Issue 9, 2013

"Can you, should you be consumed with how you walk?" in the *Boston Globe Magazine*,
Connections, August 17, 2014

Published by Little A, New York

www.apub.com

Amazon, the Amazon logo, and Little A are trademarks of Amazon.com, Inc., or its
affiliates.

ISBN-13: 9781542044745 (hardcover)
ISBN-10: 154204474X (hardcover)
ISBN-13: 9781542044738 (paperback)
ISBN-10: 1542044731 (paperback)

Cover design by David Drummond

Printed in the United States of America

First edition

For Mom, who taught me that love can evolve,
and for Paul, who lights dark spaces

"The Truth is rarely pure and never simple."

—Oscar Wilde

Contents

AUTHOR'S NOTE

Can you trust an author who writes a book of supposed truths and calls it *The Lie*? After so many lies, it was important for me to write a book that is, to the best of my recollection, a telling of my truth. I have consulted emails, notes, and memories to construct this memoir. Because it is a work of creative nonfiction, I have changed names and identifying physical characteristics of people who are a part of this story, and re-created dialogue that is true to the spirit of what was said as I recall. I have interrogated the Bill who used to be, and poked the holes in the story he is telling you, in the hopes that you will come to trust me.

PROLOGUE

Your face has meant a lot to me, and now I've found out it's a lie.

The email came from a woman I had never met. I would have considered it spam, but it was too well written, and there were no links for erectile dysfunction pills. She had read my blog, looked at my pictures, and now she was devastated.

She was not, in fact, the first woman to contact me about this. The Facebook friend request icon had bloomed red the night before, and behind door number one was another stranger, Helen. Now, with this second woman, I did what I always do first and expanded her profile picture, my willingness to accept someone's friendship based on the openness of their face and the shape of their smile. Head tilted slightly to the side, a few strands of blonde hair falling gracefully over one eye, a wistful smile, and all of it softened with a forgiving filter—it was a textbook selfie. I've watched my daughter Claire strike this pose so many times, I'm convinced she can do it in her sleep. Once, when we were engaged in an argument, Claire wedged a selfie in between the words, "You've ruined"—head tilt, smile, click—"my life!" But I didn't recognize this woman from Canada, and so I waited a respectable thirty minutes before clicking "Confirm."

Are you familiar with POF?

The Facebook message appeared seconds after I accepted the friend request.

I am not, I replied.

Plenty of Fish is a free online dating site.

I unfriended her. I blocked her. I checked to make certain my antivirus definitions were up to date. We had no mutual friends. She must have been a Canadian sex-line operator, eh?

But now, here was this email from another woman describing how she had had a four-year online relationship with someone who did not even exist and had assumed the identity of a forty-four-year-old man who was grieving the death of his wife. I was not certain why two women within a short span of time had contacted me; perhaps it was just a coincidence, but if the first email was a tremor, the second was the full quake.

I probably sound crazy. But after a short Google image search, I came across you.

When I put two and two together, I unblocked Canadian Helen on Facebook and sent an apology. I told her I thought I knew why she had contacted me, and she replied by sending a URL. After I clicked on the link, I expanded the profile picture, head tilted toward the camera, chin down to strengthen the bearded jawline, eyes slightly scrunched. It was a textbook selfie, and it was me.

But it was not me. He listed his age as ten years younger and his height as three inches taller. He was single, not looking for anything serious. His personality was inexplicably listed as *athletic*. I felt flattered. I felt creeped out. I felt like someone had broken into my home, but I was unable to name or know what he had touched or stolen. If two women within twenty-four hours had contacted me, how many others had he scammed?

I right-clicked my profile picture and selected "Search Google for images." That was when I discovered that my face floats to the top, above ten million results, for the search term "forty-year-old white man." I had used a selfie in an article I published that was forever married to this search phrase. The title of the article was "Loving My Selfie," and, ironically, the article was about how learning to stop hating who I was on the inside helped me to love who I was on the outside.

But now I found that I was Dieter Falk on the social network VK in Berlin, and I was John, the president of a luxury property management company, in Kentucky. On LinkedIn, I was Richard, a car dealer in the Greater Boston area, and I was Peter, an IT consultant in Melbourne, Australia. On Yelp, I was Alfonso in Waterbury, Connecticut, griping about the local Kmart and the shitty, one-star service. I was Kalledsson, a nature lover on a Swedish dating website, and IsThisHowYouDoItNow?, a single, divorced Canadian man on Plenty of Fish. I was not just one man, but many. I was everyone and no one, and I was panicked.

But the truest link to my picture was the one that led back to me, the real me, the one who had been writing about his life and posting it online, the man who shared intimate details on his personal blog, *The Authentic Life*, with a world of strangers. Why had I become the "forty-year-old man face" of deceptive online dating?

It was the universe's poetic response or perhaps a cosmic joke. For most of my life, I had pretended to be someone I was not, and now I had become the one others pretended to be. It was as if the essence of my own deception took shape and continued to live a life of lies, duping women into love and then robbing them of their joy. The phantom me was a strange reflection that mirrored too many similarities of the man I used to be. What we put out into the universe comes back to us, but who can predict the amount of time it takes to make its return, or what form it will assume? My lies had taken a trip around the galaxy and, after a decade, long after my first marriage had ended, came back to haunt me.

Why were these women contacting me? What was fueling them to put in the work to find the man behind the image? The first question they all asked me was some variation of "Do you know me?" They were hoping to God that there had been some fraction of truth to the scam, that their feelings and experiences had been known and validated, that their relationships had not been a complete lie. I was the one who had to say, "No, I'm sorry, we really don't know each other." It was then that I began to look back at the story of the lie through the lens of catfishing.

As women contacted me, I realized the question for me was not why a person would pretend to be someone they are not, but, when our supposed truths are unmasked for lies, What do we do with all of that pain and lost hope?

PART I

CHAPTER ONE

METAMORPHOSIS

Franklin, Massachusetts, 2006

The urban legend says if you place a frog inside a pot of boiling water, it will immediately jump out, but if the water is cool and you gradually turn up the heat, it will fall asleep and will not attempt to escape. In essence, it will be boiled alive, unable to recognize the slow change. Before our world exploded one night in a Walmart parking lot, it simmered.

It was a Saturday morning, and I woke up early, my wife, Katherine, still adrift in a cloud of Ambien. Our daughters, Olivia and Claire, ambled through foggy teenage dreams, hours to go before the sunrise of reality. Maggie greeted me at the bottom of the steps, wagging tail, full bladder, and *Love me* eyes. She nudged my hand with her long, brown snout and then yawned, letting out a yip.

"Shh, girl, let's go outside," I whispered.

The two of us padded through the kitchen into the family room. I unlocked the sliding glass door and pulled it open. A slap of cold air greeted us, and Maggie's eyes squinted against the affront, her long tail curled between her legs. The sun struggled to rise above the bare trees as she turned her head to look at me, eyes pleading for me to open the door to Virginia.

"It's OK, girl, go on," I said.

Out she went, trotting and sniffing the frozen grass, moving in circles as she narrowed in on the spot.

I closed the door and skated on the hardwood floors in sock-covered feet to the front-hall closet. I grabbed my workbag, stood still, and glanced up the stairs while listening for signs of life—nothing.

Heart pounding, reach inside and grab the brown lunch bag. Take it to the downstairs bathroom. Go to the back door. Let her in.

"Not now, girl," I said, altering our weekend-morning cuddle session as she begged me again with her cold, wet nose and shifted her head under the palm of my hand.

I closed the bathroom door, waiting to hear the dejected tick-tick-tick of Maggie's nails as she walked down the hall to the family room and the thud of her body slumping onto the doggie bed. *Good girl.*

I unfolded a sheet of paper and reread the numbered steps. *1) Twist the needle on the syringe until it clicks. 2) Sterilize the top of the vial with rubbing alcohol, and hold it upside down. 3) Remove the needle cap. 4) Fill the syringe to this line with air. 5) Puncture the rubber top with the needle, careful to keep it below the level of the liquid. 6) Push the air into the vial, and pull the fluid out.*

Tap, tap, tap.

I pulled my pajama pants down and twisted my body to get a glimpse in the mirror, avoiding the eyes looking back at me and focusing instead on my bare right cheek.

I picked up a cotton ball, placed it over the opening of the rubbing-alcohol bottle, and drenched it. I pulled my pants down a bit more and pressed the coolness against my skin in the upper-right area of my buttocks. The clinical scent of the alcohol stung my nose. I took a deep breath and then hesitated. Was I really doing this?

One

Two

Three

Bam!

Deep breath. Quick sting. Push in the plunger. Pull the needle out. Careful, don't bend it.

For a moment, I stood in the bathroom, waiting for something. Would an air bubble enter my brain, or would my heart explode? When neither possibility occurred, I gathered up the evidence, buried the spent syringe and cotton ball in the bottom of the kitchen trash can, and took the garbage bag to the garage.

Boxes. The garage was still filled with so many unpacked boxes from our move back to New England six months ago.

We didn't leave anything behind. We packed it all up and brought it with us, including my insecurity in bubble wrap, and unpacked as soon as we reached our new home. Like Maggie, my insecurity twitched and scampered about the house, begging for attention and nipping at my ankles. Katherine had gathered up her bottles of medications and brought those along too, her mental state a constant companion, the two of us locked in a fatal embrace.

I walked into the family room and sat down on the sofa. Maggie jumped up and put her head in my lap. I rubbed the silky soft spot on top of her head, between her ears. One day she was living in Virginia and the next in Massachusetts. In her mind, it was that simple, with no idea how many thousands of events convened to bring her to this place. This was where we were now, and there was nothing she or I could do to alter it. I lifted her snout in my hand and looked deep into her eyes.

What I saw was pure love, and at that moment, it was all that mattered to her. I knew what it felt like to be so single-mindedly filled with an obsession that it consumed all other feelings. I was. And I was standing on the edge.

One
Two
Three
Bam!
I jumped in headfirst, turned up the heat, and let it boil.

CHAPTER TWO

DARUMA

When Olivia was two years old, she would giggle in her sleep. Katherine and I would tiptoe into her bedroom and peer in to see her small body lying there—dark tangle of hair, ivory skin, eyes closed, and a grin spread across her face. There was so much joy inside her tiny body, it oozed out even as she slept.

Both Katherine and I wanted children; we wanted to create beings who were the best of us, vessels filled with hope for the future. I remember sitting with Katherine at a table in a restaurant with Olivia in a lace-trimmed dress and hand-knitted booties. She was nestled in a baby carrier we had placed on the table between us. The server asked us for our order, and because nothing else in the world existed other than this beautiful creature we had created, we did not hear the server the first time. She smiled, tapped me on the shoulder, and asked, "First child, huh?" Startled, we laughed and replied, "How could you tell?"

Those were the sunny days on Dellwood Drive in Greensboro, North Carolina. We were playing house, then, Katherine and I. When I was twenty-three and she twenty-two, we married each other, running away from our past and hurtling headlong toward the bright promise of the future, one year in Florida and then a return to North Carolina.

For a while, we found contentment in that tiny house, our energy channeled into painting, furnishing, and feathering a nest. Soon, Olivia came along, and in the halo of light cast from a solitary lamp at 3:00 a.m. in our small family room, bleary-eyed, I would glance down at Olivia, milk spilling from the side of her mouth as she cooed and smiled back at me.

Katherine had stopped taking antidepressants during her pregnancy. I was deeply concerned, but her psychiatrist said, "Perhaps this pregnancy will help her bloom." And, indeed, her skin glowed, her hair became lush, and a sense of happy forgetfulness settled in, as evidenced by the purse often left behind, keys misplaced, and beverages abandoned on top of the car. The pregnancy also emboldened Katherine and ushered in a protectiveness in her that I had not witnessed before. When a gaggle of young neighborhood boys stopped in our yard and one of them proceeded to unzip his pants to relieve himself, Katherine, broom in hand, charged through the front door, shouting, "Hey! Keep away from our flowers!" and they scattered like ants.

When Olivia was two years old, I accepted a job with a start-up bank. The hours were long and the responsibility great. As the sole breadwinner, I felt the intense need to provide for my small family and to prove to everyone our success. When I was a kid, I looked up to my older brother, Alex, with an almost religious devotion. My three brothers and I would sit on the curb of our street in Greensboro, North Carolina, sipping Slurpees from the 7-Eleven and sharing our dreams with each other. "I just want two point three kids, a wife, and a house in the suburbs," Alex said. I had learned by the time I reached the age of reason that my dreams were not fit to share, and so I mythologized my big brother's. I came to believe it was the only dream that would make me happy and help me become a man.

But Katherine seemed to resent my time away from her and Olivia. Tension began to supplant joy, and after one intense argument, Katherine packed up Olivia and walked out the door. (I can't remember what the argument was about. If I told you it was about A, Katherine would tell you it was about B, but the truth is, such arguments are always about C and what lies beneath.)

"You're a terrible parent!" I yelled after her, but not before I noticed our elderly neighbor standing on his front porch, attempting to avert his eyes. That statement has seared itself into my brain. It was a projection, of course. I despised the flaws I saw in myself. When Katherine returned, I apologized, and then we began to make love. When I asked her about birth control, Katherine told me that she had had her period earlier in the week. A couple of months later, she showed me the results of a positive pregnancy test. I did not believe we were ready for another child. If the first pregnancy with Olivia helped Katherine bloom, the tension and fighting during the second one caused her to wilt.

After Claire was born, Katherine begged me to work part-time. "I just can't handle two children on my own," she said, and so I turned my promising seventy-hour-a-week job as a bank executive into thirty hours a week, and then they laid me off. My mother-in-law had groceries delivered and secretly gave me monthly checks, which I both appreciated and despised. It was a new and different type of emasculating shame. Becoming a man required you to pay for it through hard work. Monthly handouts and food deliveries threatened to erode that façade and lay bare my shame. If I could not provide for my family, of what value was I?

When I finally found a new job, we moved from that tiny house in Greensboro, North Carolina, to Roanoke, Virginia, and settled into a restored craftsman home with quarter-sawn oak floors on Maiden Lane. It was a neighborhood with wide front porches, creaky porch swings, and cement sidewalks that buckled in spots from the gnarled roots of spreading oak trees. On summer nights, Olivia and her long, dangling legs would push the swing back and forth, making a seesaw sound layered above the constant drone of whirring cicadas.

An old Japanese maple tree grew outside of Olivia's bedroom windows on Maiden Lane. As Olivia and Claire grew, the delicate red and purple leaves returned each spring, shimmering against the blue of the sky. When my company in Roanoke filed for bankruptcy, I searched far and wide for another job, finally settling on one in New England. "Just give it a year," I told Katherine. On the day of our move to Franklin, Massachusetts, I walked through the empty house in Roanoke, checking for things we had forgotten to pack, and stopped at Olivia's door. She was sitting on the floor in the middle of her room, tracing the outline of those leaves in her notebook.

"Olivia, it's time," I said.

"I don't want to go," Olivia replied.

"Sweetie, you have no choice."

She didn't answer.

"Now!"

She burst into tears, and I wrapped my arms around her.

"Claire and I will save our allowance and come back to buy this house," she cried.

———

There was an indentation in the mattress where Olivia's body lay at night. When we moved to Franklin, we should have spent more on better quality, but money always slipped through our fingers, and when Katherine's grandparents passed away, her mother lost the family business too. I sat down on Olivia's bed and looked around her room to see the world from her angle, through a sixteen-year-old girl's eyes. Here was Petie, her beloved and well-worn stuffed animal. In blue overalls and cap, he looked like the comical offspring of a country mouse and a teddy bear. When Olivia had squeezed the stuffing out of it, we secretly switched it with an identical one. There were no posters of boy bands or teenage movie idols hung on her walls. She lived in a different world of fantasy, one filled with mythical creatures from another land. There were her Japanese anime dolls, lined up neatly on her bookcase: Sailor Moon, Sailor Jupiter, and Sailor Venus, the plastic representation of teenage girls in traditional schoolgirl outfits, who battled evil.

On top of her desk was a Japanese Daruma doll, a round, red, bearded papier-mâché toy. I had given it to her for her sixteenth birthday.

"Color in the left eye so that he can see your wish," I told her, referring to the Japanese legend.

"When does he get his right eye?" she asked.

"You promise him full sight once your wish is fulfilled," I told her. One big black eye stared back at me.

I picked up one of her notebooks from a stack beside the bed, laid my head down on her pillow, and curled my body into the curve of her mattress. I closed my eyes and searched for remnants of her dreams that might still be lingering in the air, like the flickering dust particles sifting through the shaft of winter light cutting through the window over her bed.

I opened my eyes and leafed through the spiral-bound pages of Olivia's notebook. I knew these were her private thoughts, her diary, but I was searching for clues to find the missing happiness. Perhaps she too had secrets, and those were the seat of her melancholy.

Instead of writing words, Olivia drew pictures, "manga," a style popularized by Japanese video games and movies, the characters of her fantasy life. Her pencil drawings were of young girls her age with large eyes and hands clasped over their chests, valiantly defended by warrior princes brandishing swords in some galaxy far away. She would spend hours in her room, drawing these pictures.

"Olivia, you need to appear less vulnerable," Claire had advised her the other morning.

"What do you mean?" Olivia asked.

"You need to be like me and not care what other people say or do," Claire said.

"Oh yeah, right. You wear what everyone else wears and look exactly like all of the other plastic girls. No thanks," Olivia scoffed.

"Suit yourself. I tried, Dad." Claire gave up quickly. I had asked Claire if she could help her older sister fit in and make new friends. It always seemed so easy for Claire. When we first moved to Franklin, within a week, Claire was traveling in a pack with the other popular girls.

Claire, now fourteen years old, had learned the art of survival. Each morning, she would straighten her curly chestnut hair, take off her glasses, pop in her contact lenses, squeeze into tight jeans, and layer a knit sweater over a camisole from Aeropostale or some other officially sanctioned teenage-girl clothing store. It was less of an outfit and more of a suit of armor.

"What's my hair doing?" Claire asked me.

"Nothing, it's just lying there," I replied.

"OK, good, let me know if it does anything," she said.

I looked up at her hair and wondered what it might attempt to do.

"What?" she asked, eyebrows arched.

"Nothing," I said, shrugging my shoulders.

"You're looking at my hair!"

At night, her hair, like her dreams, would come back to life as curled-up, brown wavy snakes, only to be tamed and singed back into submission the next morning with a flat iron. While Olivia always slept peacefully, Claire wandered from room to room at night, literally over-turning furniture in her sleep and battling phantom demons in her dreams.

Olivia, wearing a T-shirt with "I like chocolate cake!" in white lettering, looked sideways at Claire, ran her fingers through her short bob, and said in a mocking, perky tone, "On Wednesdays, we wear pink," referring to a line describing the herd mentality of cliquey teenagers from the movie *Mean Girls*.

"Are you going to drama class today?" Claire asked Olivia.

"No, why?" Olivia narrowed her eyes warily.

"'Cause you're going there now." Claire flipped her hand up next to her ear, palm facing outward, *Talk to the hand*. Within seconds, doors were slammed, tears were shed, and Katherine shot me a glance that said, *Damn you for making us move back here*.

Katherine's aspiration was to become a wife and a mother, to have a family that she could claim as her own and one that would claim her—her dream and the one I had mythologized dovetailed. But, when your hopes are dependent upon others, compromises must be made. "You're always packing and unpacking," I heard her mother say to her once. Perched in the northeast corner of the country, seven hundred miles from where we used to live, Katherine would often say, "I feel like we're living on the moon."

This was our return to Franklin, a second chance to make it work. The first time we moved to New England, I asked Katherine to give it a year, just one. "You can do that, can't you?" She counted the days, and on the 365th, when I came home from work, Katherine said, "We gave it a year. You can work here until you find a job in Roanoke and then come back to us. We're going home to Virginia." And so she did, taking the girls. This was our life, a series of impulsive gestures, followed by regret.

During that time, I was alone in a way that I had not been for more than twenty years—seven hundred miles away and for the first time truly alone with the secret that separated me from my family. I moved into a tiny garden-level apartment in a cinder-block building in Marlboro, Massachusetts. A folding table was my dining-room set, cardboard boxes my nightstand, and a mattress on the floor, my bed. At night, I lay awake, listening to the foreign words the Brazilian neighbors spoke, and I would catch whiffs of exotic food scents seeping through the dingy white walls. Every other weekend, I would fly to Roanoke, cling to the girls, and plead with Katherine to come back; she'd plead with me to find another job and return to them in Roanoke. Our marriage was not broken, but fractured; never mind the iceberg floating just beneath the surface. Perhaps, I thought, the miles and time in between could mend its brittle bones.

But I worried about the girls. Once, I called on a Friday afternoon, and Olivia answered the phone. "It's a good day," she said. "Mom has been acting kind of stressed, and you're coming home for the weekend."

It took six months and biweekly visits to a marriage counselor to convince Katherine to come back to Franklin. I even prepared a spreadsheet that detailed how much better we would fare financially. I listed additional benefits, such as a lower crime rate and better schools. I was the Franklin Chamber of Commerce. My math was fuzzy, but it was the meticulous and calculated presentation that really convinced the counselor that I had my shit together and Katherine was like a leaf in the wind. After a lifetime of being an impostor, I could manipulate a situation, though I was not proud of it.

On the day of our final marriage-counseling session in Virginia, Katherine was late, and so I took the opportunity to make a confession to the counselor.

"I feel so guilty," I said.

"No, no, no, no, no," the counselor said, deep furrows riddling his forehead. He was tall and lanky with a bald head and a meticulously trimmed beard, so perfectly stubbled and with such a strong jawline, I felt envious. If I had a jawline like that, I thought, I wouldn't care if I was bald. He peeked through the open door, glanced down the hall, and then closed it so that there was only a thin crack of light. He lowered his voice and said, "Guilt is a useless emotion."

Ask me, I thought. *Just fucking ask me why I feel so guilty.*

For most of my life, I had run away from the truth, but it was always there, just around the corner, forever hoping someone would call its name. After all these years, I could not summon the truth myself, but I grew tired of its calling after me.

"But we're uprooting the girls again," I chose to reply.

And then, inexplicably, he started to perform jujitsu, or tai chi, moving his legs and arms in slow, deliberate arcs.

"Yes, you're jerking them around a little, but your marriage is stronger now," he said.

He stopped in some sort of warrior pose, or maybe it was something from *The Matrix*, his legs and arms stretched out in straight, horizontal lines.

"You've made the decision; now stick with it. Your daughters depend on you."

He clasped his hands in a Namaste pose. For a moment, I thought he might hold out his hands and ask me to choose between the red and the blue pill.

OK, our marriage *was* stronger now. It was just a matter of belief, young grasshopper. I could do this. Hadn't I always?

And so, here we were, back in Franklin, where everyone was of either Italian or Irish descent. On both sides of the white line on Union Street, the town would paint a green and red stripe—the colors of the Italian flag—during the feast of Saint Rocco in August, and serve up fried dough and homemade pasta under small white tents on the village green. Every bar or liquor store plastered paper shamrocks on the windows and displayed wooden clocks in the shape of Ireland on the wall. If your last name was Bissanti, Pizzi, Brady, or Donegal, you belonged. If it was Dameron—our last name—you were lost.

After we moved back, both of the girls attended new schools. When we took Olivia to Franklin High School on the first day to register her for classes, I stood behind her and watched her answer questions posed by the guidance counselor. She merely nodded her head yes or no, and I struggled to keep from responding for her. Her eyelids were heavy, and she gathered her oversized hoodie jacket about her like a shield.

Katherine had given her an antihistamine to combat her allergies. I wondered if she was nervous, or drifting off into another world with the help of the allergy medicine to deal with the stress of a new school. Her hands were like her mother's, smooth alabaster, and when she gripped the pen to write her name, they trembled. I remembered thinking then that the way she formed her letters, the way she made the loop of the *O* in her name, was from now on her adult handwriting. She became her name. Olivia, the sound of the syllables cascading like raindrops and her hazel eyes the color of the lonely New England sea.

When we took Claire to her middle school on the first day, she smoothed her hair and pulled it back into a ponytail. She wore a purple V-neck sweater over a lacy white camisole and her mother's pearl necklace.

"You look so pretty," the school receptionist said to Claire.

Like Olivia, Claire grew into her name and wore it well. Claire, the name, like the girl who carried it, was sunny and tropical. She had dark hair, chocolate-brown eyes, and olive skin that bronzed in the sun, whereas Olivia's pale skin was prone to burn.

When one daughter conforms to the norms of society's sense of beauty, and the other shirks them, you constantly find yourself struggling to simply accept compliments from strangers without dividing them in half and distributing them equally. *Both of my daughters are pretty,* I wanted to reply even in Olivia's absence.

———

I flipped the page of Olivia's notebook, and when I saw the next drawing, a lump grew in my throat. There on the page was a picture of two girls kneeling, face-to-face, and holding hands. Written in big loopy letters encircling them were the words "I will never forget you," over and over again. I recognized the drawing as Olivia and her best friend, Laura, from Virginia.

Olivia had turned sixteen two months after we moved back to Franklin. Sweet sixteen—the term conjured up the image of a gaggle of girls in party dresses beneath twinkling lights, cupping their hands to one another's ears and whispering about the boys on the other side of the room, but we had left all of Olivia's friends behind in Virginia. A week before her birthday, after pressing Olivia for a list of friends and coming up empty-handed, we turned to Claire.

"She mentioned a girl named Harriet," Claire said.

"What is she like?" Katherine asked.

"I don't know. She's always pulling her hair out," Claire replied.

"What do you mean? Is she frustrated?" Katherine queried her.

"No, literally, clumps of her hair are missing. She has bald spots," Claire said while examining the tips of her hair for split ends.

"But she's sweet, right?"

"Not really. She has a foul mouth." Claire was beginning to lose interest. "She says *fuck* a lot," she continued.

"Hey!" I said, and then added, "We don't talk like that."

"Sorry, Daddy." Claire smiled sweetly.

When Claire trotted out of the room, Katherine whispered to me that she was going to pick up Olivia from school the next day and ask her friend, if she could find her, to come to Olivia's birthday party.

"What the fuck? Her friend sounds like trouble," I said.

"Hey!" Katherine said. "It's the least we can do for her, and don't forget we have our marriage-counseling session on Wednesday."

Like the girls, our marriage, the one we had convinced the counselor in Virginia was strong, was sagging again, and we were unable to keep up our ruses while attempting to conform to the shape of our new surroundings.

Each week, we met Arlyn in her southwestern-themed office decked out with boldly colored geometric-shaped throw rugs, a Kokopelli clay statue playing his flute, frozen in his playful dance, and a white-noise machine on the other side of the door. Katherine would opine about my lack of affection and the girls' struggle with the move. I would offer up the stress of my job as the reason for my distance.

"But sex has been a semiannual event for years, Bill," Katherine would say.

"It takes two to tango," I would volley back.

"You know I need you to initiate it," she would serve up.

"Remember that night, two weeks ago when I asked you?" I said, referring to a time when I knew she was too tired. Game, set, and match.

But it wasn't a game. It was real life. I was damaged, and I was passing that damage on to Katherine, making her question her own desirability. It was a Pyrrhic victory in which the price I as the victor paid to win was everything. There are many nights I find myself, pained, still wondering what years of being married to a man in hiding—a man like me—does to a woman. At our wedding, we each held a candle in our hands, and then together, we lit a common one. There was some back-and-forth discussion with the priest over whether we should then blow our two individual candles out, signifying that our union made us one, or let the two candles continue to burn, signifying that we were still two individuals together in one marriage. We decided to blow the two candles out and let the common one burn. It was like the salt covenant of ancient times in which an agreement was sealed by two people who took a pinch of salt from their pouch and placed it in the other, signifying that the promise could never be broken until the two were unmixed. The crystals of our twenty years were combined forever, and no matter what, Katherine could never separate the grains to their original state. When the girls discovered that we were attending marriage-counseling sessions, Claire furrowed her brow and said, "Oh my God, are you guys getting divorced?"

"No," we both said, laughing it off.

Turning my attention back to Olivia's notebook, I flipped through the pages and stopped where she had sketched a rough drawing of a nude male. She couldn't quite get the gist of the anatomy, but the intention was there.

"She likes boys," I whispered, and let out a deep breath. Life would be easier for her.

I closed the notebook. I thought about Olivia's sweet sixteen birthday party. We went bowling at the candlepin lanes, served pizza and a supermarket sheet cake. We were able to round up two girls to attend. Poor Harriet wore a hat to cover her mangy head, and her friend Katie was sweet enough but said very little. Claire flirted with some boys in the lane next to us and cringed when Olivia and her friends started doing the chicken dance.

"Dad, why can't Olivia just act normal?" Claire whispered to me.

"She is normal. Your sister is her own person," I replied.

"Whatever," Claire said.

I turned a phrase over and over in my mind. The marriage counselor had said, "If the parents are strong, the kids will be fine."

"How screwed up are we?" Katherine had asked the counselor.

"I've worked with so many couples who have many more problems than you, drug addictions and infidelity," she said.

Katherine breathed a sigh of relief. It's funny how counselors never seem to ask the most basic questions. I did not tell her that I had begun injecting illegally obtained substances into my body, nor did she ask. I also did not tell her about my recurring dream in which a faulty brake pedal failed to stop our minivan from hurtling headlong into the abyss.

"Don't tell anyone your wish," I said when Olivia opened the gift of the Daruma.

"What should I wish for?" she asked me while coloring in one eye.

The truth, I wanted to say. But instead, I told her the next best thing: "Wish for your heart's desire."

CHAPTER THREE

COFFEE NAME

We stopped walking for a moment, and the world was quiet except for the faint tinkling of snowflakes falling, like crystal glass breaking at a great distance. I looked down the dark snow-covered street, breathed in the cold air, and exhaled, watching the steam of our breath mingle and dissipate. A halo of light surrounded the streetlights, and all of the angles, now softened—the pine, shaped like a Christmas tree with white, heavily weighted branches; the steeply pitched A-frame roof of the village colonial; the serpentine outline of the car in the driveway—merged into the landscape.

Enzo rested his arm on my shoulder and pointed his index finger at the scene. "Look at that, Billy. There's nowhere else in the world you'd want to be now, would ya'?"

His voice danced in the snow, curling up at the end as if a soft breeze had suddenly caught it before it landed. There was a buzzing inside my head, like the music from the bar had rumbled around and left an echo. The snow was gathering in my eyelashes and resting on my head. If we stood there long enough, we would have merged into the landscape.

"The only other place I'd want to be is inside a bathroom," I answered him.

"We're just a block from home."

"That's a block too long."

"Then go behind that tree, ya' idiot." He laughed while pointing at the pine tree.

I looked at him and considered whether he was joking. This was someone's front yard.

"Go on now. Nobody's awake at this hour."

I moved as quickly as I could across the front yard, taking exaggerated steps like a giant. The snow came up to my knees. When I reached the tree, I fumbled with my zipper, and the cold air was surprisingly refreshing as it drifted across the part of my body that was a stranger to the snow.

"Don't be writing your name," Enzo shouted, and I started laughing like I was in church, trying to contain laughter from the funniest joke in the world.

"I—I'm—writing your name, ya' idiot, E-n-z-o . . . ," I shouted in between laughter as my body weaved back and forth, the balance compromised by the effort to stand still as the world continued to spin and the sense of relief from the release of the alcohol-infused stream.

When I finished, I turned around and realized that Enzo had vanished. "Fuckin' idiot," I whispered, and started laughing again as I stumbled down the street toward his home.

Enzo and I worked together in a business park off Interstate 495 in Franklin, he in engineering and I in IT. The first time I met him, I thought he looked fearsome. He was tall and angular, his hair was too blue-black, the skin too smooth, the jawline too sharp, and the eyes too bright green. It would not have surprised me if fangs appeared when he smiled.

"*Enzo*—is that Italian?" I asked.

"First generation," he replied. I reached back into my mind and pulled out a snippet of Italian.

"La sicilia è piccola," I said.

"Molto bene. You've been, then?"

"No, but hopefully one day."

While he was Italian, originally from Italy, most in the Boston area were several generations removed. He was an Italian in a land of echoes. I was a Southerner in a land of Northerners. But still, he was a member of a tribe, and I desperately wanted to belong. Our connection was rooted in a familiar feeling of displacement. Here, we were the diaspora.

He offered up his friendship readily, in a way that I had never experienced with a man before. I could count on one hand the number of close friends I had, without even uncurling my fingers. Once you got past the wall around our marriage, there was the one I kept up around me. Enzo ignored the walls and walked right through them.

He was like Michael, a boy I became friends with in high school. On the first day of biology class, Michael sat behind me, tapped me on the shoulder, and whispered jokes in my ear, without even introducing himself. It was as if we were friends before the introduction was made. Enzo was like this. We moved from pleasantries, *"La sicilia è piccola,"* and "I was born in North Carolina," to jokes.

Me: "How do you get an Italian on the roof? Tell him the drinks are on the house."

Enzo: "What're a redneck's last words? 'Hey, y'all watch this!'"

I'd laugh about the way he couldn't speak without using his hands, and he would jest about the way my name had multiple syllables, "Beee-uh-iil." While women could give each other a peck on the cheek or a hug, this was forbidden between American men (or those Italian men who had been Americanized). Making fun of each other was the safest way to show our affection, and we picked on each other ruthlessly.

It wasn't until after Katherine and the girls moved back to Virginia that Enzo and I began to hang out with one another outside of work.

On the weekends when I did not fly back to Roanoke, I developed a Friday-night routine, sad and lonely as it was. I'd drive through the center of Marlboro and stop at Chin's Garden restaurant to pick up Chinese takeout. In my tiny cinder-block apartment, I'd eat sticky sweet-and-sour chicken from a Styrofoam container by the flickering light of the TV and wash it all down with cheap vodka and tonic. One Friday night, I heard a horn blare, and then I peeked through the slats of the mini blinds at an old, green pickup truck in the parking lot. A group of Brazilian men in dark Levi's jeans came running out of the apartment building, whooping and hollering, and jumped into the back of the truck. The night stretched out before them like a lugubrious promise.

I walked around my apartment, glancing at the white kitchen cabinets, at the peeling linoleum floor, at the empty walls, and turned on the bare overhead light bulb in the bedroom. On the cardboard-box nightstand was a photograph of Olivia and Claire. Both of them wore winter gear, standing in front of a snow fort in the yard of our old house and grinning goofily like two kids do when school is canceled. Olivia wore a red knit cap and a green puffy jacket, and her arm was draped around Claire's shoulder. Claire's glasses were all steamed up. I picked up the photograph, wiping at Claire's glasses like I could somehow clear away the fog.

And then I made a decision. I worked up the courage to text Enzo. Hey, what r you up to? After a painful five minutes, I received a reply. Heading to the North End for a drink, join me?

The drive to Boston from Marlboro was an hour. I looked around my apartment, and then through the mini blinds at the empty cars beneath the parking lot lights. I changed my clothes and decided to join him for a drink, just one.

The drink turned into three or four, maybe more, between us, perhaps a gallon. I was giddy with the company. I confided in Enzo that Katherine and the girls had moved back to Virginia, something I had not told anyone at work. "Come on, Billy. Let's have another, and we'll talk through this. You'll sleep in our spare bedroom, hmm?" he told me, and so began a new weekend routine.

During my marriage, I never pursued a *boys' night* or a *poker night*. I already knew Katherine would resent them. She was jealous of relationships that existed outside of our marriage, as if there were only so much of me, and she didn't want to offer up a slice to anyone else, including extended family. I had not seen my mother for years, but that was a more complicated story.

Did I fail to pursue those relationships outside of my marriage because of Katherine's jealousy, or was it because if I did, I would expose the impostor? It was perhaps easier to think that Katherine kept me locked up, but if she had a duplicate set of keys, my mother and I had the original.

Once, Katherine and I were sitting at a bar on a "date night," a chance to get away from the children when they were toddlers, for a few hours. We began chatting to a stranger sitting next to us, the alcohol had melted the invisible wall between us. Katherine told the man I had no male friends. "Would you be Bill's friend?" she asked him. It sounded so desperate, and it was so pointed, the question, that it impaled me. "All I need is you," I whispered to her, and for a while, this seemed to be true enough. At times she would ask me what I was thinking about, and I would respond, "Nothing." She'd sigh and say, "It must be awfully lonely in that head." She must have wondered how my head could be so empty, when a wife and two daughters were so willing to fill my heart.

But I was aching for male companionship, and one night, during dinner, I showed one too many cards. I made a comment about Enzo, some trivial detail about his accent, or what he was wearing, and Katherine rolled her eyes. "Another story about Enzo," she sighed. "You're so infatuated with him."

"No, I'm not," I replied. But it sounded too defensive, and it was too late.

I built a wall around my friendship with Enzo, hiding it, but the things we hide become desperate to be seen. When I phoned Katherine the next day and slipped up by mentioning that I had spent the night at Enzo's house, she was incensed.

"Why on earth would you sleep at his house?"

"Isn't it better than driving home drunk?"

"You got drunk?"

"Well, not drunk really. I mean, I had a couple of beers and a limoncello."

"A limoncello? What the fuck is that? When did you become Italian?"

I took a deep breath.

"Are you there?"

"I'm here, and you're not. Why does it matter if I slept at his house?"

"Men don't sleep at other men's houses, especially when they're in their forties. Jesus Christ, Bill, act your age."

"It isn't just Enzo's house, you know. He's married and has a child."

"All the more reason you shouldn't be getting sloppy drunk and sleeping at his house."

"I wasn't sloppy drunk," I mumbled, rubbing at the beer stain on my shirt.

"Bill, I'm just trying to hold things together here, and you're running around town with Enzo. He's ten years younger than you. Don't you think he just feels obligated? Don't you think he finds you, I don't know, pathetic?"

I looked around the apartment, at the nearly empty bottle of vodka on top of the refrigerator, at the take-out box on the kitchen counter, sticky red sauce running down the side, and then up at the dirty half window.

"Bill, is everything OK?"

"Yes, of course, it is." It was, wasn't it? Of course, it was. "I guess I just miss you and the girls," I said, picking up the picture of Olivia and

Claire, touching their sweet faces. I wanted to rub that damn fog away. Was Katherine making certain that Claire's glasses were clean?

On those Friday or Saturday nights, when I went out with Enzo, I would call Katherine just before I left. "I'm really tired, going to bed early," I'd say, and if she tried to call me while I was out, the next morning, I'd tell her my phone battery had died.

After I convinced them to move back to Franklin, the time I spent with Enzo diminished, and I was sorely missing those nights out with him. During one of our marriage-counseling sessions, I mentioned that I would like to have a night out on my own.

"Why?" Katherine asked. "Aren't we enough?"

"Of course, but sometimes, a guy needs to talk to another guy."

"About what?"

"I don't know, guy stuff."

"For an hour or two?"

"I don't understand why there would need to be a time limit."

"What could you possibly do with more time than that?"

"I don't know, talk."

"About what?"

"Someone wants to be with you, or they don't," Arlyn broke in, and then continued. "You can't make Bill want to be with you, Katherine, and if you're forcing him, then it won't be authentic. Let him have a night out."

She reluctantly agreed.

On the scheduled night, I tried on multiple shirts while getting ready. Claire walked into our bedroom and noticed a small pile of them on the bed.

"Aw, Dad's got a bromance going on," she said, smiling.

"No, I don't," I replied, and then asked sheepishly, "What do you think of this shirt?"

"That's a cute top," Claire replied, inspecting it, head cocked to the side.

31

"Men don't call them tops," I scoffed.

"OK, precious, that's a pretty blouse," Claire laughed, and then walked out.

I took the commuter rail in and joined Enzo at a small, loud bar in the North End.

The entrance to the pub was through a small alley, where drunken men and women were smoking and gabbing.

"Look at my new coat, Enzo. Don't it make me look like Jenny from the block?" a woman in a white faux fur coat asked.

She was middle-aged with short, reddish-brown hair, and she turned from side to side, modeling and rubbing the smooth fur with one hand. She exhaled a puff of smoke from the corner of her mouth while holding a cigarette up between two fingers, just above her right shoulder, and raised her eyebrows, waiting for a reply.

"The spittin' image!" Enzo replied.

"Ah, go on now," she replied, laughing.

"Who's yer friend?" she asked, glancing at me sideways and sizing me up.

"This kid? He's a good guy, but he's from the South. He married his sister."

"Pity," she replied.

"If she looks like Jennifer Lopez, then I'm fuckin' Liam Neeson," Enzo whispered to me while placing his hand on the doorknob. I was intrigued to find out what man Enzo considered to be the pinnacle of good looks.

When he opened the door, music tumbled out, and as we stepped inside, laughter bubbled above the din. On one side was a massive wooden bar that extended the length of the front room, and behind that were wall-length mirrors, punctuated by four marble columns. In the middle of the bar was a circle of beer taps. Spotlights illuminated the glossy wooden top like a huge advertisement, *Drink up!*

Enzo ordered two beers, and when I tried to pick up one of the glasses and began to sip, he held his hand up.

"Now wait, Billy, a toast before we drink," and then added, "Jesus, Billy, I thought you rednecks were less hurried about things."

"What would you know about the South?" I asked.

"Plenty, I've seen *The Dukes of Hazzard*," Enzo said, pointing his finger at me.

"I can see ya', Billy, with Daisy Dukes on"—he narrowed his eyes—"that are *just slightly* too short, jumping into the General Lee and giving everyone that Sharon Stone peekaboo moment."

Enzo grabbed the two beers, and we moved to a tall empty table on the other side of the room. He handed me a glass and then lifted his up.

"To the General Lee," he said.

"To spicy meatballs-a!"

Clink!

The beer went down quickly and combined with the buzz and freedom of the evening; I knew that the glass would soon be empty.

"It's good to have you back, Billy."

"You don't think I'm pathetic?"

"Of course I do, but, Jesus, Billy, you've been eating all of your meals."

"I've just been using weights instead of swimming," I replied, thrilled that he noticed.

"Giving the banana hammock a rest, huh? The men must have lodged a complaint about your paradin' around the locker room in your Speedos," he said.

"I don't *parade* around in Speedos. They're called jammers. Triathletes wear them," I replied. My tone sounded too defensive.

Enzo laughed and slapped me on the back, realizing that he had found a sore point, and picked at it a bit more, like a kid with a stick poking at a cat backed into a corner.

"OK, Billy, call them what you want, pajamas, grape smugglers."

"I'm empty," I said, ignoring him and my face becoming red. I turned and walked to the bar, attempting to get the bartender's attention. Two women who appeared to be in their late twenties or early thirties sat on barstools next to an open spot.

"Excuse me," I said to the women, and smiled widely. "I'm just trying to get a drink." I was turning on the charm, cranking up the Southern accent.

"No problem," the one closer to me said as she cocked her head to the side, her long, brown hair falling across her shoulders. "You're not from around here."

"North Carolina, originally," I replied, elongating the *i* like sweet taffy.

"Oh, I love North Carolina. Everyone is so friendly there," she said.

The bartender appeared, and I placed the order for two more beers and then turned to the women. "What can I get you?"

"You're wicked nice. We're all set," the brown-haired girl replied, smiling.

I looked back to see whether Enzo noticed me talking to the women. But he was busy speaking with Jenny from the block. She laughed, placed a hand on his shoulder, and then walked away. I looked at his profile. *If I had a jawline like that.* I turned back to the bar, grabbed the two beer glasses. I took a deep breath and walked back to Enzo's side. *Men don't act jealous of other men,* I thought.

"Ah, you're a good man," Enzo replied when I handed him his drink.

"So, the girls are doing well?" he asked.

"Claire is doing well," I replied, and then added, "But Olivia is still adjusting. I think she'll be the child that I always worry about."

Enzo tilted his head to the side, a swath of black hair falling across his forehead, and gave me an upside-down smile, placing his hand on my shoulder. A current ran through me.

"Katherine and I are going to counseling," I said.

"I'm sorry. Are things that bad?" Enzo asked.

"Nah, we're just working through the adjustment, the move, and getting advice on the girls." I shooed away the heaviness. "Just a matter of time, that's all."

"Anna and her family came over from Italy when she was just a teenager. Had to pretend that she was only visiting and left behind all of her worldly possessions, which weren't many. Her grandmother gave her a clock radio for her birthday, and she couldn't bring it," Enzo said, recounting his wife's story of coming to America.

"You know, Billy, when you love someone, in a way, you want to become them."

Enzo took a sip of his drink, and I wanted to ask him what he meant by that last statement. Whom was he referencing? But then I looked at my watch—a few minutes before midnight.

"Fuck," I spit out, and then pulled out my phone—three missed calls.

"Watch the language, Billy," Enzo laughed. "It insults my virgin ears." He slapped me on the back.

"I missed the train. Katherine will kill me," I said, and dialed home—no answer.

"There's nothing you can do. You'll sleep in our spare bedroom. She'll understand," Enzo said, trying to calm me down.

"No, she won't," I replied, and my mind raced. "You don't understand."

Men don't sleep at other men's houses.

"You'll take our car in the morning and be there before she wakes up. Problem solved," Enzo said. "One more for the road now, huh?"

I wavered, but then Enzo ordered two more, and when I looked around the bar, I saw laughing faces and heard the same Italian singsong lilt in each of the conversations. But more than that, I saw freedom and escape. The train was gone, and I was too drunk to drive. A man in front of the bar, on the floor, was performing push-ups, while a couple of men stood next to him, counting and laughing. It was as if someone had released a barrel full of Italian monkeys and they were running loose, hands above their heads, swinging from chandeliers, jumping off stools, and shrieking at the top of their lungs. There was so much joy that it needed to be shared. I wanted to be a part of it.

When the lights came on, we tumbled out of the bar and weaved our way through the snow-covered sidewalks, shoes slipping and hands cupped to mouths, blowing alcohol-laden breath to warm our fingers. While Enzo paced ahead, I slowed down to look up at the snow falling, fat, dark flakes, like ashes drifting down from some volcano. The blue-gray city sky was a dome above us, like a scene from my favorite childhood picture book, *The Snowy Day*. How I used to dream about walking through a faraway, quiet, snow-covered city street when I was a kid. Life was easier then, wasn't it? It didn't seem so simple for the girls now. Olivia and Claire didn't even want to play in the snow anymore.

Once when the girls were toddlers, Katherine and I wrapped them up in layers and blankets and pulled them on a sled through the street when a surprise early-spring snowstorm blew in. We heard crashing, and then we saw it, pine trees running with sap as the sweetened spring soil warmed up. The shallow roots that could not keep a hold of the earth. It sounded like thunder as the trees fell all around us. I grabbed Katherine's hand, and we ran with the girls back to the safety of our little house on Dellwood Drive. We blew warm breath onto their small feet and hands and drank hot chocolate, our perfect little family. This was the way Katherine liked it. Our family close.

For Katherine, our family was as beautiful and precious as an ice palace, a fortress in need of protection from the capricious whims of nature and chance. Katherine learned as a child that families fall apart, that she could be given up for adoption as a baby and placed into a family where at an early age, the father would die and a grieving mother would become the queen of frozen hearts, until someone would come along to claim her, and that person, she hoped above all hopes, would never regret his decision.

When we built the snow fort in the photograph that sat on my nightstand, the girls, ten and thirteen, still delighted in the snow before we thrust them into the isolation of New England winters. The four of us climbed inside with a battery-powered lantern, just sitting there and smiling in muffled wonder. Maggie furiously dug her paws through the side, terrified that we had slipped beneath the surface, drowning in a sea of snow. With the house collapsed around us, we were laughing and spitting out snow and yelling, "No, Maggie, no!"

"*Sbrigati!* Hurry up, ya' idiot! You don't need to be eating snow," Enzo shouted.

When I reached him, he was standing in front of a Chinese takeout restaurant, the warm yellow lights spilling onto the mounds of white. He opened the door, and I looked at him, a goofy grin on his face, and my heart skipped a beat. The tinny bell registered our arrival. My stomach growled, and I said, "God, I'm starving."

"Ai-yah," the woman responded.

"I'm sorry, but we'd like two orders of sweet-and-sour chicken, crab rangoon, and um, those pancake things. Sca—scallion pancakes," Enzo slurred.

"Name," the woman responded.

"Larry," he said.

I narrowed my eyes and looked at him.

"It's my coffee name," he said. "Nobody in America understands it when I say *Lorenzo*, much less *Enzo*."

The woman returned with a large brown paper bag, grease stains on the side. Enzo grabbed the bag, and we exited, pulling our coats closed, and hailed a cab. From that moment on, the night moved in chunks. We were stepping into the taxi and then stepping out of it at the top of the road. Enzo resting his arm on my shoulder as we melted into the landscape. Me standing in the snow, urinating behind a tree. I was laughing and then stumbling down the street. We were devouring the sweet-and-sour chicken in the kitchen, and then I was lying in the spare bedroom in the basement, looking up at pulsating glow-in-the-dark stars and planets pasted onto the ceiling. The bed drifted on storm-tossed seas as scenes from the past flickered in my head.

During our separation, when I was living by myself in Marlboro, I'd often drive the hour-long trip into the city and eat alone at a McDonald's, a few miles from Enzo's house. I'd text him, Hey, I just happen to be in your neighborhood! After ten or so minutes, I'd get a reply, Driving home from dinner. Feel free to stop by. My heart soared, but on other nights, I'd get, Sorry, have plans, and my heart would sink.

Pathetic. Not because I was ten years his senior, but because I was unnamably lonely.

I would message Enzo, often multiple times a day, the connection like a lifeline that kept me from drowning. Do you miss me? LOL.

Fucking pathetic.

Would I have convinced Katherine and the girls to move back to Franklin if Enzo had not been a factor? Would I have returned to them in Virginia?

After I did convince them to come back to Franklin, we packed up the car to return to Franklin, and it labored to move forward with the heavy load of our belongings, a family of vagabonds on the lonesome road, searching for home. In the cool of the morning, a mist lent the neighborhood a dreamy feeling. An old man walking his dog smiled and waved. A lace-fringed white curtain fluttered its goodbye through a second-story bedroom window. The crispy scent of bacon sizzled in the air. Claire turned to glance back and said, "Virginia is so pretty. I don't know. Are we doing the right thing?" We gazed through our separate car windows at what we were leaving behind. My reflection shuddered back at me and then darkened when we passed beneath the canopy of an ancient oak tree, and I shivered like a leaf in the wind. The cold fingers of doubt tapped my shoulder. Twelve hours and seven hundred miles later, when we crossed the Massachusetts state line, the engine sighed, and Katherine's shoulders slumped. I squeezed her hand, the shitty stench of guilt rising to my nostrils.

This was the dividing line, the point when I knew I could not go back, that the lie had gone too far. I had placed my desire above the health of my family, jerking Katherine and my daughters back and forth. "Welcome to Massachusetts," the sign read. It might as well have said, "Welcome to Hell."

Once, one night before we moved back, when I was alone, and when I had no one to visit and nowhere to go, I drove to the video store and pretended to consider various movies, even though I knew which one I wanted. I waited for the other customers to get their DVDs and leave before I grabbed it and walked up to the cashier. My hands trembling, I slid the box across the counter, title side down.

"Do you want popcorn or candy?" the cashier asked, nodding his head toward the selection.

"No, just this please," I said without looking up.

He turned the video over, glanced up at me, and said, "I need your membership card."

I thought his stare held a certain conviction as I fumbled through my wallet, and when I looked up after retrieving my card, I caught him regarding my wedding band.

When I returned to my tiny apartment, I poured a hefty amount of vodka into a glass, placed the DVD into my laptop computer, and sat in the single chair next to the small folding kitchen table.

A dusty little town, the longing twang of a guitar chord, and the desolate landscape of Wyoming were all it took for me to know that Ennis Del Mar and Jack Twist's relationship was doomed from the start. When it ended, one dirty, bloodstained shirt lovingly folded into the other, it ended me too. It felt shameful to watch that video, like I was watching porn, but perhaps even more sinful, because shame made gay love feel more pornographic than actual porn.

I turned my head to glance through Enzo's basement window, half-covered with drifts of white. The snow had stopped falling. I looked back up at the throbbing stars and wondered, If I had the chance to change my name, to change who I was, what would my coffee name be?

In that moment of clarity that comes at three in the morning when the snow muffles the noise and the landscape you thought you knew transforms itself, your mind finds a single point, and you can't escape it because the angles are softened and you are left without the generosity of distractions. *When you love someone, in a way, you want to become them.* It was fucking pathetic, but God help me, I was obsessed with Enzo. No, no, no, no, no, it was more than that.

I had fallen batshit, crazy, in love with Enzo. Exhibit A, the shirt he lent me after a night out that I never washed or returned because it smelled of him, neatly tucked away in the back of my closet. Next to it, a brown paper lunch bag of syringes.

And then as if my mind had chosen another identity, another name, it prodded me. *Come on, go ahead and say it. Just admit it.* The dogged thought furiously clawed at the walls, the house collapsing all around me, until I spit it out, "Shit, I'm so gay."

CHAPTER FOUR

LOCKER ROOM TALK

There is a code in the men's locker room. Do not touch another man when he is undressed. Do not talk about things that are pretty or fabulous or sparkly. If you must talk, limit it to sports, the weather, or politics. Do not look below the waist, yet somehow compare your penis to every other man's penis. Do not talk about how your hair "just will not cooperate," but you question whether his hair is thinning more than yours. Talk about losing that gut while placing your hands on your belly, even if you have nothing to lose. Do not ask if your ass is fat. You are a man.

I started lifting weights in our unfinished basement because I was too embarrassed to be seen struggling to lift dumbbells at the gym. The girls had given me a bench and a weight set as a birthday gift, which collected dust and acted as a prop for boxes and clothes for years. It came with an illustrated sheet of twenty-five exercises. After dinner, I would slink down into the cellar, like a teenage boy, and struggle to curl twenty pounds. There was no mirror to check my form, just the cement walls, and the low rafters. It was as if I were trying to lift the entire house above me, with all of its secrets and its silences. Occasionally, I would bump the low ceiling when hoisting the weights over my head. I'd stop and listen for one of the girls to yell, "Dad! What are you doing down there?" I'd shout in reply, "Sorry!" and go back to struggling alone in the damp cellar that smelled of cardboard and mildew.

I set the bench up near a bare bulb that cast a bright circle of light and plugged in a CD player that I kept on low so that it wouldn't disturb Katherine, who was stretched out on the couch above my head. If you were to slice the house in half and present it as a diorama, you would see a skinny middle-aged man in the basement, legs shaking as he lifted a barbell. On the first floor, a woman lay silently on a sofa by the flickering light of a TV, and above her, one daughter sat huddled at her desk, sketching in a notebook, and the other in her bedroom, talking on the phone, each of us clinging to our form of escape.

The weights represented something I could not say out loud. It was all balled up inside me, the years being the gangly kid who never seemed to grow into a man's body and the yearning that grew inside of me. It was the hopelessness of feeling trapped and the anger of being unable to set myself free. Everything seemed out of control, but the more weights I added to the bar, the more I noticed the nascent bulge in my biceps. With every curl, like with every injection, there was a sense that I could control something, mold my body into someone to be desired and my life into one that I could bear to live inside.

And yet, how I longed to be held in a way that I had never experienced. It was more necessary than water and air, this need; it was a physical hunger. When I made the promise at twenty-three years of age forsaking all others, I could not know how loneliness would make my skin become like parched earth, thirsting for the touch of another man. At night, in my dreams, my want would summon up a shadowy lover, but the intensity of my desire would cause him to vanish. In the morning, I awoke hungry, with nothing to fill me.

When I was thirteen, I would spend hours staring at my reflection in the upstairs bathroom of my childhood home. I would lean against the toothpaste-encrusted sink, turning my head from side to side in an attempt to figure out what made a face handsome. Was my face handsome? I wanted to know. Maybe it was just too thin, or maybe my eyes were too small. My blue-black hair hung in long, straight, oily bangs to hide the acne on my forehead, a pizza face with a mouth full of metal.

"Open the door, doofus!" my older brother, Alex, would shout while banging on the door.

"I'm going to the toilet, dickhead!" I'd scream back, and reach over to flush the toilet.

"He git it from his mama," was the saying in North Carolina. My mama was an expert at a questioning look. She would flit from the mirror in the hall to the gilt-framed living-room mirror, stop to look sideways, curl a strand of hair between her thumb and forefinger, and query me, "Do I look like Ali MacGraw? Everyone says I do."

She was tall with dark brown hair cut into a bob just like the 1976 Ali MacGraw—not the early 1970s one dying from leukemia, with the long ironed hair, macramé belt, and hunky boyfriend whining about how "Love means never having to say you're sorry."

I would stop playing the piano and reply, "Yeah, sure, Mom, a dead ringer."

"No, Bill, now seriously, don't you think so?" she'd ask while tossing the end of a knockoff Hermès scarf over her shoulder and framing her face between her two thumbs and index fingers, two *L*s forming the viewfinder of a photographer's camera.

"I said yes," I'd say, and start playing again, Beethoven's Moonlight Sonata. Scribbled in the margins of the sheet music were the words *shut up!*, a musical note of instruction left by Alex, who was ignoring us both while he strangled his guitar in an attempt to master "Stairway to Heaven" by Led Zeppelin.

"Dickhead," I whispered.

"Well, there's no reason to get nasty," my mother would reply, and move on to another mirror with better light.

"Now, try to play it all the way through again without stopping this time, even if you mess up," she'd offer from the other room, and I'd drop both of my hands onto the piano keys. I had *messed up* at a recital before, and she fled, leaving me to walk home alone, my incompetence sparking in her a sense of betrayal. She was unable to face the other parents. "I just didn't know what to say to them, Bill. How could you do this to me?"

My weaknesses were my mother's disappointments, and there were myriad ways to shame her: being too skinny, too pimply, too poor a performer, too effeminate. As a child, I learned that I was a direct reflection of my mother's status. Social standing was a time-honored tradition in the South, and I had been steeped in its boiling waters. Add a heavy serving of Catholic guilt, and it was a toxic mixture. Had I passed this on to my own daughters as well? Was it possible to be an unhappy father and still raise a happy child, or did shame make my love poison?

After my father left my mother and married Robin, someone who was much younger and blonder than she, the question of her beauty became more persistent. When people compared our physical similarities, my mother would respond, "It must be our weak chins." She'd tug at the skin on her neck, pulling it tight.

"I'm prettier than Robin, don't you think so?" she'd ask.

"Of course," I'd reply.

"Do you love me more than her?"

"You know I do."

"She's not your mother."

"I know."

"Her skin is so bad. She just covers it with gobs of makeup; you know that, don't you?"

She was the queen of insecurity, and I was her heir.

She'd turn back to inspect her skin. I would lock myself in the bathroom again and pop the pimples on my face until it resembled a Martian crater field.

When I didn't secure myself in the bathroom, the swimming pool was my escape. Every Tuesday night at the weekly swim meets, I'd stand on the starting block, watching the honeycombed lights quiver on the bottom of the pool and wait for the gun to sound. I looked over at the boy next to me, lean, tan body with long, downy-haired muscled legs and broad shoulders. The boy threw a beefy arm up over his head, pulling the elbow with the other hand down behind his head to stretch his arm, and then he pulled the top of his Speedo swimsuit out to tighten the strings and stuffed them back in, revealing a triangle of white skin and a shock of dark pubic hair. The boy shot a competitive glance back at me.

Don't look, faggot.

One

Two

Three

Bam!

The sting of the frigid water felt like needles, forcing me to take short, quick breaths. I threw my arms over my shoulders in front of me: *One, two, three, four, breathe, one, two, three, four, breathe,* kicking as hard as I could, the sound of the shouting voices materializing every time I turned my head to the side to gulp for air. *Go! Go! Go!* When I put my face back in the water, the sound vanished. No more questions of beauty, no more accusing looks, no more dickhead brothers. I was in my watery world of dancing light and wavy black lanes that led to nowhere and everywhere.

I climbed out of the pool, my chest heaving and water dripping from my thin body as I walked to the bleachers. I looked up at the times on the board—first place!

When I reached my mother, she stared straight ahead, eyes hidden behind dark Jackie O sunglasses, cigarette perched in the corner of her mouth. Her frosted hair matched the chilly statement.

"You're so damn skinny, Bill."

She watched the boys strut in front of us, removed the cigarette, blew a puff of smoke, and pointed at them with the smoking ember. "You need to press weights, like those boys."

Press weights. That was how she phrased it. I hated the way she said that. If I had a pound of muscle for every time she told me I should press weights, I'd be Arnold fucking Schwarzenegger. But that skinny, insecure kid was still inside me. And he was awakened by Enzo. And so, we started *pressing weights.* Yes, that would set everything right and prove everyone wrong. It was a place where I could stuff my love-anger-hate into an obsession. And another benefit? I would look good. I'd look so good, Enzo couldn't help but notice.

One evening, a month or two later, after putting all of the weights on the basement barbell set and going through all of my reps, I returned upstairs and sat on the sofa, resting my arm behind Claire's back while watching TV.

"Dad, the muscle on your arm hurts. It's too hard," she said, reaching behind her back and pushing my arm to the side.

The next day, I joined the YMCA up the hill from my office. I was no longer emaciated, just thin, so it was time to move my underground grunting routine into the daylight.

The first time I went into the gym was like returning to high school physical education class, the testosterone so palpable it grabbed you by the neck, though the guys were slightly older and indeed more filled out. There was a group of men with V-shaped torsos who carried gallon jugs filled with a liquid that looked alarmingly like urine. They adhered to a dress code of black, white, or gray colors and sported sleeveless T-shirts stretched across their superhero chests. They also wore the occasional skullcap or tousled "I just rolled out of bed" hair that must have taken hours to style. Sometimes, they would lift up their shirts while standing in front of the wall of mirrors, pretending to adjust a waistband or an errant earbud cable, but their eyes were on the reflection of their washboard abs. *If I had abs like that.* They would greet each other with a graze of the hand, just the fingertips, and walked as if their tightly coiled muscles made it difficult to bend their knees, arms hunched in front like gorillas.

As I did in high school, I clung to the perimeter. I blended into the exercise machines and peered from the corner of my eyes, like Jane Goodall hiding behind the tall grass, at the Vs in their natural habitat of free weights, beyond the chain-link fence that marked the boundary of their territory. Often they labored alone, but sometimes one would tap another on the shoulder and ask if he could spot him. A stack of plates would be pushed onto the bar, and then one would lie down on the bench as the other stood straddling his head, holding his arms out to guide the bar as it was pushed up with a primal grunt and groan, a bench-press orgasm.

"Yeah, yeah, come on bro', you can do it. Push it, push it!" the other V would offer encouragement.

I deposited that image into the spank bank.

The first time I ventured into the Vs' territory, only a couple of them were in the yard. One was a muscled black guy in his forties, with a short, rounded Afro. He always wore a red tank top that strained at the seams with skinny straps that barely covered his nipples. He had fingerless gloves and a weight-lifting belt, and his exposed shoulders looked like two basketballs. He kept to himself, and there was some unwritten but understood rule that he was the top V. Now and then, he would offer a fist bump or a grunt to a lesser V, but he always flashed a stellar white smile to any woman who might approach.

The other man in the yard was a smaller muscled white guy with thick shoulders and arms, dark wavy hair, and short legs that did not receive as much attention from the weights. He moved around the yard with vigor, running circles around the top V, who would be curling the equivalent of his body weight. Here he was on the bench press, there he was performing push-ups, and then he was lying facedown on the rubber floor, kicking his feet and stretching his short bulging arms out in front of him like a grounded Superman. Occasionally, he might say something to the top V while laughing and get a grunt back in reply. It was like watching a miniature bulldog tottering around a mastiff, yipping for attention.

Because I was new to the yard, they glanced at me when I timidly entered and then continued their repetitions without a greeting. I approached the bench press and tried to figure out how it worked. My weight set at home came with end pieces that screwed on at the ends, which held the weights in place against a plastic sleeve. But this bar looked different. Because I did not want to appear a novice, I hurriedly placed two forty-five-pound plates on either end of the bar and lay down on the bench, looking up at the massive metal rod above my head. When I attempted to push the bar up, it felt too heavy, but I took a deep breath and heaved anyway. The right side went up, and the left tipped down as I watched one plate slide in slow motion off the bar and crashed to the floor. My face became red as I moved my hands and arms up to my head in a defensive gesture, like a teenage girl swatting at a bee. When I removed my hands from my face, I quickly looked around and saw Big V peering over his shoulder, snarling.

"Hey, bud, use these clips to hold the weights in place," Little V said.

He had jogged over and was standing next to me, holding up a circle of metal that looked like a spring with two handles. He squeezed the stems several times to illustrate how they worked.

"Thank you, I'm new to this," I said, embarrassed to admit it.

"Hey, at least you're skinny and haven't gained weight like a lot of older guys," he said, and I winced at the backhanded compliment.

For years I endured comments from people, typically women who thought they were doling out compliments. "What I wouldn't give to have that skinny body," or "My arm is as big around as your thigh."

"Maybe you should try lifting only the bar first. It's forty pounds by itself," he said, sliding the other plate off. Then, seeing my expression, he added, "Or maybe these twenty-five pounders."

"Thank you," I said as he slipped on the plates and made a show of attaching the clips by holding them up for me to see and then slid them over the bar. "Place these clips and the weights side by each," he said in a Rhode Island accent. "I see a lot of these young guys liftin' these big weights, and they can't even reach above their shoulders to pull on a shirt," he said, shaking his head. But that was precisely what I wanted, to be so big that a small moon might orbit me. I wanted to create my own gravity, one that would be strong enough to attract Enzo.

"Slow and steady wins the race. Let me know if you need anythin' else," he said, turning around, and jogged back to his spot in front of the mirror.

After the initial tumble, I began to learn how to use the weights, and within a short time, I was going to the gym daily and on the internet nightly, checking out muscle-building forums. Each week, a different transformation story would be highlighted. Here was pale, sickly "before Vince," holding a newspaper with a date on it from three months ago, and there was "after Vince," spray tanned and posing with forty extra pounds of muscle, two saucer-shaped breasts, melon-sized biceps, and trapezius muscles like steel cables. Underneath the pictures was Vince's story, how he went from zero to hero, with all of the supplements, diet tips, and exercise routines he used. I memorized these. There was some numinous quality to these stories as if everything in life fell into place once the perfect proportions were realized.

In addition to regular meals, I would mix up protein shakes with ice cream and guzzle them down. Katherine seemed to accept all of this, knowing that I despised shopping for clothes because they invariably hung from me like garments flapping on a clothesline. Even in summer, I rarely wore shorts because my legs were so thin. Perhaps she also secretly desired a husband who weighed more than she did.

I was going to the gym now with earbuds plugged in and a single-minded determination. I downloaded music, angry music, Incubus, Pearl Jam, Army of Anyone, and turned up the volume. I entered the yard and nodded to Little V, who nodded back. On the bench press, I placed the forty-five-pound weights on either side, pushed up, and performed eight reps with no hesitation. I slid on two additional twenty-five-pound weights and completed ten more reps. I was sweating more now when I worked out. It soaked through my shirt, and across my back a ripple of acne formed.

"My pores are clogged from the sweating," I said to Katherine when she questioned the appearance of the acne on my chest.

"You have cleavage now," Katherine remarked, looking concerned.

Claire would ask me to flex my biceps, then squeeze the muscle with her fingertips and jerk her hand back as if she were touching the rock-hard body of a corpse with rigor mortis.

"Ew-uh, it's so hard, Dad!"

At work one day, a female coworker glanced at me and asked, "When did you become so buff?"

Good, people were noticing; it wasn't just me.

One evening, I was standing in the bedroom with a measuring tape, taking the daily measurements of my biceps, chest, thighs, and calves, and then I pulled my pants down to get a proper measurement of my waist, pants around my ankles, pushing the top band of my underwear down. Olivia walked by the bedroom door, stopped, and then screwed up her face. "Oh my God, Dad, what are you doing?"

I jerked up my pants. I knew what it looked like, a man holding a measuring tape near his crotch. "It's not what it—I was just measuring my—my waist," I said.

Did that sound any better?

I was crossing the line, but the line was so far behind me now that I lost sight of it. If Katherine felt like we were living on the moon, I felt like I was drifting untethered through deep space, so lonely and isolated that I was losing touch with reality. On the weekends, I'd go to the gym after I finished my chores; the grocery-store shopping, cleaning the house, the yard work. All of this had become too much for Katherine. *I have allergies, Bill. I can't breathe any of that stuff in, and you know my back just can't handle it.*

There was a ready supply of prescription medications when I needed the occasional break from reality. We were both coping with the isolation, our *skin hunger*, as scientists have coined the phrase, in much the same way. Katherine's sadness was the result of my loneliness, and after our children were born by cesarean section, she endured pain in her lower back, which never seemed to dissipate. She went to the doctor and had the prescriptions filled, and I started skimming from the top. "I think the drugstore shorted me," she would say. It was another way in which I deceived her. Katherine confronted me about an empty pill bottle, and I confessed, telling her that there was a problem employee at work, and I took one or two, to ease the stress. "Bill, you took an entire bottle of Valium that was prescribed to me. No one does that just because of a problem employee." She was searching for answers, perhaps as terrified as I at what the truth could be, but I assured her that it was a momentary lapse of judgment. I backed off on the intake and split the pills to make them last, slipping into the comfortable world of numbness once or twice a week. It was as if we were playing a game of Jenga with our lives, each of us taking turns to remove the blocks, but both silently agreeing not to pull the one that would cause our world to crash. I would have called the pill-taking self-medication then, but when I look back through the harsh lens of reality, my chemical relationship could only be labeled as an addiction.

I had gained twenty-five pounds in two months and was drinking protein drinks, cleaning my dinner plate, and then finishing the girls' leftovers. One night, when I was mixing up bananas with ice cream, milk, and protein powder, the girls, sixteen and fourteen then, stood in the kitchen and began to joke about my drinks.

"Time for a protein shake," they kept saying over and over, wiggling their bodies and shaking. This normally would have struck me as slightly annoying, but now, for some reason, it enraged me. Primal anger of unknown origin bubbled up, and it was as if I were a bystander watching this other man become red-faced as he growled, "Shut the fuck up!"

Katherine walked into the kitchen where the girls were standing, stunned and motionless.

"I'm sorry, work has been stressful," I apologized.

Later that evening, when the girls went to bed, Katherine placed her hand on my back and asked, "Bill, what's wrong with you?"

"Nothing." I jerked away.

"You'd tell me if anything was going on?"

"What do you mean?" I asked.

"I don't know; there's just something different about you," and then she leaned toward me and sniffed. "You even smell different." She paused a moment. "Is everything OK?"

No, it was fucked. It had been for years, but how could I say that now? I had brought them back here, made promises. I had taken the red pill or the blue one, maybe both of them, and fell down the rabbit hole. The girls depended on me. They all depended on me; they always had. But I couldn't get Enzo out of my head. Wouldn't it just be better if he was gone? Yes, yes, then things could go back to normal, albeit an approximation of normal. But, no, no, no, no, what would my life be like without him? The thought of him and these weights were the threads that kept me stitched together, even as I was bursting at the seams. Nothing would ever happen between the two of us, but I could dream. *Jerk off to some gay porn and get it out of your head,* I told myself. Then a prayer, *Dear God, that's it. I'm done. I got it out of my system. I'll never do that again. Amen.* I'd never cheat on Katherine, never had. I had made a decision long ago to be straight. There was no reversing course. Our lives were built on that decision.

"Yes, everything is fine," I replied to Katherine.

The next day, I went to the gym, plugged in my earbuds, and walked into the yard. Big V was standing next to the water fountain, and as I passed, he reached out his hand, fingertips extended. Stunned, I looked up at his face, and he nodded to me. I nodded to him and brushed my fingers against his. I walked to the weight benches, with a slight smile on my face, and then I wiped it off as I joined the other Vs.

"You've bulked up since you began lifting, bud. What is it, fifteen, twenty pounds?" Little V asked.

"About thirty," I replied, but I knew it was precisely thirty-seven pounds. Before Bill was a weak, sickly 155 pounds; After Bill was 192 pounds of someone else, of someone he was always meant to be.

"Good job, bud," he said, slapping my hand.

I slid one forty-five-pound plate onto the bar and then grabbed another and slid it next to the first one, side by each. I went to the other side and pushed on two more forty-five-pound plates. Fuck the clips. I turned up the volume on my iPod and lay down on the bench. Each press burned like fire through my arms and chest, cauterizing the wounds, pushing that skinny, insecure kid down, telling him to be quiet, just shut the fuck up. And then I turned up the music until I couldn't hear him asking why we were doing this. I turned it up louder so I couldn't hear him whispering to me about the men in the showers or about the shape of Enzo's handsome jaw or the piece of clothing I had stolen the last time I was at his house.

One, two, three, push it!
Four, five, six, are you wearing his underwear now?
Seven, eight, nine, keep going!
Ten, eleven, twelve, what are you, a faggot?
Thirteen, fourteen, fifteen, fuck you!

Just as there is a code for the locker room, there are rules for taking steroids. You plan the cycle out meticulously, purchasing everything you need for the twelve weeks ahead. You do not tell anyone. You inject in the downstairs bathroom when your family is sleeping. You withdraw money from your dead father's IRA and wire it to the offshore supplier in Moldova, some eastern European country where werewolves and vampires haunt the night. You eat as much protein as you can handle, and then you eat some more. You lift weights. You *press* the shit out of those motherfucking weights. You work out every day. You gain weight, ten pounds, twenty pounds, thirty pounds. You use the weights as a surrogate for everything that is missing or fucked up in your life. Your neck becomes larger than your head. Your shirts no longer fit. You nod to the other Vs. They acknowledge you. Your arms and back become riddled with acne. If you are careful, your balls do not shrivel up, and you do not grow tits.

You remind yourself that pain is weakness leaving the body, and you have so much weakness you need to be freed from.

You slip into the skin of masculinity and stuff it full of muscles so that no mama can ever question her boy's manhood. You fist bump and grunt, "You da' man."

You are a man. Yeah, sure, bro', that's what you are.

CHAPTER FIVE

STOP THE CLOCKS

Greensboro, North Carolina, 1984

When Katherine and I first met on a chilly night in 1984, I couldn't stop staring at her eyes. Yes, they were beautiful, hazel with flecks of amber floating in the irises, but there was something else in them that resonated with me, a sense of being lost. We met through a mutual friend, Luann, who would later tell me that Katherine was adopted. I have heard since that adoptees often recognize each other and form a connection by casting a spiritual life buoy out to one another. I was not given up at birth, but I felt like a motherless child.

"Did she just leave the house barefoot?" I asked when Katherine walked out the door.

"Probably, she's crazy like that," Luann replied.

I had returned from a summer spent in Colorado with my aunt several months prior and was still reeling from everything that had happened there and my mother's tight grip, when I called Luann in an act of desperation to get out of the house. Luann and I had been friends since grade school, and she always had a crush on me. I knew this because when Katherine left to purchase Miller Lite at the neighborhood 7-Eleven, Luann said, "You know, Bill, I have always had a crush on you."

She took a puff of her cigarette, tilted her head up, and exhaled a column of smoke.

"I know," I replied.

She laughed, whacked me on the arm, and then pushed her glasses up on her nose.

"But when we kissed, it felt like I was kissing my brother." She shuddered.

We were in high school and both drunk when we kissed. My mother was working the night shift at the hospital, and I threw a White Russian party. Luann told me then for the first time that she had a crush on me, but I already knew it. I thought if I kissed her, I might feel something that was missing, and so I did, and then she vomited a milky white stream of vodka, Kahlúa, and cream.

"I'm glad you called me," she said, and then added, "It's been so long since I last saw you, and I already had plans with Katherine, so thank you for tagging along." She turned her head to the side, blew out another puff of smoke, and said, "I can tell that she likes you."

We were sitting on the brown shag-carpeted floor in the family room that Katherine shared with her mother in Greensboro, North Carolina. Three or four clocks were hanging on every dark paneled wall. Each of them set to a different time.

"She seems great, but—" I said, looking up at the clocks, and before I could finish my statement, Luann replied, "She is great."

Katherine opened the door and walked in. She was wearing a blue-and-green Mexican peasant blouse over dark jeans. My mother would later say she had "such a pretty face," in her usual Southern way of delivering a compliment in place of saying what she actually thought—that she could stand to lose a few pounds. Her dark brown, curly hair was shoulder length, and I knew if I felt it, it would be crunchy from the hair spray. Her skin was a flawless ivory color, and I couldn't tell if the beauty spot on her right cheek was real or drawn. She pulled a six-pack of beer out of a brown paper bag and held it above her head, "Ta-da!" Luann and I glanced at each other and laughed. When I looked down at Katherine's bare feet, she followed my gaze.

"Shoes can be so constricting," she said. "Don't you think?"

We went to a traveling carnival in the parking lot of Carolina Circle Mall on our second, or would that have been our first date? On a ride called the Zipper, Katherine sat next to me. I watched her scream and laugh, alternating between sheer terror and pure joy as the cage we were in lurched and flipped. Her curly hair blossomed upside down surrounded by a halo of neon red and orange carnie lights. A lipstick container bounced around us, pinging against the cage, like a small moon in a wildly irregular orbit. When the ride finally came to a stop, I picked up the lipstick, and as we stepped uncertainly onto the solid ground, I handed it to her.

"That's not mine," she laughed. "Do you think that's my color?"

I looked at the pink container and then at her red lips and then back up to her eyes. And there it was, that look of lostness and also the same thing I saw in Luann's eyes at the end of my White Russian party. She wanted me to kiss her, and so I did, but she did not vomit.

The kiss was like an echo, and on the other side would be our marriage, our children, and the lonely sound my name would become from both of our mouths. But in that moment, the excitement of the ride was still coursing through us, and the smell of popcorn and corn dogs mixed with the screams of roller-coaster passengers lent the air a thrill. I glanced around the carnival at girls holding on to trophy stuffed animals with one arm and the other wrapped around their trophy boyfriends. I wanted so badly to be like those boys, and so I took Katherine's hand, and like a lost buoy in the night, she took mine.

And just like that, we were dating, once a week at first. On Friday nights, we'd go to Hooray Harry's, a college-dive bar, a routine that became two or three nights a week over time. Early on in our relationship, she called me late at night, sobbing after a fight with her mother over some small matter. I offered to come over, but she said, "I just needed to talk to my boyfriend."

Was that what we were, boyfriend and girlfriend?

We began to share our dreams with one another. Katherine wanted to be a hairdresser in a chic Manhattan salon, and I, after college, wanted to immigrate to Australia, mostly because I had wanted to be like Mel Gibson after seeing him in the film *The Year of Living Dangerously*. I practiced speaking with a flat Australian accent, and Katherine attended Leon's Beauty School, cutting my hair in her kitchen for practice.

It was then, sitting in the center of her kitchen, that I noticed that none of the hands of the clocks in the family room and on the kitchen walls ever actually moved. They were frozen in time, still set to the night we had first met.

"My grandfather started a wholesale clock company out of the trunk of his car," she said. "And now it's grown into this huge family business. Largest clock and watch-part company in the world."

The clocks were purely ornamental, Katherine explained, and she wanted nothing to do with them. Her father worked for the clock company until he died when Katherine was five years old. Her birth mother had given her up for adoption so that she could have a two-parent family with a stay-at-home mother. But her adopted mother returned to work at the family business to support the fatherless family. When Katherine dropped out of college, it was expected that she would join her mother, putting together "assortments," tiny kits of clock and watch parts in little plastic bags for eight hours a day. This was the job at the family business reserved for women, while the men ran the company.

"As if that's the only thing a woman can do," she sneered as she nudged my head forward and snipped my hair.

We both wanted to run away for different reasons. Katherine desired to escape the role cast for her, and I wanted to assume one that until now I had not considered. At the end of our dates, we'd kiss;

the heavy, mouth-open, tongues-meeting type of kiss. I was reaching deep down, throwing myself into the role—Mel Gibson when he pulls Sigourney Weaver out onto the veranda during a fancy party and plants one on her—and I thought, *I could throw myself into this.*

I introduced Katherine to my older brother, Alex, and his fiancée on a double date. We played pool in the back room of Hooray Harry's, and when Katherine and I began to lose the game, she climbed up onto the table and lay on it.

"I don't want to play anymore," she said.

I saw the look of disdain spread across Alex's face, and later when we were alone, he said, "She seems kind of immature." And so I stopped calling Katherine. Our multinight weekly dates began to trickle down to one and then to none, until later when I decided to call her because I needed a date for Alex's wedding.

"When I didn't hear from you, I thought you wanted to break up with me," Katherine said.

"No, of course not. I've just been too busy with school and work. That's all," I replied.

"I'll go with you, but I can't risk getting my heart broken. So we'll just go as friends."

On the day of Alex's wedding, she wore a pink satin dress with shoulder pads and an impossibly narrow waist. She had a long strand of pearls looped several times around her neck, and her hair pulled back and tied with a bow. It was pure 1980s fashion, like a royal Carrington from *Dynasty*, the TV show, but the result was an hourglass figure transformed by the weight she had lost. All of my brothers took notice, including the groom himself, my older brother, Alex.

"Damn, Bill, she looks good!"

Weddings, like carnivals, are intoxicating events. There are the thrill of the crowd and the magic in the air, the freak-show aspect of standing up and ogling the bride, and then at the reception, drinking the actual intoxicants. When Alex pulled off his bride's garter belt, he stretched it back like a slingshot, closed one eye, and aimed it directly at me. When I grabbed it with one hand, he laughed and said, "You're next."

But next it was Luann, and after her another friend, and then Katherine's brother. All around us, weddings were popping up like wildfires—1980s weddings with large crowds, multiple bridesmaids and groomsmen, shoulder pads and big hair, and I could feel the heat.

We were sitting at the bar in Hooray Harry's when I started talking about Australia again and explaining to Katherine the point system for immigrant visas. She took a sip of her beer and then put it down. She wiped a tear from one eye, and then a few more replaced that one.

"What's wrong?" I asked.

"You're going to run off to Australia and leave me behind," she sobbed.

I looked around the bar. More than anything, I wanted her to stop crying, and so I said, "But who said I was going to leave you behind?"

With that, her face brightened as she grabbed my hand. When I took her home that night, she ran up the stairs and told her mother that we were getting married and then moving to Australia. I looked up at the clocks and willed them to move backward, but they refused to budge.

When you step into a roller-coaster car, it's thrilling, and just before the safety arm clamps down, you think for a split second about jumping out, but then before you know it, it's too late, and you're lurching forward.

Katherine's mother pulled me aside that evening.

"Are you sure you can afford her?" she asked, and then added, "She's expensive, medically speaking."

I looked at her quizzically.

She lowered her voice. "There's nothing wrong with her. It's all up here." She pointed to her head, and then she took off her engagement ring, this huge stone, and handed it to me. "Get it reset," she said.

And then we were picking out china patterns and wedding invitations, and setting a date.

A month before the wedding, my mother pulled me aside and said, "Call the wedding off. We can sit down and do handwritten notes," as if thoughtfully inscribed letters on tasteful stationery could stop a speeding roller coaster in its tracks. My mother said, "Her family is wealthy, and I just don't want you to become complacent." This was her Southern way of saying, "You're settling." There was a room full of gifts that had already arrived, and people had already made travel plans. Wasn't this what my mother wanted? My mother was complicated, and it would take years to unravel her mysteries. She wanted me to find happiness, I know this now, but it was a version of her happiness. She did not believe I could be happy being myself, nor did she believe that Katherine was a suitable wife. Wasn't this what I wanted? Was there any other option? It seems so ridiculous to say it now, but I just couldn't say no.

When I was in high school, I came home drunk late one night. My mother was standing by the front door, tugging her robe closed.

"Breathe," she said, holding her nose out.

I puffed a tiny breath, and she jutted her nose farther out. "Breathe again."

I opened my mouth, making a loud "huh" sound as I exhaled deeply. Her eyes grew wide, and then she slapped me.

"How dare you come into this house knee-walking drunk."

Within a week, I was sitting with her in the office of a psychologist, Dr. Street. He was the father of one of my classmates and spoke with a Southern drawl. He grabbed my arm.

"Do you mas-tuh-bate?" he asked me.

"What?"

He tightened his grip around my skinny arm, his hands working like a vise.

"It's perfectly natural. You do it too, now, don't you, Mary?" he asked my mother. He didn't let go of my arm.

"Well, I mean," she stammered, tugging at the top of her blouse.

Dr. Street smiled at me, digging his hands into my arm, and asked, "Are you going to tell me to stop?"

"I don't know," I replied.

"Your mama tells me you mas-tuh-bate more than normal. That your sheets are all sticky."

I looked at a smudge on the wall and willed myself to become small, to become that dark spot and disappear. His hands kept tightening, but I said nothing.

"What do you think about when you do that?"

I was gone now, somewhere deep inside the wall. I left my arm behind. I peered from behind the drywall to see if my mother might pull out the pictures I had drawn as inspiration for mas-tuh-bation.

"You have a problem with men," he said, and let go of my arm with a flourish. "You don't know how to say no."

What had my mother told the doctor? She had convinced me that I needed to see him because of my "alcohol problem." One night of drinking, but he was grasping at something else. Did I have a problem with men, and what men was he referring to? My father? He left when I was twelve. I know that I did have a problem with men who grabbed my arm and asked about masturbation, and the only way to make this end was to agree with everything he said.

He pushed back into his seat triumphantly. My mother picked at a thread on her blouse with one hand while patting the back of her hair with the other, her eyes avoiding mine. I looked down at my shoes. I wore long-sleeved shirts until the black-and-blue finger marks faded.

During the wedding rehearsal, Katherine wanted the bridesmaids to stand in order by height. She whispered this to the priest, and he replied, "Well, they're right there. Why don't you tell them?" But she couldn't do it. I could see her hands trembling. These were friends and relatives, but she was too timid to address them as a group, and so I saw something else in her that drew me. Another mask that I could wear in addition to becoming her husband was that of a caretaker.

"Can y'all stand in order of height?" I asked the bridesmaids.

The night before the wedding, I lay awake in my childhood bed at my mother's house, staring at the ceiling. It was August, and the air was dense, but I had the windows open instead of turning on the air-conditioning unit because I wanted to hear the crickets whirring and the frogs croaking in Buffalo Creek. I used to go *creek walking* and catch tadpoles and crayfish with my childhood friends in that creek. In many ways, I was still that young kid, and now I would be walking down the aisle. I knew it felt wrong, and I was seized with panic, but what felt more wrong were the ugliness and sin I was trying to leave behind.

When we were teenagers, my older brother, Alex, helped one of his friend's neighbors carry a piece of furniture from his car into his house. "Be careful," my mother admonished Alex. "He's a homosexual." Alex's eyes grew wide, and he said, "But he had such a strong handshake." *Pedophile* and *homosexual* were words used interchangeably in my youth in North Carolina; in certain places, they still are.

Fear of eternal damnation, the fear of ridicule, the fear of being labeled a faggot and being beaten to a bloody pulp as I had seen happen to classmates who were unable to hide their queerness had created a fear and internal homophobia so great that it eclipsed all others. If shame and self-hatred were a creek, I had been thoroughly soaked in it. And here I saw redemption. My brother Alex seemed so happy, and my brother Christopher was in love with a girl and would soon be engaged. This was the way forward. This was what Billy Graham had promised about renouncing homosexuality in his column right next to my favorite comic, *Funky Winkerbean*, in the daily newspaper. "It is never too late to return to God. That does not mean it will be easy to renounce your present lifestyle and begin to live for Christ again. The Bible is clear in its condemnation of homosexual activity."

This would be the last time I slept in that bed on Latham Road, and it felt like I was crossing a threshold that could not be uncrossed. I had graduated from college in May and never heard back from the Australian consulate. The fancy salon in New York was too much of a pipe dream for Katherine. With Australia and Manhattan no longer possibilities, we set our sights on the only place that offered me a job far away, a bank in Tampa, Florida. I was twenty-three and Katherine just twenty-two. We were barely adults, but at that age, time was purely ornamental. I could not grasp what *forever after* meant, and if I was going to be lost in time, there would be someone by my side.

CHAPTER SIX
EVERYTHING IS FINE

Roanoke, Virginia, 1995

Katherine knitted her hands together and paced across the porch, the threat of snow charging the atmosphere and her breath misting in the frigid air. She wore no coat, just a pair of jeans with a blue-and-black untucked flannel shirt. When she saw me pull into the driveway, she raced down the steps and ran up to the car. I rolled down the window and looked down at her bare feet turning ghostly white in the cold.

"He found her!" she said.

"Who found who?" I asked.

"Her! The Searcher found my mother!"

For years, Katherine had looked in vain for her birth mother, combing through high school yearbooks in local libraries from the early 1960s for pictures of girls who might have borne a resemblance to her.

"There, doesn't she look like me?" she would ask, plopping the book in my lap and pointing at a black-and-white photograph of a young girl with bouffant hair, a dark blouse, and a strand of pearls around her neck. Katherine would turn her head and stare off wistfully into the middle distance, like the girl in the picture. She could have been every girl on that page.

"I guess," I replied, and when I noticed the disappointed expression, "Yeah, sure, that could totally be your mother."

The Searcher was a shadowy figure we heard about through a connection of a connection in an adopted children's support group, which Katherine attended regularly. Katherine provided her birth date and the few known details of her adoption to the Searcher's agent. She was told to wait. It could take months or even years. But her search continued, scouring public records, visiting the adoption agency, and looking at high school yearbooks in surrounding towns.

Soon after we were married, when we lived in Florida, Katherine was convinced that a checkout clerk at the local Publix supermarket was her birth sister, though she had no proof that her biological parents had another child. It was the way the girl stared at her, Katherine said, like the checkout clerk felt it too, a lost connection finally found. Sometimes, I thought Katherine might stumble and fall backward into the black hole of her missing genetic history. The search for her mother became all-consuming as if when she was found, the puzzle would be complete.

We both had these secrets in our past, and when Katherine began digging to uncover hers, I couldn't help but notice how much they both haunted us in many of the same ways. But even as she kept uncovering hers, I piled more earth on mine, for fear that it might cause our unraveling. The feelings of loss that could have bonded us were actually pulling us apart. Katherine wanted me, the man who she hoped would never give her up, as her birth mother did, or regret taking her in, as it sometimes seemed her adopted mother did. I wanted someone who could never be. We both had wants. The difference was, I knew the truth whereas Katherine was searching for hers. Truth is power, but for me, that power was wholly crushing and for Katherine, it was the lack of it that seemed to flatten her.

"If we get two thousand dollars to the Searcher tonight, I can find out where she is," Katherine said, opening the car door and sitting down in the passenger seat.

"But we don't have two hundred, much less two thousand," I said, looking up at the dilapidated roof tiles and the peeling paint on our house. "And besides, how would we get the money to him tonight?"

"I have to talk to her. I have to talk to her now!" Katherine said, using the back of her hand to dry her face as her chin quivered.

"We'll get it somehow, but not tonight." I reached up to wipe the wetness from her cheek. "Who's watching the girls?"

"Martha," Katherine said as she swiped my hand from her face and then pointed to our next-door neighbor's house. Her head dropped forward.

The money for the Searcher would come from her adoptive mother, June. "Maybe now she'll get some peace," June said while tearing a check from a register and handing it to me. She lowered her voice and peered over the glasses resting on the end of her nose. "You know, she told me she couldn't sleep because the sound of your heartbeat keeps her awake at night."

A year after Olivia was born, Katherine sank into a severe state of sadness. She would often ask, "Is everything OK?" She would ask this perhaps thirty or forty times a day. "Yes, everything is fine," I would reply, but it wasn't, and we both knew it. There was always a part of her that sensed something beneath the surface.

"Do you think she's going crazy again?" June asked.

"She wasn't crazy. She was sad," I replied, and unknowingly she was a woman constantly in search of her footing in a marriage she did not know I had built on quicksand. "Everything is fine," I added.

"I don't know how you put up with her," June said. Neither one of our mothers could accept us for who we were, and that feeling of a parent's rejection endeared Katherine to me even more. Katherine did not play by the rules her family had laid out for her, and this offended them. Katherine's adoptive mother often said, "I always wanted a little boy," and then she would add, "Oh, and a little girl too," as if Katherine were simply the additional piece that made up the pair.

"Well," I said to June, "I love her." It was more of an indictment than a statement. It angered me that Katherine's mother would say something like this about her daughter, and it tugged at my primal wound of rejection.

But I did love her. It was a bit of the craziness, the part of her that refused to be tamed and obey the rules that I did love. It was her pilgrim soul, the woman who alternated between screaming and laughter on a carnival ride. In her thirties, as a young mother, she became tattooed for the first time, when no other young mothers in our bougie neighborhood would consider such a thing, a moon and three stars on her shoulder, a yin-yang symbol at her ankle, and an ankh symbol on her wrist. She would not participate in a religion that did not believe in equality, something not too common in the early 1990s. When we were shopping for a new car, the dealer made a disparaging remark about an Asian family, and Katherine became incensed. "I want to speak to someone in power!" she yelled at him, and then spoke with his manager about the remark. What happened to the girl who was afraid to speak up at her wedding?

One evening, as we were strolling down the sidewalk after a celebratory dinner in downtown Roanoke for my work promotion, Katherine asked me if I was excited. "Yes, of course," I replied. We had left the girls, who were five and three years old then, at home with a babysitter.

"Well, let me hear it!" she said.

"I'm excited," I said.

And then, without warning, she screamed. Startled, I looked behind us to see if anyone was watching or listening.

"Katherine," I whispered while grabbing her hand.

"I'll do it again, unless you show me how excited you are."

"Aaah," I squeaked out, and when I looked at her, she was inhaling, ready to let out another scream, and so I beat her to the punch.

"Not bad," she said, and then she screamed again, and so did I. We did this, like two loons calling to each other until we reached our car, and then we sat in the front seat, laughing.

I wanted to be as free as Katherine had become, but letting go of those inhibitions would release the secret I had kept in for so many years. In my thirties, I had locked myself into the panic room. But, away from our hometown, and now in Virginia, Katherine seemed to find some confidence and freedom that had been missing. And soon, she would discover more of the mystery.

After we wired the money into the Searcher's account, his agent provided a name, an address, and a phone number. I took the girls to the park and left Katherine alone to make the call.

It was an *Oprah Winfrey Show*–worthy event—mother and daughter reunited after more than thirty years apart. Katherine did have a birth sister after all, though she had never lived in Florida. Her mother married her birth father two years after giving Katherine up for adoption, and together, they had another child.

They visited often, backfilling in the history so that Katherine no longer felt like an island. Their relationship blossomed. There were trips to each other's homes to meet extended family, cousins, uncles, and nieces. There were dinners with laughter and wine and remarks about Katherine and her sister. "My goodness, you two could be twins." It was all going so well. But when you begin to dig into the past, you're likely to discover things that were intentionally left behind or forgotten. But as the weeks passed, there was a change in Katherine's psyche, and I had no idea why. Her contentment dissipated, and Katherine began to become agitated, ill at ease, and she started to feel an intense pain, like menstrual cramping, that would not go away.

"We're not alone in this house, Bill," Katherine said one day, looking sideways as she lowered her voice. She glanced toward the back door in the kitchen.

"What do you mean?" I asked.

"He watches me while I'm cleaning the dishes," she said.

"What? Who is watching you?" I asked, suddenly livid that a Peeping Tom was standing by the window and staring at Katherine and the girls.

Shortly after we moved into the house, a next-door neighbor was raped in her home. She convinced the rapist that she needed to urinate halfway through the act, and he let her go to the bathroom. When she escaped by squeezing through the tiny bathroom window, she was wearing only a T-shirt as she ran screaming and tumbling down the hill to the fire station. The image haunted me. And if I felt fear, I could only imagine what Katherine must have felt during the day when she was alone all day in an old house with the girls who were four and two years old then.

"I don't know who he is, or was. He died in this house," Katherine said.

A chill ran through me, and I stood up while glancing into our small den that converted into a playroom. Olivia was wearing a light blue pajama shirt and a pair of panties. On her feet were plastic shoes that we bought at the Disney Store in the local mall. When she stepped from side to side, little lights embedded into the heels flashed and played the tune, "Beauty and the Beast." Claire laughed as her sister danced around the room.

"Are you saying that our house is haunted?" I asked.

"He stands in the corner, there," Katherine said, pointing to a dark corner of the kitchen by the back door. "He doesn't speak. When I turn to look, all I see is a shadow. But I can sense that he's angry."

The unknown was lurking around every corner. She also began to experience physical pain in her joints along with the mental pain of reconciling her adoption, a rapist hiding in the bushes, and the mystery surrounding the secrets that I kept.

She called a psychic—1-800-psychic—who told her to get rid of all of the digital devices in our home. The clock radio in our bedroom was replaced by a child's wind-up clock with a manual dial, little panda bear arms for clock hands, and a grating bell for an alarm. It was the type of clock that was smashed by a sledgehammer in the cartoons the girls watched.

"They're a conduit for spirits, Bill," Katherine said when I quizzed her about the disappearing electronics. She looked at me as if this were something I really should have known, and then she lit a stick of sage leaves while waving it around the kitchen.

"This is the year 1996," she called out, looking up at the ceiling. "Your loved ones are waiting for you in the light."

But the light was being siphoned out of our home. A chill settled, and I began to feel like the line between this world and the next, between sanity and insanity, became fuzzy. I feared that I might stumble and fall into the other side. Was our house haunted? I could not answer the question, but I could believe there was an entity seeking a resolution for past wrongs.

"Is everything OK?"

"Yes, everything is fine," I replied.

Over several months, Katherine's sadness morphed into anger. When I would return home late from work, she would chastise me. "How many times have I told you that you need to be here at five fifteen? Not five twenty or five thirty." And when I received a promotion at work, she became furious. "You'll never be home now. You're abandoning us!"

One night, after visiting an office in another city, my manager drove me home. Katherine was waiting on the porch swing. She was smoking a cigarette, and the tip flashed red in the blackness as we walked up the steps.

"Hey, I'm sorry I'm late," I said.

Katherine was silent, her jaw set. She stood up as the porch swing creaked and rocked back and forth on its own. She walked over to us and then without warning, punched me in the gut. I doubled over. She snubbed the cigarette out on the railing, opened the door, and walked inside. My manager placed his hand on my shoulder and said, "Don't worry about it. I didn't see anything."

"Is everything OK?"

"Yes, everything is fine."

A mysterious illness began to attack Katherine, pains that settled in her joints, shortness of breath that necessitated an ambulance ride in the middle of the night, but when the doctors searched for a diagnosis, the specter illness was nowhere to be found. In many ways, the search for the basis of her illness mirrored the search for her birth family. There were professionals who had the answers, but she had to fight and work around the system in order to uncover the truth. Physicians dismissed her pain, and adoption agency counselors did not believe that knowing where Katherine came from would offer her any benefits. This disbelief on the part of professionals seemed to exacerbate the intensity of Katherine's feeling of being deceived.

When the removal of the electronics and the crystals hanging in the windows failed to deter the angry spirit, Katherine called our pastor to perform a blessing on our house. Afterward, when I walked him to the door, he asked me to step outside with him.

"Do you believe your house is haunted?" he asked.

"I guess it's possible," I replied.

"Don't you think something else might be haunting Katherine?"

That night, Katherine had a dream that in a past Victorian life, her husband committed her to a psychiatric hospital, a snake pit, so that he could collect all of her money, but a kind doctor took pity on her and attempted to help her. She glanced sideways at me. "I don't know if you were my husband in that life or the doctor." I couldn't help but wonder if Katherine was searching for the shadowy figure of another secret. Was I the ghost who was haunting our marriage? How many secrets could Katherine uncover, until the sheer weight of them caused her to collapse?

I was struggling with a new job, a despondent wife, and two young daughters, attempting to find a balance, trying to keep things together, but bleakness and a sense of dread filled the house. The boiler rattled late at night. The century-old bones of the craftsman groaned. A mouse made a nest in our oven and was burned alive.

"Why did my mother give me up?" Katherine asked me, the joy of reconnecting grating against the reality of a lifetime of absence. Katherine was struggling with the reality that parents make decisions that affect the outcome of their children's lives, sometimes in negative and damaging ways. Katherine's birth mother gave her up, but kept her sister. What decisions might we make that would affect our daughters? What decisions had we already made that could not be undone?

"Your birth mother gave you up so that you would have two parents," I replied.

"But my father died when I was five years old," she cried.

I was terrified. What other ghosts were we summoning forth?

When I could no longer put off a training class in Washington, DC, for work, I told Katherine I would be gone for five days.

"No, I can't handle that right now. I need you here," she pleaded.

"Everything will be fine."

But on the second day of training, I watched a woman walk into the classroom and hand the trainer a note. He looked up at me and said, "You have an urgent call."

I walked out of the classroom and picked up the phone.

"Hello?"

"Bill, it's Alice." My coworker's voice quivered. "I don't know how to say this. Katherine is, well, she needs you to come home."

The drive from Washington, DC, to Roanoke, Virginia, is a four-and-a-half-hour trip. I made it in under four hours. When I walked through the door, Alice, who lived in our neighborhood, one street over, was in the den with two McDonald's Happy Meals for the girls. Olivia and Claire shouted, "Daddy!" I picked them both up and gave them a hug and a kiss. Alice nodded her head toward the closed kitchen door. "Eat your Happy Meals," I told the girls. "Be good for Daddy."

I walked into the kitchen, closing the door behind me. Katherine was in a nightgown, and her eyes were red, her face puffy.

"Is everything OK?" she asked.

"Everything will be fine," I replied.

"I can't get my thoughts straight." She started sobbing.

I took her to the hospital and admitted her. They told me to go home, that her stay would be like a vacation, an opportunity to find some calm.

She was paired with a suicidal roommate, a mother in her thirties, Virginia. When I visited Katherine the next day, they had already become fast friends, bonding over the humiliating experience of giving up sharp objects and other implements of self-destruction and not being allowed to use the bathroom alone.

"How do you make pancakes?" Virginia asked me. "Katherine tells me they're delicious. That you make them every Saturday morning."

There was something watchful in her eyes, like a cat that was ready to pounce. It unnerved me.

"I use a boxed mix, but I pour in a little half and half cream and—"

"I use yogurt! That makes mine better!" she cut in, looking triumphant and glancing over at Katherine.

Later that night, I received a call from Katherine.

"They searched my room and found something, Bill. It's not mine. I want to come home."

"Who searched your room? What did they find?"

"That gay nurse—he found a piece of broken plastic hidden in my clothes," she said. "I can't stand him, the faggot."

I winced.

Virginia would confess to breaking off the plastic from a light fixture, placing it in a pile of Katherine's clothes, and tipping off the staff. "It was the way she bragged about her husband's damn pancakes," Virginia conceded.

"What would she do if anything ever happened to you?" Alice asked me when I returned home from one of my daily visits to the hospital.

"Nothing ever will," I said, scooping Olivia and Claire into my arms. "I will never leave them."

Alice pulled on her coat and walked toward the door. Outside, snow began to fall, slowly at first and then increasing in intensity. The boiler rattled, and the wind howled. She turned the crystal knob, and the door creaked open. A gust blew a flurry of snowflakes into the house. Alice turned to look at me, this young father, clinging tightly to two young, squirming girls and drying his eyes on their sweet little pajama shirts.

To Alice, I was the kind doctor of Katherine's dream who took care of his patient, but the truth tugged at me. Had I dragged Katherine and myself into the snake pit? Insanity is the inability to distinguish fantasy from reality. Could I see the difference? I thought I could, but I honestly believed my secret thoughts and desires were disordered and if acted upon would condemn me to hell and ruin all that we had built.

Later that year, in September 2000, a man named Ronald Gay would walk into the Backstreet Café, less than two miles from our home, take out a gun, and empty the bullets into the crowded bar, killing Danny Lee Overstreet, aged forty-three, and wounding six others. Several patrons would not give their last names for fear of losing their jobs for being at a gay bar; one would go to work with a bullet in his back. The shooting would not be charged as a hate crime, because Virginia statute did not include sexual orientation as a protected class. The shooter would say that being taunted about his last name made him want to "waste some gay people."

Family, religion, and society had robbed and destroyed me, and it created a ripple effect that caused Katherine, already grappling with losses of her own, to lose control too. I must become a better husband and father, in order to pay a penance for my disturbed thoughts. I would play the kind doctor, while deep down knowing I was the horrible husband.

Insanity is the inability to distinguish fantasy from reality.

"Is everything OK?" Alice asked while standing at the door.

"Everything is fine."

CHAPTER SEVEN

DADDY'S HOME

Franklin, Massachusetts, 2007

"You need to come home now," Katherine said.

It was 4:30 p.m. This was not a request. It was a command.

"What's wrong?" I asked.

"We need to talk. Just get here."

My office was a five-minute drive from home, in a business park just off Interstate 495. As I drove down Pond Street and passed John F. Kennedy Elementary School, I recalled another rushed trip I made when Olivia was three or four years old. She had been playing with a plastic cup, tripped, and fell on it, causing it to splinter and slice her lip, which required stitches. The tone of Katherine's voice was different from that phone call, harsher, more accusing. There was no blood pouring from a child's lip, but the anxiety that gripped me was the same.

I opened the front door and stowed my workbag safely in the front-hall closet and did not unbutton my coat. When I walked into the kitchen, I found them sitting there silently. There was no greeting.

The stools we purchased for the kitchen counter were too high. When you sat on them, your knees brushed the underside of the counter, and it looked as if you were floating just above the expanse of the white counter in front of you. The straight backs of the metal chairs forced a stiff posture, and there was nowhere to put your hands but straight in front of you, usually clasped together, as if in prayer.

Katherine sat in the middle; Olivia, now sixteen, flanked her right side and Claire, who was now fourteen, was on her left. I stood across from them, separated by the great white cloud of laminate. The only sound in the house was the ticking of the grandfather clock. Through the kitchen window, I could see Maggie running and barking, defending the backyard against intruder squirrels. The sun was setting as the rooms in the house became wrapped in shadows. During New England winters, darkness fell early, and a crimson stain split through the evening sky.

I glanced at each of their tight faces. Katherine slowly unclasped her trembling hands and held out a vial of amber fluid in the palm of her right hand.

"What is that?" I asked. The color drained from my face.

"Don't play dumb," she replied, and then asked, "Why don't you tell us? It came in the mail, addressed to you."

I steadied my expression and lifted my gaze slowly from her hand up to her face. She narrowed her eyes, searching the creases in my forehead for traces of guilt. Her jaw set like the underbite of a bulldog. I turned to look at Olivia. Her chin was wrinkled, and it quivered, but her hazel eyes were cold. Claire could not look at me. She turned her head away, her long brown hair shielding her face like a curtain when I attempted to make eye contact with her.

"You have no right to open my mail!" I exploded.

As if my outburst pierced some membrane, the girls' faces became washed in tears.

"How could you involve the girls?" I accused her, no longer able to plead my innocence but determined to make a case against her.

"We thought it was some late Christmas delivery, Bill. The handwriting on the envelope was so odd. When we opened it, *this* was wrapped in a foreign newspaper," she replied.

Claire sprang from her stool and ran to the front hall. I knew where she was going, and my heart began to race.

A scuffle of chairs and suddenly we were all standing in the foyer as Claire, hunched over, pulled my workbag from the closet and rustled through it. I felt that, like the tell-tale heart, the bag pulsed with its secret contents. Whenever the girls asked if I had a pen or paper or some other item that might be inside it, I would quickly grab my bag and prevent them from rifling through it. I kept the secret by my side, always. I took it to work with me in the morning and brought it home at night, tucking it away in the back of the closet.

When I was young, my father would shout, "Daddy's home," when he returned from work. My brothers and I would punch each other in the arm and stick out our feet to trip each other as we rushed to the front door to greet him. Our hands would search his pockets. The lucky one would find a package of Juicy Fruit gum.

Claire pulled out a crumpled brown paper bag and stood up slowly. She opened the bag while peering inside and then pulled out a cluster of hypodermic syringes held together with a small rubber band.

"Oh, Daddy," Claire whispered. Her small fingers began to uncurl as if the contents might be contaminated. A fresh set of tears streamed down her face.

I looked at her small hand, the delicate fingers now with peeling pink polish on the nails. I had a part in making that hand. It was the same one that I would hold in the middle of the night, my arm hanging over the side of the bed and her hand reaching up to clutch mine. When she was small, she would often come running into our bedroom in the darkness and jump into the bed. Finally, after many sleepless nights, we told her she could no longer crawl into bed with us. If she was scared, she could bring her sleeping bag in and lie down on the floor next to our bed, but she was not allowed to wake us. Somehow in the middle of the night, our hands always found each other.

Katherine took the bag and the syringes gently from her hand as I attempted to grab them. She held them behind her back with one hand, while pulling the girls closer to her with the other.

"I need those," I said, trying to make my voice sound calm. "Give them to me. They're mine."

She brought the bag from around her back, looked inside, and pulled out a shiny foil package of pills.

"What are these?" she asked.

I hesitated and then slowly said, "Clomid. If I don't take them, then . . ." My voice trailed off as I looked at Olivia and Claire.

"Then you'll grow tits," Katherine said, sparing no coparent respect. I winced.

She had done her research, which meant she had suspected before today. Did she suspect anything else? Did she go through the files on my computer? Did she find the history of gay porn? Did she discover the numbered steps detailing a steroid cycle stack? Or did she wonder why this man she thought she knew so well wanted to change himself so drastically?

Just a few weeks ago, when I stepped out of the shower, I could sense her looking at me. From the reflection in the mirror, I could see her gaze wander over my back and saw the quizzical look on her face as she regarded the constellation of red bumps that riddled my shoulders.

I rarely let her see me naked. At night, I slept fully clothed in sweatpants and a T-shirt and sometimes a sweatshirt. When I showered, I locked the bathroom door behind me. My father urinated standing up with a burning cigarette in his mouth and the bathroom door wide open. Let the entire world see his manhood. A multitude of women had seen it through the years. But I never let anyone watch this private act. My body was perpetually afraid it would betray my queerness.

After the shower, I quickly pulled on my sweater, but it fit too tightly. She had called me on it then, keeping the question veiled. "What are you doing to get so big?"

She walked over to put her hand on me, and I flinched.

"Why do you never touch me anymore?" Her voice was angry, and the edges tinged with pain.

This was usually the cue I needed to initiate intimacy. I grabbed her hand and attempted to pull her in for a hug, but she moved away, jerking her hand back and crossing her arms.

"We don't even kiss anymore," she said. "Is it because of my weight?"

"No, no, it's not that, well—I mean," and here I crossed the line as if not crossed before. *Sex has been a semiannual event for years, Bill.* She was zeroing in on the secret, and it was getting more and more challenging to keep. I could stop taking the steroids, but this other secret, I could not quit. Would she begin to question my fascination with Enzo? It was as if there were a hum, a whispering, like a pattern you pick up in the static from the TV, when the network is off the air. *Do you hear that? Hear what? No, no, I don't hear anything at all. There must be something wrong with you. You should have your ears checked.*

And then I said it. "I mean, you could probably stand to lose a few pounds." She went slack-jawed as if my words had slapped her. And they did. I threw a punch filled with my self-hatred directly at her.

I tried to recover. I began to list all of the reasons for my distance: *work is so busy; I'm still trying to fit in here; I'm worried about how the girls are doing in school.* I made a mental calendar entry to have sex with her, not that night as that would have been too suspect, but a night in the near future. I would need to find some inspiration, a mental image to hold on to, check out my favorite porn sites, and then purchase some wine on the way home. Take out the trash, pick up some milk, mow the yard, have sex with the wife. It was always on the bottom of the list.

"Your neck is bigger than your head," she said then, studying my body.

I told her it was the protein shakes and that I was lifting more weight. This was true, but only part of the truth. I did not tell her that I was at the end of a cycle and now my body had stopped producing testosterone because I had supplied it with a ready and abundant source through a syringe. Clomid—I needed to wake up my testicles by taking a drug that infertile women consumed to stimulate their own body's hormone production. I was taking pills so that my balls would not shrivel up and so that I would not grow "bitch tits," as the weight lifters called them.

And now, in a final act of emasculation, Katherine was standing in front of me with our daughters, holding those pills beyond my reach. She was not going to give them back to me. I knew this. I would ransack the house later when they were gone. In a fit of rage, I would turn over the mattress of our bed and search through the drawers of the dresser. Maggie would follow me through the house, nipping at my ankles as if it were some game.

"How in the hell did you get these?"

You could buy anything on the internet, including a new body. I lurked in the bodybuilding forums. Late at night, there I'd be with a glass full of vodka and Valium on my tongue.

Katherine and I were using the same coping mechanisms, seeking an escape from our different worlds of pain, though hers came through prescribed medications from medical professionals and mine were self-prescribed. After a lifetime of pretending, I was better at hiding it, and as a man, more easily forgiven than a mother, for the same offenses. The pills were a way to silence the beast and the more it growled, the more I fed it, but I have to wonder if I had not become addicted to the pills, would I have so easily slid into the steroids? What I also did not notice then was that as my dependency on the tranquilizers grew, Katherine's judgment sharpened, and mine began to fall apart. We were a delicate balance. When one of the scales tipped down, the other nudged up. And as I spiraled down, that is when I started shopping for a new body, legs like this, arms like that, a superhero chest that stuck out like that one. I wanted a body like that; I did not *desire* the bodybuilders, I told myself, but if I did, I could find videos of that too, and after I watched them, I vowed it was the last time, never going to do that again. I prayed for strength, dredging up the words my mother had used in our prayers together to help rid me of this sin, another pill on my tongue, like the perverted body of Christ. Amen.

Once, I became hallucinatory from the combination of alcohol and tranquilizers while obsessively searching for images on the internet of home remodels late at night to avoid going to bed. This was before I became obsessed with reshaping my body. I found a room that I liked, but someone was haunting the picture on my computer monitor. He was turned to the side, trying to hide, but *see, right there, he moved!* I slowly turned my head from side to side, and his eyes followed me like one of those old portrait paintings. His body was flat against a column in the room, but his face was deformed, and his big, protruding dark eyes could not hide. They watched me, judging me.

"When and where did you inject yourself?" Katherine asked.

I hated her for asking these questions in front of the children. I felt as if she were drawing up the battle lines and amassing her troops.

"In the downstairs bathroom, when you were all sleeping," I said, surprised by my honesty.

There was a stunned silence as the vision played out.

"I can't stop shaking," Olivia said while staring at her pale, quivering hand as she held it out. For a moment, we all seemed transfixed by this. Her hand seemed to glow, her fingers so unmarred and tender. There was the light of youth pulsing through them, and here I was, her father turned monster, threatening to take that light away.

When Olivia was five or six years old, Katherine and I picked her up from preschool one day. As we were driving home in our minivan, Katherine smiled devilishly, turned to look back at Olivia in the middle seat, and asked her if she had a boyfriend at school. Olivia shyly said no, but that when she grew up, she was going to marry Daddy. Her innocence charmed me.

"Aren't we lucky to have such a strong daddy?" she had asked then.

Not much longer after that, I took Olivia to the neighborhood park. There was a long, polished silver slide that she was too scared to go down by herself, though she wanted to master it. I told her that I would go down the slide with her, but she was still wary.

"I won't let you go," I said.

After she considered it for a while, she told me she was ready. We slowly climbed up the steps together, and when we reached the top, I put her in between my legs and wrapped my arms around her tiny body and rested my chin on the top of her head, breathing in the scent of her warm, dark hair. We sat beneath the leafy green branches, surveying the other children running through the park from a bird's-eye view. The breeze turned leaves and lifted single glowing filaments of Olivia's hair into the sun.

"Are you ready?" I asked her.

"Don't let go, Daddy," she said, placing her hands on top of mine.

"Never," I said.

We pushed off, and immediately I realized something was wrong. We began to descend at a pace faster than I could control. Someone had waxed the slide. As the hard-packed soil below came toward us at the end of the slide, I realized that if I continued to hold on to her, I would not be able to control myself. When we hit the ground, my body would end up on top of her tiny body. I had to make a choice.

When I looked into the eyes of Olivia and Claire now, I felt something slipping away, my hands unwrapping from theirs. It drained from me and dissipated in the crack beneath the front door like the vanishing sunlight.

If this were a film playing out and the camera panned, you would see a family of four standing silently by the front door with no sense of whether they were coming or going. Pulling farther back, a set of upset kitchen chairs lying on their backs, and then drifting above the house, the gnarled branches of leafless trees hovering over the roof, where chattering squirrels pranced and mocked a barking dog. Just beyond this house were other similar homes where warm yellow lights began to illuminate windows and the headlights of cars cast yellow triangles in the dark driveways. Behind the doors of those houses, you might hear the muffled cries of excited children running toward the front door, holding out their hands and shouting, "Daddy's home!"

CHAPTER EIGHT

SINKING SHIP

If we were in a boat and it capsized, who would you save, our child or me?
Katherine first asked me this question early in our marriage, when
the children were merely hypothetical. Even back then, she was a
woman in love with the hard questions. In years to come, it would be
her willingness to ask me the hardest question of all that would finally
force me to stop lying and give her the hardest truth.

I replied, "Our child, of course."

"Wrong," she said.

"Then I would save you both."

"But you can't do that. You have to pick one."

I hated the question, the rules around it, and the thought of our
child sinking below the surface while I trod water, struggling to hold
on to Katherine and helplessly watching our child go.

After Olivia was born, Katherine sat propped up in our bed, surrounded by the wavy blue comforter with white pillows piled behind
her back. I handed her a bottle and began to iron my work clothes.
Katherine looked down at Olivia suckling the expressed breast milk.

"If we were in a boat and it capsized, who would you save, Olivia or me?" she asked again. This time, our child was flesh and blood.

I hesitated.

"You would save Olivia, of course," Katherine said.

But what if I was unable to hold on to anyone?

Would I save myself?

CHAPTER NINE

THE LOST GOLD MINE

Central City, Colorado, 1982/Franklin, Massachusetts, 2007

It's strange how two memories in your life, separated by decades, can touch, as if the years have curled into one another, forever locked in a fatal embrace, tethered together by a defining moment. I can't see one now without the other. I'm a beaten-down middle-aged man driving a minivan by the village green on my way to the Walmart in a cold, New England town. I'm young and full of promise, driving a white pickup truck up a steep Rocky Mountain road as the summer sun rises.

Just before I met Katherine, when I was nineteen years old, I lived with my aunt Sheila for the summer and worked as a tour guide at the Lost Gold Mine.

Every morning, we would rise earlier than the sun, jump in the pickup truck, and drive in silence from Denver toward Saddleback Mountain. There was only one crooked road that led up to Central City before gambling took hold there. At Highway 6, we'd switch back and watch the sun come up over the Rocky Mountains, filling the truck cab with a blast of yellow light too hard to ignore. The tips of the pine trees and high canyon walls would catch hold of the sunlight, and just like that, it would ricochet and splinter into a million points of light upon the ripples of Clear Creek, where it slowed down and spread out many times wider than it was deep. Unable to hold our silence in the midst of the morning's honesty, my college roommate, Mike, shifted the truck into a lower gear, looked out the window, and said, "I don't like the way men look at you here."

As we turned onto Main Street at the entrance of Black Hawk, the town still quiet in the hollow of the cool morning, I looked at Mike and asked, "What do you mean you don't like the way men look at me?" knowing full well what he meant.

"Like you were a piece of meat, all of Allen and Stan's friends," he replied, emphasizing the word *friends* that gave it an illicit weight.

"Oh, well, I think they're looking at you," I said, trying to shift the attention.

We were both working as tour guides at the Lost Gold Mine, a tourist trap set at the top of Eureka Street up high in Central City. The mine was owned by an unlikely gay couple, Allen and Stan, who were friends with my aunt Sheila. They agreed to hire us sight unseen based on Sheila's recommendation. "Bill's adorable," she told them, and within a month, Mike and I had driven cross-country, during summer break from our college in North Carolina to live with Sheila.

For five bucks a head, we would lead a group through a hundred-yard tunnel tucked away behind a metal door in the back of a gift shop. It was brimming with authentic Western memorabilia imported directly from China. The conclusion of the tour was a plea, "Thank you, ladies and gentlemen. I'd like to point out the tip bucket on your way out. I'm working my way through college, and that's my little gold mine!"

My ingratiating request usually guaranteed a modest tip, but Mike's halting, deadpan delivery would often net him a disgruntled reply, "Consider it lost."

Mike and I shared a room in my aunt's two-bedroom 1950s ranch in a tidy Denver suburb. I suppose the best way to describe Mike was beefy, with a head slightly too small for his body. Most of the time, we worked the same shifts, but occasionally he would wake up early, grumbling to himself, and slam the door shut, unhappy to be making the trip alone. On one of those days, Sheila skipped work and announced that the two of us would take a sightseeing day trip to Colorado Springs. She worked as a bartender at a golf course clubhouse, but she had bigger dreams and a bank account full of money to back it up from a sexual harassment lawsuit settlement. "My boss walked into the supply room with his pants down and told me to suck it. Look who's sucking it now," she said. She winked and exhaled a cigarette smoke ring.

Sheila was a tall woman with permed curly brown hair and big, round brown eyes framed with fake eyelashes. She had a sexy low voice and smoked long, skinny Virginia Slims cigarettes, held at the tips of her first and second fingers, like the 1940s film star Bette Davis. Blue jeans and T-shirts were the extent of her fashion choices. She could make anyone feel at ease, but could not do the same for herself.

I loved her intensely.

Before I left for Colorado that summer, my mother warned me about her sister. With all of our dead ancestors peering down from their oil portraits, my mother in her starched nursing whites sat erect in one of the wingback chairs and regarded me as if consulting a terminally ill patient. She gravely announced, "I want you to know that Sheila is"—she hesitated, then lowered her voice—"a lesbian." Her face winced as if she had bitten into a lemon. I imagined the police breaking down our door and arresting my mother on the spot for uttering that word, her sensible orthopedic shoes dragging and her hair a frightful mess as she was carried away sobbing and screaming, "I won't say that word again, I promise!"

A half smile crept onto my face.

"Don't let her change you," she commanded, and then asked, "Are you listening to me?"

"I'm sorry, Sheila is a what?"

I could not resist.

As we rode south in her white Mustang toward Colorado Springs, Sheila took a quick drag from her cigarette, hesitated, held it up and away from her face, and then glanced at me. "Have you ever had an experience with a boy?" She then blew smoke through her pursed lips to the side like a curling question mark.

"Sort of," I said, hesitating.

"And was it delightful?"

"It was confusing," I replied.

"You are who you are," she said. "I'm going to buy a bar. One of *those* bars, although you can't drink when you own one."

I knew what kind of bar she was talking about but had never entered one. In the 1980s, they were nondescript buildings with blacked-out windows on the edge of town and were given fancy names like the Exit, which is exactly where we ended up that evening. Sheila parked the car in the bar parking lot, turned to me, and said, "I'm going to introduce you as my son, because calling you my nephew implies something else." She looked me in the eyes, took my hand, and said, "Don't be nervous, honey."

But I was. Here in the middle of nowhere, I worried that someone might see me and label me.

When we walked into the bar, the contrast between light and dark was startling. As my pupils dilated, I felt the stare of hungry eyes zero in on me like lions focusing on a gazelle timidly approaching the watering hole. We sat down at the bar. The bartender wandered over, smiled at me, cocked his head, and asked how old I was.

"How old do I look?" I innocently asked.

"Old enough to go home with me tonight," he replied.

I made a mental note to say twenty-one the next time anybody asked.

He pushed two drinks toward us and said, "From your admirer," while glancing toward the end of the bar.

"Don!" Sheila shouted, throwing her hands over her head and jumping up from her barstool.

I watched Sheila run laughing toward the man she knew named Don. He looked to be in his early twenties. Sheila motioned for me. As I walked toward them, I could see that he had blue eyes. If there was a faster way to get the alcohol into my bloodstream, I could not find it and tipped the rim of the glass into my mouth, feeling the shock of the ice hit my teeth and a slight dribble run down my chin.

"Don, this is my son, Bill. What do you think of him?" Sheila asked, holding her hands out like a model presenting valuable merchandise on a TV game show.

"Cute," Don replied, and offered his hand. I quickly wiped the drink off my chin with my hand, brushed it against my shirt, and then shook his hand.

"The hell he's cute, he's gorgeous." Sheila winked at me as she put her arm around my shoulder.

Don turned to me and asked directly, "Why do gay men have lesbian friends?"

"I don't know," I replied, glancing at Sheila who was rolling her eyes.

"Someone has to mow the yard," he replied, slapping my shoulder.

I laughed, without really knowing why. Don would continue to tell me jokes in rapid-fire succession until Sheila eventually said half jokingly, "Don, enough. You're making him dizzy!" I don't know if it was the jokes, the attention from Don, or the vodka tonics, but I was intoxicated. Time lost its meaning. And it was like for the first time in my life I had stopped dragging the stone in me up a mountain. I froze in both the relief and danger of being seen. It was the beginning of the evening, and suddenly it was late night. The bar buzzed with activity and the deep bass beat of the music. Laughter bubbled over the hum of voices.

"You're good-looking, for a man," I heard a woman who had joined us shout over the din. I turned my head to look at Don.

"She's talking to you," he said, and then rubbed his knee against mine. *Boys don't touch each other like this.* I heard my mother's sharp voice.

"I have to go to the restroom," I said, and stood up, attempting to find my balance, altered by alcohol and honeyed attention. That was when I felt Don's hand holding mine, his hand dragging time to a halt.

We opened the bar door and stepped out into the night. There was a truth in the deafening silence that washed over a person at two in the morning under the starry Colorado sky. The beat and hum still pulsing through our veins, we walked to his car, Don's arm around my shoulder, mine around his waist, and then his lips on mine. The air molecules became charged, and I felt as if I were at the basin of Phantom Canyon as a cold wind blows in, and a June snowfall glitters on the red canyon walls, and then at the top of Royal Gorge on a suspension bridge, staring dizzily a thousand feet below at the Arkansas River cutting through time. When time started up again, our foreheads were touching, and my arms rested on his shoulders as we breathed deeply, the distant beat of the bar behind us and the moonlit sky stretched over the silent Rockies. And then I heard the hum become Sheila's words, like the recognition of an alarm in a dream. She was walking quickly toward us. "He's not sure yet if he's gay, Don!"

But there was no more confusion. I knew. All it took to confirm was a single kiss.

On the last night before I returned home to North Carolina, I woke up late at night, the remnants of a lurid dream lingering in the air, the pickup truck climbing a red mountain road so steep that it tipped back upon itself before tumbling into the dark abyss. As the dream vaporized, I walked into the kitchen, my heart still racing in my chest. Sheila was sitting at the kitchen table in the dark, an open bottle of vodka in front of her as she clutched a cigarette that mysteriously clung to an entire length of ash. Her gaze was fixed somewhere in the middle distance. Not wanting to startle her, I turned around and headed back to my bedroom. "Uncle Dan was like us," she said without looking at me.

"What?" I asked.

"My uncle Dan moved to California where he could be himself. I told your grandmother that I was like Uncle Dan," she said.

I walked into the kitchen and sat down across from her, the moonlight filtered through the blinds painting her face with horizontal shadows.

"'Sheila Marie, when are you going to find a good man and settle down?'" she said without blinking, mimicking my grandmother's voice. She returned from her memories, and her face gathered recognition of the present. She placed the burned-out cigarette in the ashtray, cupped my face with her hands, and said, "In a previous life, I was pregnant with you, but the ocean swept us away." She believed in reincarnation and that the people who surrounded us now were the same ones who surrounded us in our past lives, but in each go-around, we assumed different roles. On some ancient shore, Sheila lost me before she could give birth, and in this one, she was terrified of losing me again. Looking back, I can see that Sheila was struggling, and so was I. We needed to cling to each other, so that if the world erased us, we might get another chance. She saw me for what I was, something unfinished.

She pushed herself up from the table, walked to the window, lifted a single slat to peer through it, and said, "God, I hate going to bed at night. I always feel so alone." She pulled out another cigarette from the pack, lit it, inhaled a quick sip of smoke, and then released it while saying, "Now you're leaving me too."

In the morning, I got dressed in the clothes Sheila had bought for me, packed my bags, and tiptoed into her room. She was still sleeping, or she was passed out. When I nudged her, she mumbled some unintelligible words but did not budge. I tapped her on the shoulder repeatedly, each time pushing her more firmly. Finally, I said, "If I don't go now, I'll miss my flight." She sat up with a start, like a corpse popping up after rigor mortis sets in.

When I walked off the plane in North Carolina, my mother cocked her head. She hugged me and then placed her hands on my shoulders, holding me at arm's length. "You look different, more filled out," she said. She looked down at my shoes and then slowly moved her gaze up, like she was analyzing an outfit on a mannequin, her lips pursed and their corners turned down.

"New clothes," she said.

But it was what she did not say, her Southern way of saying something in place of saying what she thought, *Those are homosexual clothes.*

I slept in my childhood bed that night, my feet hanging over the edge, and stared up at the ceiling, thinking about the stars in Colorado. I touched my body the way Don had.

In the morning, my mother was sitting alone at the kitchen table, her back to me, and I looked at the nape of her neck. One of my earliest memories was sitting in the back seat of the station wagon, my father driving and my mother sitting next to him. She smoothed the hair of her new pixie cut with a white-gloved hand as we crossed the bridge over Buffalo Creek. Our new house on Latham Road appeared above the dashboard, and I kept watching her fuss with the hair on the back of her neck, wondering what the expression on her face might reveal.

"Mom, Sheila and all of her friends are just like me. The love they have for each other is the same," I said. She didn't turn around, just reached up and patted her hair. I sat down at the table and glanced at her face. It was the same grimace I saw when she uttered the words *lesbian* and *homosexual.*

"I knew it the minute you walked off that plane," she said. "Sheila dressed you up in those *clothes.*" She looked down her nose at my shirt, and then she continued in a high-pitched, singsong mocking tone, attempting to imitate my aunt Sheila, but sounding nothing like her. "It's OK, Bill, just go ahead and be *gay!*"

She had never accused me of being gay, preferring other scare tactics like *effeminate.*

Don't put your hands on your hips like that. It looks effeminate.
Those flip-flops make you look effeminate.

I didn't say I was gay. I couldn't be that strong. I was testing the waters, and now I was drowning, and she knew it.

"Do you want to be a woman too?" she asked.

I winced and began to retreat. "Mom, I'm not gay. I think, maybe, I'm confused."

She cast aside her Southern euphemisms and went straight for the jugular. "It's disgusting is what it is. There is nothing natural about it. Let's pray."

The torture would continue for months. It was calculated and surgical, like the removal and irradiation of a gay tumor. Conversation therapy doesn't always occur at a facility. Often, it takes place at the dining-room table.

I couldn't be who I was without Sheila, and the ocean of space between us swept us apart. I returned to the closet, and Sheila returned to the bottle. Neither of us was strong enough to maintain the path we cut together along Clear Creek.

Sheila died in the middle of the night from a sudden brain aneurysm when I was in my thirties. She was living in a trailer park in Florida alone, except for the two dozen or so exotic birds that she was breeding as her next big moneymaking scheme.

I did not cry when she died, less because she would not have wanted it, and more because I felt like I did not deserve to. It was another thing that Sheila and I had in common, how our secret kept us far away from loving ourselves.

———

Twenty-five years later, Katherine sits next to me, in the passenger seat of our minivan, and fidgets with her hair. The families who settled this small New England town built stone walls at the edge of their existence. Hundreds of years later, the boulders crisscross fields and tumble into the woods, staking long-forgotten boundaries. I drive our minivan in

silence past the pumpkin-colored village colonial, past Oak Hill cemetery bordered by a crumbling fieldstone wall, and pull into the Walmart
parking lot. "Just park the car now, Bill. I have to ask you this, or I'm
afraid I never will." When I turn off the ignition, Katherine's question
pierces the heavy silence.

"Are you gay?"

The air in the van is too heavy. Through the vehicle's window, I
see a family of four open its car doors. They take each other's hands,
shuffling across the pavement. They disappear into the dark and then
reappear beneath a yellow circle illuminated by a parking lot light. Their
questions, I imagine, are easier to ask and to answer. *Do we need more
paper towels? How much milk is left? Will we make it back in time to watch*
American Idol?

She waits. Doesn't she already know the answer?

It has always been there, but I kept it cordoned off for all these
years. I built my life on *No*. That life is crumbling now, and neither of
us can keep pretending I can support it.

"I don't want to be," I reply. An answer that is truthful, but one I
hope won't bring all of the walls down.

For a moment, the world stops turning, and we stop breathing. Our
whole lives suspended in the silence that a shattered secret can make. I
exhale as she inhales.

"Oh God," she says, and looks through the car window. Her body
slumps under the weight of the words, filling the van like water.

"Oh God, oh God, oh God, I told myself to be ready for the
answer," she says. "But how could I prepare for this?"

But I know, the hardest things to prepare for are sometimes the
things that we already know. Despite the rubble I've made, a lightness
tugs at me, pulling me up as Katherine sinks below the surface.

For the first time, I see that nineteen-year-old traveling that one
crooked road along Clear Creek.

And he sees me.

PART II

Nun will die Sonn' so hell aufgeh'n

als sei kein Unglück die Nacht gescheh'n.

"Now the sun wants to rise as brightly

as if nothing terrible had happened during the night."

—Friedrich Rückert

CHAPTER TEN

KINDERTOTENLIEDER

Sound travels in waves.

In college, I was seduced to the tune of Mahler's *Songs on the Death of Children*. Before I met Ryan, I heard him. He was the embodiment of the piano music he produced, intense, angular, and beguiling with doleful brown eyes. I was a freshman, nerdy, and confused. He pulled the record from its sleeve, *Kindertotenlieder*, three German words crashed together to form a single melancholy one—children, death, songs. He placed it on the turntable and sat down next to me on the sofa. "Listen to this beautiful anguish."

The music began, a single oboe, simple, slow, stripped down, and then a woman singing counterpart. It was a beautiful, mournful anguish. Ryan ran his hand up the inside of my leg and said, "Mahler's wife begged him not to compose this. Do you know why?"

"No."

He ran his fingers through my hair.

"She thought that if he did, their child would die."

He brushed his fingers across my neck.

"Do you know what happened?"

"Nope."

He unbuttoned the top three buttons of my shirt.

"He composed it, and their daughter died."

A glockenspiel from the record sounded the death knell.

A sound wave is a disturbance that moves energy from one place to another.

The wailing I heard coming from behind Katherine's and my closed bedroom door reminded me of the anguish and devastation I first heard on that scratchy record player in Ryan's apartment decades ago. It was the sound of a woman whose entire life had crashed around her, and she was trying to scream her way out of the storm. Her song had begun with just a single, stripped-down note. *Are you gay?*

"Katherine, open the door, please."

Her sobs became louder.

"You'll wake the girls. Please, just open the door."

In sound, the disturbance is a vibrating object.

That evening with Ryan had begun innocently enough with a haircut. He offered to cut my hair at his off-campus apartment. He prepared a candlelit dinner, and afterward, we were smoking pot and listening to a woman wail about the death of her children while Ryan attempted to undress me. It was tragically romantic. And it was so wrong.

"Wait. This doesn't feel right," I said when his hand went for my belt.

"OK," he said, and pushed his other hand down my shirt from the other direction.

"Yeah, that doesn't feel right either," I replied.

What I wanted to say was, *I don't know what to do. I don't know how any of this works. Do men kiss?* I felt like a girl. I felt helpless. There was nothing or no one to guide me. But I couldn't say anything, because it was wrong, and I felt a sickening dread, a maelstrom of guilt and sin swirling around me.

When sound originates, it displaces a molecule.

We did not go into the store that night, Katherine and I. She said, "I just want to go home," and stared through the window. I could feel it, that sense of loss I had created in her. She was looking around at the foreign landscape, at the crumbling stone walls and the old village colonials, someone else's history, other people's lives. *I feel like we're living on the moon.* I knew what she was thinking. After more than twenty years of marriage, we finally knew each other's thoughts. *Where is home?*

This molecule, in turn, pushes the molecules surrounding it in three dimensions.

"I just need to let my roommate know I'm going to be late," I said, and rose from the sofa. Ryan turned the volume down and walked into his bedroom while I listened to the phone ring and ring. On the other end was a pay phone in the residence building, and I knew at this time of night, it would take at least thirty rings before a student would begrudgingly walk down the hall to answer it.

Ryan reappeared, wearing a short tan robe, the pale white skin of his chest and his long legs exposed. He whispered in my ear, "Any luck?"

Someone picked up the receiver, and I listened to it clang against the wall. I heard footsteps squeaking, the sound diminishing as they disappeared down the hall. Ryan walked over to the record player, turned it off, picked up the vinyl record, and nimbly placed it back in the sleeve.

"My legs are so tight," he said as he bent over to touch his toes, his robe rising. I looked up at the ceiling. He walked over to me and glanced at my crotch. I was hard, and I was tugging at the tail of my shirt to cover it.

"I like you, Bill," Ryan said.

"I like you too," I replied.

"No, I mean I *really* like you." His face was inches from mine. "You're different."

"Ryan, I can't. People will talk about us."

"Well," he said, walking to his bedroom door, "let's give them something to talk about."

The disturbed molecules create a ripple.

When we pulled into the driveway, Katherine raised her head and looked up at the house, at the moonlight illuminating dewy cobwebs in the trees, and then I heard a swift intake of breath and then a retching sound. Her hands fumbled for the door handle. "Are you OK?" I asked. The door flew open. She bent over and heaved.

The ripple causes the eardrum to vibrate.

I stood there listening to the silence on the phone and then looked around the room. I couldn't do this. I grabbed my shoes, put them on, and ran out the door. "What happened last night? I waited for you to join me in the bedroom," Ryan asked the next day, but I ignored him. I broiled in anguish. I told my classmates that he had made a pass at me, that he was a predator. They shut him out, protecting me, and told him, "This seat's taken," when he tried to sit at our table in the cafeteria. He became a pariah.

When the ripple reaches our ears, the body converts it to electrical energy.

Katherine unlocked the bedroom door and stared at me, eyes red, beseeching, her hair wild. She turned around, walked away from me, and then slumped onto the bed. I walked over to my side and undressed. We lay awake in the position that we always took, her hand resting on the pulsing vein of my neck. The girls slept in their beds, unaware of the change. The moon circled the earth, and spiders threaded gossamer strings.

The electrical energy travels through our nervous system where it is forever stored in our neurons.

After Ryan left college the following year, when he was just an echo, I met Marie, a transfer college student from Georgia. We had sex in my dorm room. *I don't know what to do,* I thought, and she guided me. She returned home for the holidays for an abortion, my first child gone.

Sound alters us. It is physically impossible to remain the same after listening to a few strains of Mahler's Kindertotenlieder, *or to your wife's songs on the death of her marriage.*

CHAPTER ELEVEN
NEVER CAN SAY GOODBYE

Our lives dangled from a tether pinned to a date on the calendar: May 27. The girls would have the weekend to recover, we reasoned. The moment Katherine and I picked the day, it felt like a betrayal. We knew something that the girls did not, something that would forever change their lives, but we played the roles of husband and wife, father and mother as if nothing had changed. On that day, we would execute the plan surgically. Get it out there quickly, in one sentence or two. Any words after that would pile up at their feet.

In the weeks leading up to that day, the last traces of winter melted, leaving behind salt and sand on the shoulders of the roads and the grass glowing green. Yellow, red, and blue kayaks skimmed the surface of Beaver Pond like water bugs, and the girls ditched their heavy winter coats. The world, it seemed, was lightening up, despite our best efforts to darken it.

One night, Claire screamed out, "Dad, come up here quick!" I ran up the stairs to her room. She was sitting on her bed, pointing at some dark little spots in the corner of the bedroom ceiling.

"Get them, Daddy!"

Fourteen years old and she was still terrified of spiders. I grabbed some toilet paper from the bathroom and squashed them, one by one.

"See, they're gone," I said.

"But, they'll come back," she said warily, pushing her eyeglasses up on her nose.

Who would kill the spiders when I was gone?

Katherine and I bonded like hostages might. We became close to the secret that had become our captor. It held us together in the grip of its silence.

For a while, the relief of telling someone the truth was like loosening a relief valve, and I felt a wave of love for Katherine after having released it, and she responded to this.

Strangely, it felt like we were the only two people in the world who could console each other, as if we were the only ones who had ever been through this crisis. For weeks, we stayed up late, talking to each other about how our marriage could continue, how we could work things out, because neither one of us ever truly imagined another reality could exist. After all these years of taking care of Katherine and the girls, how could I stop? I had always worried that she would hurt herself if I left, but was I hurting her more by staying? I'd come to realize that little by little, over the years, I'd stolen her joy. It was not in one fell swoop, like the husband who cheated on his wife with another woman. That was one single, deep cut that could be stitched up, and though the scar might remain, the flesh healed and returned to life. She was in love with a ghost, and every time she looked at me, she could sense but not name her own haunting.

Katherine retreated into the closet with me, my secret becoming hers. She was the first person to ever know me completely. She caught a glimpse of the spiders lurking inside of my closet, at the web of insanity I had been weaving, building over decades, and it terrified her. And as her fear turned to anger, she began to divulge my secret to a close circle of relatives. When it became clear that there was no fix, it all began to unravel.

"All of these years, I've stood by your side, and now I'm going to be cast aside? I have no skills," she'd say. "What are we going to do?"

Life up until I came out was certain. I would hold on to my secret and live out my days taking care of her and the girls. It was a decision I had made in my early twenties, and I couldn't have imagined it any other way, and I was sure Katherine could not have either.

I kept waiting for Katherine to ask, "Is everything OK?" In times of great stress, she would ask this question. I never knew what prompted the question. It just came on, and it was like someone who had to wash their hands twenty-five times or turn a light switch on and off eighteen times to make certain their family would not perish in some fiery crash.

We'd lie in bed, staring at the ceiling, and I'd wait, but the question never came, because finally she knew the answer, the one I had been keeping from her for decades, the insidious whispering overheard in the static on the TV, the wispy ghost standing in the kitchen corner, vanished. Everything was not OK. But now I needed to know, and so I said, "Perhaps we can stay together." It was a way of holding on to something when our future seemed so uncertain.

"If we split up, there is no way we can afford to live up here, Bill," she said one night. "I've hired an attorney."

"Maybe we could stay together, and I could, you know, date?" I asked.

"You've got to be fucking kidding me," she replied. "Don't even give me an image of you with another man, Bill. I can't handle that."

While our life was in limbo, we made a final trip together to our marriage counselor, Arlyn. Driving down Pond Street to her office, trees sprouting chartreuse leaves and yellow daffodils nodding in the warm spring breeze, Katherine, without turning to look at me, said, "You know that Jonathan is Olivia's boyfriend."

"What?" I asked.

"He's always at our house. I'm going to kill him if he doesn't keep his hands off her," she said.

"But what about Jeff?" I asked.

"Oh, Bill, how can you be so blind?" Katherine asked, and then added, "Jeff and Jonathan are friends. Jeff wanted to become Olivia's boyfriend, but Jonathan beat him to it."

I smiled, thinking of boys fighting over Olivia. When Jeff first appeared at our house, I was happy that Olivia had made a new friend, although concerned that he always wore all-black clothing and his long, brown hair was pulled back in a ponytail. But he was kind, good-looking, and polite.

"All of my friends' parents love me," he had said, and Olivia rolled her eyes.

"Oh, Jeff," she replied, and playfully swatted his shoulder.

It was the first time I had seen her flirt. Soon after, every time Jeff was at our house, Jonathan, short and thin with dark wavy hair and a thin mustache, a *dirt stache*, Claire called it, was always at his side. Claire had multiple boyfriends in her short span, but always broke off the relationship and would dismiss it with a wave of her hand, saying, "I don't have time for that. Boys are stupid." But Jonathan was Olivia's first boyfriend.

"Good for her," I whispered.

"Haven't you noticed how she's grown her hair longer and started wearing clothes like the other girls?" Katherine asked. I had been so wrapped up in our own turmoil that this escaped me.

"But if I walk through the living room and see those two sitting so close again, I swear. Maybe you should have a talk with those boys and set them *straight*," Katherine said.

I glanced at her, and a faint smile passed across her face.

"You know what I mean. No one is going to have sex under my roof," Katherine added. This time, I ignored the unintended pun and did not turn to look at her.

When we reached Arlyn's office, we sat outside in the carpeted reception area in silence, cut off from the discussion on the other side of the door by a shroud of static emanating from the white-noise machine sitting on the floor. We watched a couple, hand in hand, exit and turn down the hall. When Arlyn appeared, I took a quick breath, and my heart began to race. She displayed a thin smile and nodded. She was short, middle-aged with a brown bob and a silk scarf draped about her neck, and her glasses rested on the end of her nose, like a schoolteacher. When she looked up, I felt as if I was being inspected, judged. After Katherine discovered my steroid use, she had a private appointment with Arlyn, from which point she began to question who I was. Arlyn had asked Katherine then, "Don't you think that a part of you always knew?"

We walked into her office and took our assigned chairs. With nothing left to prove, we did not hold hands. I looked around her office, at the crystal dangling from a length of fishing wire in the window, breaking the light into a tiny rainbow of colors, the southwestern painting of the adobe house among the distant red hills, the black, orange, and white Native American *Storyteller* clay figurine, with small children clamoring about her arms and legs.

"So, a lot has happened," Arlyn said, starting the conversation.

"Pretty much the same old, same old," I replied, attempting to lighten the mood, but no one laughed. Laughter may be the best medicine, but it stings when the wound is still so fresh.

"You know, you can have a *good* divorce," Arlyn said, getting to the meat of it.

"That's what we want," Katherine replied.

Was there such a thing as a good divorce? I wondered. And how did you build that on top of the burned-out cinders of lies, drug abuse, and repressed sexuality? Had I catfished my wife? I chose an identity to become—a straight man—but I did not possess the anonymity of the internet. I could not simply vanish, though once I came out, the husband Katherine thought she knew most certainly did.

"I need my support system back in Virginia, and we can't afford two homes up here. You can come to Virginia anytime to see the girls," Katherine said.

"You expect me to live without the girls?" I asked.

"Bill, you did it for practically a year," Katherine said, referring to my time in Marlboro.

"But, the girls," I replied, holding my hands up.

"How do you expect the girls ever to trust another man?" Katherine said. "After all these lies you have told. And God damn you, Bill, how do you expect me ever to recover?"

"You'll build up airline points," Arlyn smiled, attempting to put a positive spin on it, trying to salvage the conversation. They had already worked out the logistics. I was racked with guilt and shame. I felt powerless to argue. The girls loved Virginia, and from that safe distance, they could be far away from any ridicule my gayness might bring them.

"Bill." Arlyn took a deep breath and then said, "Can you tell me what you were thinking when you took the steroids?"

I shrank into my chair. I turned to look at Katherine, and she held on to my stare.

"The only way we're going to get through this is to be honest with one another," Katherine said.

I searched my mind to come up with an answer, but the complexity of it left me speechless.

"Are you aware of the damage they can do? Did you know that it could have killed you?" Arlyn prodded.

I assumed she had to ask these questions to rule out a suicidal patient. I thought of responding that I just wanted to look good, but I knew this wasn't what she was searching for, and only a fraction of the answer. The truth was like the light split by the crystal in the window.

Turn it in multiple directions, and another splinter of color would appear.

"I didn't care what happened to me," I finally replied.

Arlyn raised an eyebrow and turned to look at Katherine.

"You didn't care if the girls were left without a father?" Katherine asked.

"Of course I cared about that! I didn't want to die. I just didn't want to be *me* anymore." My voice broke at the end of the sentence.

Arlyn leaned over to reach across her desk and pulled a tissue from a box. She dabbed at her nose and adjusted the glasses above her red-rimmed eyes.

"I'm so sorry," she said. I didn't know if she was apologizing for causing my outburst, for having a runny nose, or for my wanting to disappear.

"I know that you want to tell the girls, but this is beyond my expertise, and I've been searching for a therapist who specializes in this, Bill," Arlyn said. "I've made a few calls and found some who specialize in coming out. They're all located in Boston. Katherine will continue to meet with me." We were splitting things down the middle.

She picked up a piece of paper on her desk, looked at it, and then handed it to me. There were several names, telephone numbers, and email addresses listed. The first name was *David*.

"I just want to ask you something." Katherine turned to look at me and narrowed her eyes. "Are you attracted to Enzo?"

I considered her question. Enzo was attractive.

"Yes," I replied.

Katherine shook her head and spit out, "I knew it."

"I just want to be honest now, about everything," I said. "But nothing ever happened between us. He's straight and—"

Arlyn leaned forward in her chair and held up her hand. "Bill, it's not necessary to divulge everything. Give Katherine time to work through these things first."

There was no road map. I did not know what to say or do. For all of my life, I had kept a guard around what I said. God, it had been so tiring translating in my head before saying anything out loud.

We left Arlyn's office and stopped at a McDonald's. We had told the girls this was our date night so that they would not grow suspicious. We ordered dinner at the drive-through, and Katherine pointed to a few cars parked at the side of the parking lot.

"Park over there; this is losers' row," she said.

I pulled the car into a spot and looked to my left. A single older man sat in the driver's seat in the car parked next to us, eating a hamburger. When I was a child, my father would pick us up every Wednesday night as a part of the custody agreement and take my brothers and me out to dinner. In the beginning, he took us to fancy restaurants and spent time with us, discussing our lives. As the years passed, the dinners simply became a check mark on a to-do list. He would rush us to McDonald's and, cigarette perched in the corner of his mouth, ask if we were finished. We'd leave, still chewing our cheeseburgers.

"Son, this is your father," he would say on the telephone when I was an adult.

He called each of us Son; it was easier than remembering our names. On the rare occasion when he tried to call me by my name, he'd say, "Alex—Chris—Damian—I mean Bill," snap his fingers, and blink his eyes, attempting to recall my name. Put a beat behind it, and it was a name-calling scat routine.

"I was just calling to see if you were still alive," he'd say.

Telephone conversations with him were as awkward as our relationship. He never would say goodbye. One minute, we would be talking, and the next, he would be gone, no goodbye, just a dial tone.

I looked ahead at the Walmart parking lot and then turned to look at Katherine. "Do you ever for a moment wish that you never asked me?"

"Yes," she replied without blinking, staring straight ahead.

"I'm sorry, sweetie," I said.

My father called every woman "sweetie," the wives, the girlfriends, the waitresses, the woman with the too-blonde hair, husky cigarette voice, and fire-red nail polish. He did not want to call a girlfriend or wife by some other woman's name. It was the same term of endearment that I used for Katherine and the girls.

When my father lay in bed dying, I placed my hand on his forehead, and my brothers sat at the foot of his bed, as we counted the seconds between his final breaths, and then, he was gone, like his phone conversations. Afterward, we sorted his belongings and found a list of hundreds of women's names. They were organized into categories: these women while he was married to wife number one, those women after wife number two, these women during the tenure of wife number three, and so on. It was a list of all of the women he had been intimate with. When he left my mother, I made a vow to stay married and never be like my father.

When Katherine and I were dating, we attended a party in Summerfield, on a farm in the country at the end of a long dirt road. Katherine sat on a wooden swing beneath an old oak tree while a cluster of young men stood around her, talking and laughing. She looked beautiful that night, her eyes flashing and her hair billowing as the group of boys playfully pushed her swing higher and higher, until she was on the edge of exhilaration and fear, of laughter and screams, her face glowing from the fireflies tangled in her hair. It was the first time I thought I could marry this girl. On the night before our wedding, Katherine and I walked through the parking lot of the Sedgefield Country Club to the rehearsal dinner. Her hair was swept up in a French twist, and she wore a purple silk dress with large printed red roses and a single strand of pearls around her neck. I thought, *This is when you feel it. This is when you are supposed to experience something uncontrollable.* But I didn't feel it. *It will come; just give it time.*

A few years after we bought our first home in Greensboro, North Carolina, I lit up the brick patio in the backyard with candles and placed a stereo speaker in an open window. It was a summer evening, and Nat King Cole's velvety voice drifted through the oak trees. I poured Katherine a glass of wine and handed it to her. The sunset kissed her face, and a warm breeze caressed her hair. Fireflies began to light up the woods behind the house as I rubbed her shoulders and looked out at the freshly mown lawn. I envisioned our children, before they existed, laughing and running through the backyard. I wanted that uncontrollable feeling to take me over. I ached because I wanted it so much, and I prayed to God to give it to me. I loved her spirit, but she needed me to love her in body and soul.

"Where did you get the money for the steroids?" Katherine asked, and then added, "I checked all of the accounts and didn't see anything missing."

I thought about my trips to Stop & Shop, standing in line, waiting to get a money order, and then mailing it. How stupid.

"From the money Dad left me in his retirement account," I replied.

"That money is ours!" she said. "And you'll pay me back every penny."

Katherine and I visited the cemetery a year after my father died, but we could not find his gravesite. I knew where he was buried, but there was no marker. I wanted to say goodbye, one last time, but instead, I ended up walking in circles, sobbing. My brother never ordered a tombstone. Even in death, my father never could say goodbye.

All of this time, I thought my father was just rude for not saying goodbye, but sitting there, thinking of that date looming on the calendar and all of the countless awkward conversations I would have with my daughters by telephone, missing the daily talks about boyfriends, what top to wear, how their hair looked, it became clear. If you never said goodbye, you could ignore that you were never there. They would have to learn how to kill the spiders themselves.

On May 27, my father's birthday, I would tell the girls who their father was, watch all of the words pile up at their feet, knowing the only one they would hear would be goodbye.

CHAPTER TWELVE

NOW YOU KNOW

The girls complained when we told them we were having a family meeting. It was not a part of our daily life, and it surprised me that they found it more of an annoyance and less of a concern.

"Can't you just go ahead and tell us now?" Claire said with one hand on her hip, wanting to spend the day with her friends.

But we stuck to the appointed hour. The clock crept forward as if someone had filled the gears with molasses. Like a stage actor, I rehearsed my lines over and over in my head. When I walked into the family room, Katherine was sitting on the sofa and looked nervously up at me; Claire sat next to her on the left and Olivia in front of her on the floor. I found my mark, took my position in the chair in front of them, and leaned forward, clearing my throat, forearms resting on my knees.

"So, girls, your mother and I wanted to talk to you." My throat felt constricted, and I took a deep breath. I looked at their faces. I wanted to remember them as they were now before they changed. Claire smoothed her hair absentmindedly with her left hand. Olivia picked at the end of a string on her hoodie jacket. Katherine glanced at the girls. They had already watched me stumble when the steroids were discovered, but somehow that seemed like a distant memory, and if they held on to any contempt, it did not appear in their eyes now.

A week before, I had my first appointment with David, the therapist our marriage counselor had recommended to me. When he sauntered into the lobby, I thought he was too handsome. He wore dark designer jeans and a light blue fitted polo shirt. I wondered how many of his patients fell in love with him.

David had advised me to say it as clearly and simply as possible and not to hit them with too many details, as nothing else would sink in. The questions would come later. When I told him I had no one I could talk to, other than him, he gave me the email address of a previous client named Hans. "He is a kind, sensitive, and courageous man, who is a father and was married," he told me, and then added, "He has made it to a more hopeful place." Was that as much as I could wish for, a "more hopeful place"?

I emailed Hans and received a long and thoughtful response almost immediately, with six or seven fat paragraphs that I jumped into. It was like a pool of words teeming with reassurance and would be the first email of hundreds, perhaps a thousand over the next year. In that first email, he detailed his journey, and how he came out to his children.

> I walked the mile that you are walking right now . . .
> It is not easy . . . but one thing I came to realize that
> there is never a "good time" to tell your wife or
> kids you are a gay father . . . At one time, I thought
> I had to choose the perfect time, but then I realized
> that would never come . . . You take the moment as
> you have planned it.

At work, Enzo had noticed a change in me, a furrow that rippled along my forehead and heavy sighs that escaped like steam throughout the day. Finally, he said, "There's something troubling you. Come on,

Billy, now what is it?" I told him then that Katherine and I were having difficulties and that we would be splitting up, but I did not tell him the reason. I shared with him that we would be discussing this with the girls over the weekend. His concern was genuine. "Ah, Billy, is there nothing you can do to work things out?" *Sure, give me a pill that will make me straight,* I thought, but I did not say it aloud. He sent a text message on Friday evening, **Good luck this weekend, Billy. I'll be thinking about you.** That simple sentiment pierced my heart.

How do you tell someone that he was one of the reasons you are making the biggest changes in your life, especially when he was completely unaware? In many ways, I wished that I had never met Enzo, or that he had been less kind. Intellectually, I knew that it was not him, but the promise of someone like him that worked like a wedge, splitting me in two. The division was complete, and I could never go back to who I was before.

"He is just a safe object," David had said to me when I told him about Enzo. "You were interested in him because deep down you knew he could never reciprocate. When you come out and begin meeting men who are truly available, that will fade away."

"What if we had never met?" I asked David.

"He was only a single factor. There was so much pressure building up, the cork had to pop, and now that it has, you can't put it back in."

Katherine and I felt that the girls would begin to notice the change in us as well. To continue to lie to them would only make it more difficult to accept when we finally did come out with the truth. And so now, I was taking that moment, however imperfect the timing.

"Girls, there is something I have been dealing with for a long time. Something I have been dealing with since I was a child." I paused and then continued. "And that thing is that I am a gay man." I waited for a response.

I scanned their faces. I knew that they held no prejudices. As parents, we taught them that everyone was equal, but I was their father, and the lie I had told had been the only story they had ever known. There was a stunned silence, and then Olivia looked as if she had put two and two together.

"Oh, so now it makes sense," she mumbled.

What made sense? Did she think that my use of steroids was typical for gay men, or did she sense something about me that was unlike the other fathers? It was not the reaction that I was prepared for.

A scene flashed through my mind from several weeks before. I was driving as Olivia, Jonathan, and Jeff struck up a conversation in the back seat. Jeff was taking part in the Day of Silence, to support his gay friends in high school. I listened intently as Jeff told them that one day every year, students elected not to speak to support those who could not speak about being gay.

"I'm proud of you, Jeff," I said from the driver's seat. Did Olivia pick up on this? Or did Jeff specifically do this because part of him knew I was struggling? Did he attempt to give me the words that I could not speak?

Or was she thinking of the day I took the girls to see a movie, and we sat behind two teenage boys? Before the movie started, we were listening to the chatter, when one of the boys turned to his friend and said, "You're so gay." Something inside of me erupted as I tapped the boy on his shoulder, my heart pounding, I chastised him for using that phrase. It was an anger born from a seed planted long ago. Before I admitted to myself that I was gay, I could listen and indeed make jokes about someone being gay, but now discrimination and prejudice hit me with an intensity that was surprising. Even when Enzo made jokes, benign as they were, I would not participate and began to harbor resentment toward him. You've gone from a majority to a minority, Hans had said in his email, and the next line resonated. You can't pass anymore.

"I don't understand," Claire said.

Katherine put her arm around Claire's shoulder, turned to her, and said, "Your dad is gay, sweetie," as if saying it a second time would make it more clear.

"But why did you marry Mom?" she asked.

"Because I loved her and because I wanted to have a family. I'm still the same person that I was yesterday; the only difference is that now you know," I said, trying to soften the blow.

"So, are you and Mom getting divorced?" Claire asked, and Olivia, who had accepted the news with nonchalance, now looked concerned.

"We're still discussing things." Katherine spoke up while looking at me. We had talked about how this might play out. If the girls asked questions, we would not shy away from the answers. "But yes, probably," Katherine added.

Claire immediately began to cry and curled up into a ball. Katherine wrapped her arms around her. I wanted to soothe her in some way, but the words were failing me. This part of the discussion was unscripted. I looked at Olivia, and her face had become cold as she narrowed her eyes.

"If you leave, how are we going to afford this house?" she asked.

"Sweetie, we might move back to Virginia," Katherine replied.

I watched Olivia's face turn pale. She closed her eyes and leaned her head back, and a weariness settled in like gravity as the reality that the truth imposed descended upon her.

"I can't move again. I can't," she said, and tears began to roll down her face. "I just made friends. You gave me that stupid Daruma doll, and it worked. I wished for a boyfriend," she sobbed.

This news sucked the wind from my lungs. All of this time, I thought her wish was to move back to Virginia, but now I had taken away everything that she had hoped for. The room became large, and I shrank into the chair. It was like a scene from a horror movie, where the hall with many doors telescopes, and the feet of the parent desperately running toward his child's room becomes mired in carpet the consistency of quicksand. I had taken the yoke that had been resting on my shoulders and placed it squarely on my children's shoulders.

Olivia stood up and said, "I have to get out of here." Claire opened her eyes and said, "I'm coming with you." They both ran from the room, and I sat staring at Katherine, both of us frozen in the aftermath.

"Should we go after them?" I asked.

"I think they need some time alone," Katherine said, holding her hand to her forehead.

We listened as the front door opened, and then it slammed shut behind them.

After Katherine's grandfather died, we sat in the living room of his home while family members and friends spoke in hushed whispers and young children were scattered about the floor, like throw rugs. Katherine looked out the window then and asked, "What are we supposed to do now? Go back to our lives, like nothing happened?" I regarded the corpse of our marriage and, not knowing what to do, grabbed on to the security of one of the mindless chores of survivors. I walked into the garage, opened the door, and pulled the lawn mower into the yard and pushed it back and forth, attempting to lose myself in the neatly cut rows of grass.

Katherine walked out of the front door, keys in hand, and I turned the lawn mower off.

"What the fuck are you doing?" she asked me.

I stared at her.

"I've got to find them," she said, and I told her I would go with her.

"Haven't you done enough already? No, you need to stay here, in case they come home."

She pulled out of the driveway, and when the van turned the corner, I sat down on the ground, next to the large maple tree, leaned my back against the trunk facing the house, and began to cry. When I was able to stem the flow of tears, I called Hans and heard his voice for the first time. It was as reassuring as the words from his email, calm and certain.

"You've just completed the hardest part of coming out," he told me, and then added, "It all gets easier from here."

"I've ruined my children's lives," I muttered. "How could I be so selfish?"

"No, you haven't ruined their lives. You've saved your life, and your children deserve a father who is a complete person, not a facsimile of one," he said.

Our conversation continued, but when the van turned into the driveway, I quipped, "I have to go; they're here." Speaking to another gay man filled me with guilt.

Katherine had driven first by the elementary school playground down the street where the girls sometimes still played on the swing set. Not finding them there, she drove to Jeff's house. When his mother opened the door, she hugged Katherine and walked her up the steps. The girls were lying on Jeff's bed as he tried to comfort them.

"Did your father tell you he was a drug dealer?" he asked them.

When they looked stunned and said no, he continued. "Did he rob a bank? Did he kill someone?"

Eventually, they would understand his line of reasoning, and I marveled at his understanding when Katherine told me this.

That night, Katherine asked me to move into the spare bedroom, where I slept on a twin-sized bed that would roll about the hardwood floors at night as I thrashed and slept in fits, the air stifling. On Sunday, Claire would go to a bonfire at a friend's house, where she would cry and confess to her coterie of friends, "My father is gay." They would console her and say that their fathers were gay too, but Claire would correct them and say, "I don't mean gay, like stupid. I mean he actually is gay." When I picked her up, she was embarrassed.

"I thought Mom was picking me up," she said, eyes darting back to her friends, teeth clenched.

It was the first time I ever felt that she was ashamed of me. It would not be the last.

The next weekend, we planned to spend Sunday together as a family, squeezing every drop of family bonding, before time ran out. Claire put the leash on Maggie, and Olivia joined her, announcing that they would take her for a walk. After forty-five minutes and no return, Katherine sensed that the girls had other plans and set out in the van to search for them. When she returned, the girls were sulking, and Katherine said she found them at the school playground where they had secretly planned on meeting Jeff and Jonathan.

"You girls know better than to lie to us," I admonished them.

Olivia looked up with cold eyes and sneered. "Oh really? You lied to us for our entire lives."

Not knowing how to respond, I said the only thing I could think of. "Go to your rooms."

But after some time, we all fell back into our daily routines, kicking the ball of our emotions down the road.

I began to strip the wallpaper in the dining room, painted the bathrooms, and replaced light fixtures to make the house more marketable. Claire walked through the dining room, stopped, looked at the progress, and asked, "Are we going to put this much effort into our new home?" Their new home would be one without me in it. I would help them move in, hang curtains, and place furniture, but who would mow the lawn or fix the leak in the bathroom sink or make sure that the doors were locked when they slept? Who would kill the spiders?

At night, when I tucked Claire into bed (Olivia had outgrown this routine), the questions would come.

"How long have you known you were gay?" she asked.

"Since I was a child."

"Then why didn't you come out then?"

"The world was a different place. Being gay wasn't an option," I said.

"But why did you wait so long?"

Why did I wait so long? Why? Because I made a promise to never be like my father. Because my mother fucked me over every single day by saying being gay was disgusting and that I would never be happy. Because I thought being gay was disgusting, and if I was gay, then I was disgusting. Because I thought I would go to hell. Because religion fucked me over by telling me my feelings were sinful. Because I was broken. Because I couldn't look at your sweet faces and say, "Sorry, Daddy can't live with you anymore because he wants to have sex with men." Because I thought your mother would kill herself. I lied for so long that I didn't know how to stop. I created an entire world, and how could I stop that from spinning?

The question wasn't why I waited so long but how on earth it was ever possible for me to come out at all. How could I come out and destroy every single thing I had worked for to build in this life? How could I take a sledgehammer and bash the everlasting shit out of everything they and I knew?

But this is not what you say to your daughter. You measure it out and try to come up with something that won't negate the love you feel for her mother and something that won't make her think she was a mistake, because they were never, ever a mistake. Because the truth was, I loved them all and I hated myself, but the two were locked in a fatal embrace and had to be separated.

"I held it in as long as I possibly could."

"So, it was like when you have to pee and can't hold it in anymore?" she asked.

"Something like that," I replied.

"Have you told Grandma Mary?"

"Not yet, I wanted you girls to be the first to know."

"Will she be angry?"

Fuck her! I thought to myself. *She ruined me.*

But this is also not what you say to your daughter about her grandmother.

"I will always love you for who you are and will always be proud of you," I said in response.

"Me too," Claire said, her voice growing thin, eyes already closed.

CHAPTER THIRTEEN

NUMBER TWO

My brother Alex and I were both born in July, he on the second and I on the sixth. My mother would split the difference and celebrate our birthdays together on the fourth. Not only did I get to share my birthday with our country but with my older brother too. There were three years between us, which was a distance wide enough so that all I could see on the horizon was Alex, like a Norman Rockwell Boy Scout, jaw set and leaning headstrong into the future. Wherever he was going, I wanted to follow.

When my father left us for wife number two, a woman who was all of the things my mother was not, young, blonde, and childless, Alex assumed the role of the patriarch with a red-haired boy's determination and moved to the front seat of the car. I would mark a line down the middle of the blue vinyl seat between me and my younger brother Christopher, eighteen months my junior, with a karate chop, saying, "Here, here, here, this is my side; that is yours." When Christopher's foot breached the border, I would alert the National Guard. "Mom, he's on my side!" But it was Alex who would issue a sidelong glance to keep us under control.

In the morning, he would herd me and my two younger brothers like a border collie, nipping at errant sheep. "Get up, it's time to get ready for school," he'd quip. "Bill, you start the shower," he'd say, and we would leave the water running between turns, my brother Christopher always getting the short end of the stick.

"It's cold!" he'd wail.

In high school, Alex started working at a Japanese restaurant, the type where chefs performed acrobatics with their knives at the table, throwing shrimp into the gaping mouths of diners who looked like clapping seals and singeing their eyebrows with pyrotechnic displays. The owner fell in love with Alex and his dedicated work ethic. He became known as *Alex-san*. Because Mr. Moto respected him, he agreed to hire me. While Alex waited tables in a tidy blue jacket, I was handed a dirty apron and told to wash the dishes. Often, Alex would come into the kitchen with a plate that did not meet his stringent standards. He would stealthily hand it to me and whisper, "You didn't clean this one well enough." Alex-san was honorable number one son. I was number two.

Though there were three years between us, my major life events trailed his by just one year. I was in a constant race to catch up. He became engaged; I became engaged. He got married; I got married. And so it continued with jobs, moves, homes, and each of us with two daughters almost exactly one year apart to the day. I had blindly followed his path, eyes down, until one day, he veered from it, and when I lifted my head to get my bearings, I found myself in a wilderness, with no clear trail markings.

"I'm not happy," he told me on the phone one day.

"Have you tried counseling?" I asked.

"There is no reason. I'm not in love anymore."

It was that clear. His marriage was over, and he had set off on a different path to find happiness. It was disconcerting. He had seemed so confident that this was the only way, and now he was leaving me on my own. I could continue on the old trail or follow his lead. Once again, a year after he had told me that he was splitting up with his wife, I found myself running behind my older brother, yelling, "Wait up, Alex, wait for me!" This time, I would choose a parallel but separate route. I had no idea if he would approve, or if he would sneer and act as if I had handed him a dirty plate.

On a Saturday morning, I closed and locked the bedroom door and sat on the floor, wedged between the wall and the bed, rehearsing what I would say. In an email, I had told him that Katherine and I were splitting up. In the back of my mind, I knew that I could back out and not say anything, which made it possible to dial his number. I did this several times and hung up each time before letting it complete, karate chopping my fist against the bed and saying through clenched teeth, "Shit, shit, shit. Just do it!"

I finally let it ring, and when he answered, I knew that I was on the hook and would have to tell him.

"Hey, Alex!" I said with so much false sunshine in my voice, he must have thought I was going to tell him I won the lottery or that I had terminal cancer.

We offered pleasantries, spoke about our jobs, and then dug deeper into our separation stories, asking about each other's daughters and how they were handling things.

"It's funny how similar things are between us," Alex said.

"Well, there is one little thing that is different about us," I said, and then added, "Maybe not that little, actually; it's kind of a big thing."

"Oh yeah?" he replied, my equivocation filling his voice with doubt.

It was as if I had handed him a container of unidentified food and said, *Here, smell this.*

"I've been seeing a therapist for a while, just working through things, and—and—here's what. I'm gay."

There was a pause. *Fuck, say something*, I thought.

"Well . . ." There was another delay. "You're still Bill. You're my brother, and I love you. I just want you to be happy."

I removed the phone from my ear and held it against my chest, muffling the receiver while filling my lungs with air. When I exhaled, it was the staccato sob of a little boy who just wanted to be like his older brother. Forty-four years of worrying whether someone would love me for the real me were washing down my face. In the distance, I heard his tinny voice. "Hello, Bill, hello?"

"I'm here," I said, picking up the phone and wiping my eyes with the back of my hand. "Thank you, Alex."

"The IT director at my company is gay too. Are all of y'all gay?" he chuckled.

I replied, laughing, while the tears still rolled, "Only the best ones are."

There must have been a part of Alex that always knew. There were the tiny clues, like bread crumbs that I dropped before I became old enough to know better and hid them.

When we were young, my mother, never the best planner, would scribble the grocery list on a scrap piece of paper en route to the grocery store. Often, it was the back of an envelope, a paper receipt from McDonald's, or the margin of a page torn from her *Redbook* magazine.

"OK, y'all, what do we need?" she would ask at a stoplight, looking up in the rearview mirror with a cigarette perched in the corner of her mouth. She would hold the pen to paper, looking like an expectant waitress. "Damn," she'd mutter as she viciously scribbled inkless circles. Pens never made the list.

"Coke, cheesecake, ice cream!" my brothers would answer as if these were actual Dameron-family staples.

"I'm not buying any of that crap," she'd reply.

"Honeycomb cereal with a Bobby Sherman record on the back," I would offer.

Alex would look sideways at me, narrow his eyes, and then punch me in the arm.

"Ow! I just like his song," I'd say, shrugging my shoulders, and start to sing. My mother would take the cigarette out of her mouth and join in, while exhaling the smoke through her nostrils, singing an octave or two higher.

Bobby Sherman had long brown hair and clear blue eyes, wore a leather choker, and had the most adorable little dimple right in the middle of his chin. I would look in the mirror and squeeze the skin on either side of my chin to make an indentation. If I held it long enough, it would leave a little line, just like Bobby's.

"Did you always know?" I asked Alex.

"I can't say that I'm surprised," he said, and then added, "No, that's not it. *Surprised* isn't the right word. I'm not shocked. I mean, you know, it's normal."

"Thank you, Alex," I said again. I could not stop offering gratitude.

"I just want to find someone I can be happy with. Someone who can be my friend and that I can love," he said.

"Me too."

We began to describe our ideal mates. It was the first time I ever told anyone what I was truly looking for.

When I would later come out to my brother Christopher, who was closest in age to me, he cried, not because he was disappointed but because of the pain he knew I had endured. It touched me, and even to this day, he ends every phone call with, "I love you," emphasizing the word *you*, to let me know that after all these years, he sees me.

"Have you told Mom?" Alex asked.

Why did everyone keep asking me this question? Was I not truly out if I did not tell the person who first pushed me out of her body?

"I tried once long ago, Alex. I just don't think I'm at a point where I can go through that again."

"Mom's changed. You'd be surprised at how liberal she has become."

I should have been heartened by this, but instead anger, like a dried-up plant, sprung to life with this drop of news. *NOW she has become liberal?* After all of these years and all of this pain I had caused, was she going to say, *Never mind?*

"I want to talk to you about your *tendencies,*" my mother said after I came home from that summer in Colorado with my aunt Sheila and told her who I was.

She had a list of words that she pulled out of her quill, *tendencies, leanings, preference.* They were all words that suggested what I felt could somehow be corrected. If I leaned toward something, then it was just a matter of pushing me a bit the other way. It was an insidious assault. A daily dose of adjustments, like those braces that kids had screwed into their legs to lengthen them. A turn every day to stretch them, barbaric.

She stood in her nursing whites on the other side of the kitchen island when I returned home for the day from college classes. My shoulders slumped, and I dropped my books onto the counter.

"Damian is in his room. He can hear you, Mom," I whispered, my eyes darting down the hall toward my youngest brother's bedroom. Sometimes I wonder if Damian did hear my mother. He certainly internalized her fear. When I came out to him, I told him God made me this way, and he responded, "I don't believe that."

"These feelings you have, Bill, they're just not normal," my mother said.

"I told you, I don't feel that way anymore," I said, having endured relentless talks about my *tendencies.*

"It was a phase," I promised.

"I've spoken to doctors, and they all say you'll never be happy being a homosexual. They told me that you would have to move far, far away, to someplace like London, and men have anonymous sex and give each other diseases."

She leaned toward me and asked, "Have you had *sex* with anyone?" She lowered her voice when she said *sex*, the same way she did when she said *gay* or *homosexual*. These were curse words, the worst of the worst.

"No!"

Her forehead was furrowed, and the corners of her mouth turned down, but it was her eyes, fixed on mine, that saw the secret, the ugliness that no one else knew. I looked away as if she could see something exposed in my eyes and searched for a spot in the kitchen that I could focus on, a place where I could hide, and my eyes rested on the water heater in the corner behind the kitchen door.

When we were children, we had a pet hamster named Tweetsie. My brothers and I would take him out of his cage and sit in a circle, our legs outstretched to form a barrier, and let him run between us on the carpet in the den. Invariably, he would escape and we would scramble to catch him, but he always ended up hiding behind that door. When my mother talked to me about my tendencies, I became small and imagined myself in the dusty corner, hiding behind the water heater.

"Do you want to speak to someone who can help you get over this? Father George?" she offered.

"You didn't tell him, did you?"

When I was just a kid, maybe nine years old, there was a movie titled *Fritz the Cat*. It was an animated film, a two-hour cartoon! When I asked my father if he would take me to see it, he stammered. My mother overheard the conversation and walked into the family room, drying her hands with a dish towel.

"Oh, for heaven's sake, Charlie. Bill, that movie is X-rated. Do you know what that means?"

"No," I replied, but her tone and pursed lips insinuated the answer—something bad.

"It's about sex. It's *nasty*."

"Oh."

Sex equaled nasty. Gay equaled disgusting. Gay sex was nasty and disgusting, and now the family priest knew how nasty and disgusting I was. How could I face him? I felt as if I had been sliced open, the raw part of me exposed.

"He's sworn to secrecy. You can talk to him one on one, or we can all pray together."

"No, please, Mom, no," I begged.

"Let's pray together now," she said, holding out her hand, and because I just wanted it to end, I took it.

"Dear Lord, help Bill get through this crisis," she began, and the next day and each day after that, we repeated the cycle, like the gay stations of the cross, until that exposed part of me scabbed over and became numb.

"Mom fucked me up, in a lot of ways. I can't take that again," I said to Alex.

"I understand," he replied.

"What did Mom say when you told her you were getting divorced?" I asked.

"She said, 'I want you to be happy.'"

My mother would stand by the water heater in the kitchen, early in the morning, when nothing but a thin line of red cut through the sky on the horizon. She would patiently wait for Tweetsie to poke his head out from beneath the water heater, nose twitching and whiskers probing. She would tear off a tiny piece of bread and gingerly place it in front of him. He would timidly approach, take the bread, and begin to nibble. She would then place tiny bits of bread in a line, each one farther away from his hiding place, and then scoop him up. He hardly fought; he was so used to being held in captivity.

I tried to imagine what the world beyond his cage must have felt like, how vast and wondrous it must have seemed in the beginning, but then how terrifying it must have felt when he realized that there were cats and other predators lurking behind every corner and no one to feed him.

My mother hated animals. We had a cat named Al that was banished to live underneath the house in the crawl space when he clawed up the furniture, and she would shoo our dog, Tiger, out the back door for the day to wander the neighborhood. Throughout my youth, there was a menagerie of mice, rabbits, hamsters, and fish that she allowed us to own. But she never loved them the way we did. It was their remnants that she could not abide, the fur, the tears, and the smells that messed up her perfect furniture. When we held up Tiger as a puppy for her to pet, she would screw up her face and offer a pat with one finger, as if we had asked her to inspect a rash.

But in the morning, we would find her clutching Tweetsie.

"Here, take this rodent," she'd say, holding him out to us.

She could have just as quickly let him out the back door, just as she could have said no to all of our requests for pets, but she understood what they meant to us. Alex had felt trapped and simply wanted to be happy. He would take the lead, and I would follow.

CHAPTER FOURTEEN
REALITY TV

On my birthday in July, the last one we would all celebrate together, the girls presented me with an oversized box covered in red, white, and blue paper. "What on earth could this be?" I asked while unwrapping it, sounding so much like my father. The girls stood next to me. Claire watched my face expectantly, and Olivia worried at one of her fingernails. When the last bit of paper was torn off, I stared at the box, and Claire stated the obvious.

"It's a TV for your new"—she hesitated, searching for the right word—"place."

All of our attention was sucked in by the size of the large tube television, as if it were a small planet and we were trapped in its orbit. They had chosen an item for my new home and then gave it to me as a gift. I wondered how difficult it must have been for them, knowing that I would soon be alone in a strange place, looking at the television, instead of spending time with them.

The gravity of the moment was surpassed only by the weight of the television itself. When I tried to lift up the box, it would not budge.

"How did you get this home?" I asked.

"We had help," Katherine replied, "the guy at Walmart and then our neighbor."

Katherine looked at the girls, and I pretended not to notice as she raised her eyebrows and tilted her head in my direction.

"Happy birthday, Daddy," Olivia said, pecking me on the cheek. She ran back up the stairs, and then Claire followed her.

"If it's too big, return it for something smaller. Do whatever you want. You seem to be doing that a lot these days," Katherine said, and walked out of the room.

I was left alone in the family room with the TV. It stared blankly back at me.

When my father left my mother, my brothers and I sat in the family room, watching TV. There was only one television and one telephone on the first floor, and they existed ten feet away from each other. Mom stretched the telephone cord as far away as possible, to the middle of the kitchen, but we still heard her sob and scream at Dad, "What am I supposed to do?"

We didn't say anything to each other, my brothers and I; we just sat there, staring at that stupid TV, too frozen to change the channel. We pretended to watch a documentary about a boy walking across the desert with the Giza pyramids looming on the horizon. He didn't talk or say hello to anyone, just kept walking, and there was some narration, but all I can remember is that lonely boy walking on a dusty road.

"Your father wants you, but he doesn't want me anymore," Mom cried, wiping her face with a kitchen towel, and I remember feeling surprised that he said he wanted us.

The birthday present from the girls remained in our living room for a few days, startling us whenever we passed, like a silent intruder, until I decided that it took up too much real estate, physically and emotionally. I wrapped my arms around the box and grunted as I hoisted it up.

It sat in the back of my car until Enzo and I drove to lunch at the Piccadilly Pub down the street from our office.

"Do you have a body in the back of the car, Billy?" he asked, glancing at the box.

"You know, it's funny you ask, because it's the remains of the last person who asked that same question," I replied.

When he stopped laughing, I told him what it was. That the girls meant well, but I didn't think it would fit into an apartment that I could afford. He tilted his head and knitted his brow in a sympathetic look.

"I'll help you return it, Billy. Come on now. We'll do it after work and then go to dinner with our Missouri guests, hmm?" He referred to our visiting coworkers from the Midwest.

The weight of keeping the secret from Enzo had been growing heavier with each day. Less so from any sense of newfound pride in my sexuality and more because every time I heard him utter a gay slur or a marginal joke, I winced.

I had made the mistake of describing another man at the office as having blue eyes. Enzo had been merciless in his joking about my noticing Ol' Blue Eyes, which bothered me like sand in my shoes. I would have been able to shrug it off in the past, but now whenever Joe the blue-eyed man walked by, I turned red and Enzo noticed, causing him to prod me even more.

Fudge packer, faggot, homo, fairy, butt pirate, poof: I used to be in on the jokes, complicit in my silence, like the massive TV in the back of my car, and after, I was quite literally the butt of them. There was no gradual adaptation. It was binary, on or off. The only difference was, nobody knew.

When we pulled into the Walmart parking lot that evening, I considered coming out to him right away, but then I imagined us, awkwardly standing face-to-face, lifting the box together and grunting.

After we lugged the hulking TV in and exchanged it for a slim twenty-two-inch LCD, I practiced in my head what I would say when we returned to the car. We sat in the front seat, and before I switched on the ignition, I turned to look at him.

"Uh, so, I want to tell you why Katherine and I are getting divorced," I stammered.

"No need to be spilling all of your secrets," he replied.

"No, it's important," I said.

With that, I could see the expression on his face change to one of concern. What must he have imagined? That Katherine cheated, that I cheated? In a way, I cheated on everyone, didn't I?

I looked through the car window. *Fucking Walmart.* I would have laughed if it hadn't been so pathetic. Was I going to lure everyone here and come out to them? Did I hate Walmart so much that I would say anything in the parking lot to avoid going into the store?

I turned back to look at Enzo, and it occurred to me then that this was the dividing line. One moment we would be friends, and the next we might simply be coworkers.

"You see, I've been seeing a therapist, and the reason for that is I'm gay."

Silence.

Enzo looked out the car window and then said, "OK."

Shit. I was prepared for laughter, or anger, or concern, but *OK* didn't seem OK.

"Do you have any questions?" I asked.

"Nope."

This went well. I exchanged the big, silent TV for a big, quiet Italian.

I turned on the ignition, and we spoke of nothing during one of the longest five-minute drives.

Dinner would have been enjoyable had Enzo not sat silently on the other side of the table looking so riddled with anxiety and had one of our coworkers from Missouri not been a complete homophobe. Other than that, it was perfect.

"We were going to go to Disney World with the kids, but we found out it was 'Gay Days,'" Rodney the Missourian said. The look of disdain wiped away any doubt that this was about as distasteful as it got.

Enzo stopped picking at his food and then looked across the table at me.

"I mean, why do they need to go to Disney anyway?" Rodney asked the group of people at the table. He assumed that we would all feel the same way. It was a common assumption that people made.

I looked at Enzo and shrugged my shoulders.

"Homos are trying to indoctrinate the kids," he continued.

I saw Enzo squirm as my face became red, and just when I was about to throw the fork across the table at Rodney, Enzo said, "Hey, hey, let's stop there. Some of my best friends are gay."

The group fell into silence, and I couldn't face it. I excused myself to the restroom.

After dinner, I drove Enzo back to work to pick up his car. I parked my car next to his. The wind was whipping, stirring up the sand in the parking lot that was left over from the winter snowstorms. It scratched at the windows, and the car shook.

"Why did you wait so long?" Enzo finally said something.

"Wait so long for what?" I replied.

"I mean, why did you get married? Why did you stay married for so many years?"

It wasn't a question that could be answered in a word or two, and it was one that I was still trying to figure out. I thought of my mother screaming on the telephone at my father and of that lonely boy walking through the desert. It was a scene I vowed my children would never be a part of.

"Enzo, being gay just wasn't an option for me," I replied.

It was an answer that only begged for more questions. The wind picked up and howled around the corners of the car.

"Are you going to tell everyone now? I mean, when some people come out, they feel like telling the whole world."

I didn't know if he was asking or advising me, or whether he was worried that people would begin to question our relationship. And when did he become an expert on coming out?

"No," I replied. "I'm just telling a few people."

"Why'd you tell me?"

I had expected this question, but it still shocked me when he asked.

"Because I thought you should know. Because I was growing tired of the jokes, tired of the whole blue-eyes thing. Are you sorry you made those jokes now?"

"No. I didn't know you were gay then," he replied, shaking his head a little, and then said, "It's difficult, because now when I look at you, all I can picture is the act."

The act? What, the way I had been acting?

"For men, that's what we think of," he expounded. "It's so"—he hesitated—"intrusive."

Oh, that act, the one I had not even had the pleasure of committing, or partaking in. However you wanted to look at it. A gust blew the sand beneath the car, causing a grating noise. We both stared through the car windows.

"When I think of you and Anna, I don't immediately think of your having sex," I replied. "I'm gay, but that's not all that I am."

"Billy, I'm always going to be your friend. Nothing will ever change that," he said, and I could see him softening, reaching out. I had misjudged the level of difficulty he would experience with this. That it was such a shock seemed surprising. Was I so convincing at acting like a straight man?

"I'm sorry, Enzo. I'm really sorry." I couldn't stop apologizing.

"Now, Billy, come on. Everything is going to be OK," he said while patting my shoulder.

What was I apologizing for? For being gay? That didn't seem healthy, and it wasn't what I wanted to convey.

"I'm not sorry for being gay. I'm sorry for"—my voice broke—"ruining everyone's lives, especially Katherine's and the girls'."

Enzo patted my shoulder again.

Had this been a television show, the camera would have focused on Enzo as he offered some bit of wisdom or humor that would have broken the silence and made everything all right. We would have hugged, or perhaps in a surprise twist, kissed. But instead, we sat there in silence and watched the sand shift until Enzo said, "We'll talk more about this tomorrow."

He opened the car door and jumped into his vehicle, and I watched him drive away. I stared straight ahead, observing the sand turn in little dust devils beneath the parking-lot light, and then it began to rain.

CHAPTER FIFTEEN
LOST AND FOUND

We could not find the keys to the van. I wandered from room to room, my head darting left and right. Maggie trotted behind me, navigating her way through the stacks of cardboard boxes.

"Where could they be?" I turned and looked down at her.

She cocked her head, her dripping red tongue hanging to the side.

"Have you found them yet?" Katherine shouted down the steps.

"Still looking," I hollered back up.

Maggie walked over to her bowl, slurped up some water, and then cantered back to me, leaving a trail of slobbery droplets.

I walked into the kitchen, grabbed Katherine's purse from the counter, and rifled through it for the tenth time. *Maybe I missed a pocket,* I thought. I threw the purse back onto the counter after coming up empty-handed.

A week earlier, I walked into the basement and found Katherine standing there, staring at the sea of unopened boxes from our move to Franklin a year ago. These were the boxes that had never been unpacked from that trip, and now, they would need to be moved again. She knitted her hands together as if she were facing a cliff and did not know where to place them to get a hold. We collected too many things during our lives together and never threw anything away. Now, they towered in front of us, like a great wall too steep to be scaled. I put my hand on her shoulder, and she immediately turned to me. I wrapped my arms around her waist, and she rested her head on my shoulder, letting the tears fall.

"I can't. I can't," she kept repeating.

"It's OK. You don't need to. I'll take care of it," I replied.

"You'll take care of it?" she asked.

Her voice was suddenly sharp and cold as she pulled away from me and narrowed her eyes. "Do you mean you'll take care of it the same way you have taken care of everything else?"

"I mean, I'll pack everything up," I answered.

"This was my dream home, our dream home. I loved this house, Bill." She cried. Tears were streaming down her face. "And I loved"—her voice broke—"us."

I wanted to grab on to her and hold her and tell her everything would be OK. But I didn't, because I couldn't lie to her anymore. I couldn't see into the future. All I could see was our life broken down into boxes.

She walked over to the small basement window and looked out at the neighborhood. When we first moved in, a neighbor, a man in his late fifties, knocked on our door to welcome us, and I invited him in. He stood in our empty living room and told us the house was regarded as one of the nicest on the block after the sunroom was added, and then, inexplicably, he stated that he thought the house had a history. Katherine and I looked at each other quizzically, and when I prompted him for more information, he was evasive.

"Water damage or something like that," he replied.

Standing there in the basement, watching our marriage crumble and listening to Katherine cry, I wondered what type of history our energy would leave behind. Would the future occupants feel a sense of sadness they could not explain when they stood by that window?

Would the house begin to sag from the weight of the misery that we left behind?

Katherine turned to look at me and wiped the tears from her eyes.

"Bill, just tell me you're bisexual so at least I'll know the last twenty years haven't been a lie."

I looked at her. She waited expectantly. My forehead creased, and I held up my empty hands.

"I can't pretend anymore. I loved you. I do love you, and that was never a lie," I said. "But I'm gay."

"You ruined me!" she screamed, and swiped a book that was sitting on top of one of the boxes, sending it sailing across the room and hitting the wall. "How will I ever be able to trust another man? And how will the girls ever be able to develop a relationship without wondering what secrets he is keeping from them? You told me that we didn't make love anymore because of my weight. You made me hate myself, Bill. You fucking ruined me!"

The words flew at me with the same velocity as the book and pierced its target straight through the heart. I hated myself, not so much for lying about being gay but for causing Katherine to question her value and her beauty. I stole a piece of her. And then I thought about my daughters and wondered how I might have broken them too. Would they ever trust a man, or would there always be a part of them that questioned his love for them?

"I have no skills, beyond being a wife and a mother. But you've taken away one of those."

"I'll take care of you and the girls," I said. "I promise."

I saw her face change. It became cold, and then she said, "My attorney will make sure that you do."

She turned, and as she walked up the steps, she said, "You can pack all that shit up."

But later, while I was at work, she went through the boxes and the other household items and marked those that were either too painful to hold on to, a plaque the girls gave to me for Father's Day with the inscription "My prince did come. His name is Daddy," a blue-and-white-striped sofa that was our last big purchase together, or things she simply did not want—a lamp, a blue fish-shaped bowl, a brass teddy bear. These items, a few yard-sale finds, and some furnishings that Hans and his partner, Gavin, donated would be the few remnants that furnished my new home.

But this morning, the girls would begin their seven-hundred-mile journey to Virginia, where they would stay with friends until I purchased what would become their house, and I would be left behind to supervise the movers who would be arriving in two days.

Sweat beaded and rolled down my back as I lifted the tail of my T-shirt, fanning myself. Seven o'clock in the morning and it was already soupy. The house was in disarray. The keys could be in any one of the hundreds of packed boxes. I walked into the dining room and stood in front of the window air-conditioning unit, held the bottom of my shirt up, and let the cold air fill it like a balloon, watching it billow, and found a moment of solace in the low drone. I let my mind wander through time.

When Olivia was four or five years old, on summer days, we would walk along the sidewalk in Roanoke, Virginia, to our neighborhood center together. The high-pitched whir of cicadas and the constant hum of air-conditioning units were hypnotic. I'd hold her tiny hand as she skipped along beside me, her skin so soft and smooth like a glass of fresh milk. A cluster of brick buildings made up our neighborhood center—Grandin Village two blocks away, a drugstore, a coffee shop, an old restored movie theater with a neon marquee. A metal exhaust vent on the sidewalk blew warm air infused with the unique earthy scent of herbs and patchouli from the natural-food co-op store. Letting go of my hand, Olivia would step on the vent and delight as her dress filled up.

"Look at me, Daddy. I'm a bell!" she would shout, her arms gently draped on the front of her dress as she leaned from left to right, her skinny legs stationary. "Ding, dong."

In the weeks leading up to the move, Olivia had stopped communicating with Jeff, and she broke off her relationship with Jonathan. She sealed herself off from the world in a cloak of anger. It was easier than saying goodbye. Jeff would call multiple times during the day, and I'd shout up the steps with my hand over the receiver, "Olivia, it's Jeff again."

"I don't want to talk to him. I don't want to talk to anybody," she'd shout.

"I'm sorry, Jeff," I'd reply, and before I could say she wasn't home, he'd mutter, "It's OK, Mr. Dameron. Just tell her I called."

We told her that this was her only chance to say goodbye. I would be moving to Waltham, and she, her mother, and sister would not be coming back to Franklin. "Fine by me." She dug her heels in.

While Olivia barricaded her door, Claire flung hers wide open. She had a beach-themed fifteenth-birthday party several weeks before and invited a group of girls for a sleepover. We wanted to indulge them with as much of a semblance of a family that we could muster. We put up cardboard palm trees in the backyard and burned tiki lamps, and the sound of island music, steel drums, and languid guitar chords drifted through the air from a stereo speaker perched on the deck. When the day melted into evening, a smear of orange spread on the horizon, I stretched out a white bedsheet and nailed it across the back wall of the house and projected a movie onto it. We sat outside on the cool grass, under the stars, as if we were at a drive-in movie theater.

"This is the best birthday party ever," Claire said while we sat side by side in the backyard, the film flickering in front of us. I leaned in and kissed her head, breathing in the scent of her so that it might become a part of me.

I looked at her and the group of pretty girls lying beneath the stars, their smooth young faces illuminated by the reflected light of the screen. Their hands reached out for one another when the movie became too frightening, and then they cast their heads back and let loose a full-throated laugh, like a toddler's laugh, long hair sweeping their shoulders. That night was tinged with sepia-toned nostalgia at the edges like an old postcard from the past with a simple message in big block letters, "Wish you were here." But *here* was more than a place; it was a moment in time that I could never travel to again.

Claire had grown into such an outgoing girl, so different from the shy three-year-old she used to be. When she was a toddler, she would take her glasses off and give us a playful look before flinging them into the air. We would wag our finger at her in mock disdain and then go searching. *Miss Mischievous* was what we called her. Once, she did this, and we looked far and wide, without finding her glasses until months later. They were wedged in an old heating radiator.

How many things had we misplaced during our moves, articles hidden beneath heating radiators, tucked into the eaves of the attic, or dropped into a clump of grass in the backyard? The new owners of this house would move in and find a piece of us here, surely. "That house has a history," the neighbors would whisper while glancing sideways at the blue clapboard colonial. The owners would sense it in the stillness, when the weak winter sunlight faded on the bedroom wall and cast lonely shadows or when the water groaned through the pipes in the upstairs shower. There was something lost here.

The thought of Claire's missing glasses brought me back to the present and the task at hand. As I walked through the house searching for the keys, I found memories tucked away behind doors, gathering like dust in the corners, wrapped in newspapers under cardboard box flaps. The more I searched for the missing keys, the more I found the past, until finally, I felt my chest tighten and then, without warning, hot tears of frustration and loss streamed down my face. I propped my back against a wall, then slid down and wrapped my arms around my legs, burying my face between my knees, like a passenger in an aircraft preparing for a crash. Here was Olivia as a baby in the wee hours of the morning; there was three-year-old Claire throwing her glasses and laughing; this was Olivia sitting on her bedroom floor, refusing to pack up her dolls again; over there was Claire lying beneath the stars. All around me were ghosts of the girls and the ghost of what had once been our life.

Ding, dong.

My insides jumped the way one might when driving over an unseen speed bump. I wiped the tears from my face with my shirt and listened. "Ding, dong," the doorbell rang again, and then there was a light knocking. I stood up and peered through the dining-room window to look at the front stoop. A middle-aged woman in a blue linen dress stood there and just behind her, shifting his weight from one foot to the other, a skinny teenage boy—Jeff and his mother. I walked to the front door, felt my cheeks for wetness, and quickly wiped my face again while taking a deep breath. I opened the door. Dolores looked up and began to speak, but paused as she absorbed the state of my face.

"Please forgive me," she said quietly, and then added, "But Jeff couldn't sleep."

Jeff stood next to his mother, his head slightly lowered, but I could see the same red-rimmed, puffy eyes that must have looked like mine. Fresh tears gathered at the corners of my eyes.

"Please, please come in. I'm so glad you're here," I said while shepherding them in.

I led them into the kitchen, and Jeff began to wander through the family room, taking in the liminal state of the house. I turned to Dolores.

"Is everything OK?" she asked.

149

"It's fine," I answered reflexively. She knew the situation. As much as I wanted to be in control and come out to people one by one, Katherine felt the need to tell everyone she came into contact with. I imagined the conversations.

How are you? an acquaintance would ask.

My husband's gay, Katherine would respond.

The bastard.

After a moment of silence, I said, "Excuse me, I'll just go up and speak to Olivia."

I walked up the steps, passing by Olivia's closed door. Katherine met me in the hall.

"Who's downstairs?" she asked.

"Jeff and his mother. He's come to say goodbye."

Katherine looked at me for a moment, and I wondered how she might react. Would she be incensed that he would not respect Olivia's privacy, or would she be thankful that he would not give up?

"I'll talk to her," Katherine said, lightly tapped on Olivia's door, and then opened and closed it behind her.

I walked back down the steps and began a polite and uninteresting conversation with Dolores, while Jeff sat silently on the sofa in the family room. We waited. I heard the stairs creak, and we held our breath. Katherine appeared in the kitchen alone, and my heart sank. I looked up at her inquisitively.

"We'll see," she said, and then hugged Dolores hello.

We heard footsteps in the hall, and then Olivia appeared, hair flattened on one side, wearing pajama pants and a T-shirt. She walked past us and into the family room. Jeff stood up slowly, wiped the palms of his hands on the front of his pants, and looked at Olivia as if awaiting word about whether a patient had made it through the operation. Olivia stood in front of him and then held up her arms, and he caved into her. They then stepped out together through the back door, seeking the solace of the backyard. I looked up at Katherine and Dolores, who were both dabbing at the corners of their eyes.

"I'll go and look for the keys," I said, excusing myself to allow Dolores and Katherine the privacy to speak. I walked through the living room, glancing through the French doors, and saw Olivia and Jeff, sitting on the edge of the deck outside. The corners of Olivia's lips turned up into a smile, and a feeling of gratitude for this boy who would not give up spread through my insides like a warm tonic.

I opened the front door and stood on the front stoop, the weight of the balmy summer air enveloping me. Looking across the front yard and down the street, I saw fathers mowing their lawns and a pair of children riding their bikes in a driveway. The smell of bacon from the neighbor's house wafted through the air.

"I don't know if I'm doing the right thing," I said to David on the phone yesterday.

I sat in my car in the office parking lot in the far corner, away from all of the other cars, next to a cluster of trees and a rocky outcropping on a hill. I watched the cypress leaves flicker green, then silver in the breeze, and called David in a state of panic.

"The right thing is rarely the easiest thing to do," he replied.

"What if this is the wrong decision? What if I'm destroying my family? What if I never meet anyone? What if I leave this marriage, and then I never meet anyone like Enzo?"

"You have already made this decision. The house is sold. Follow through on it. You need to feel the loss."

"But I feel so sad," I replied.

"If you weren't feeling sad, something would be wrong with you."

I wanted him to become an oracle and tell me what, exactly, was down the road, but instead I got the bullshit, Buddhist "Feel the loss, become one with the universe" reply.

"What if I'm never happy again?"

"What if you never tried?"

The front door opened, wiping away the conversation that was looping in my mind. Jeff and Olivia stepped out. Dolores and Katherine trailed behind them. Jeff stopped in front of me.

"Thank you, Mr. Dameron. Good luck," he said, extending his hand.

I took it, shaking it vigorously, and said, "Thank you, Jeff."

Not only was I grateful that he would not give up on Olivia, but also that he accepted me. Why did it matter what this sixteen-year-old boy thought of me?

Jeff and Olivia hugged and then vowed to stay in touch. Dolores and Jeff stepped into their car and drove away slowly, and we waved until the vehicle disappeared as it turned the corner at the end of the road.

"Did you ever find the keys?" Katherine turned and asked.

"I have no idea where they could be," I replied.

"Give me your car key, then. I don't need the others anymore," she said.

I reached into my pocket, twisted off a single key from the chain, and placed it in her hand.

"I'll go and get the girls," Katherine said.

Olivia and Claire stumbled out of the front door. I steeled myself. *The right thing to do is rarely the easiest thing to do.*

"Maybe I don't deserve to be happy. Maybe I could just stay in the marriage until the girls are in college," I had said to David.

"Everyone deserves to be happy," he replied.

"Katherine and the girls don't seem very happy."

"Maybe the girls would prefer to have two parents who are happy and live apart, versus two who are miserable together," David said, trying different combinations of phrases.

Olivia and Claire stood in front of me. Olivia held on to her stuffed animal, Petie.

"Be good for your mother, girls. I'll see you in a week," I said.

"OK, Bill," Claire replied.

"It's Dad," I corrected her.

I hugged both of them, holding on long enough to mark this moment, but not so long as to raise it to the hysterical-parent-on-the-first-day-of-school level, and watched them slip away like koi fish submerging behind the glossy surface of the tinted windows. Maggie came running from the open front door and attempted to jump into the van as the door slid shut.

"No, girl, you're staying with me." I grabbed her collar and pulled her back.

Katherine stood in front of me.

"This is it, isn't it?" she said.

"Yes," I replied.

We embraced and kissed each other lightly on the lips.

"Be careful. Stop whenever you need to rest," I said.

Katherine climbed into the van and put on her sunglasses. I held on to Maggie's collar as she whined and attempted to lurch forward. "I'll bring you to them in a week," I told her. They pulled away slowly as I walked into the middle of the street, waving my hand, and I stood there long after they turned the corner.

I imagined the stoic girls sitting in the back seat, while Katherine would look up occasionally in the rearview mirror, smile, and sing along to the radio. They would cross the Hudson River over the Tappan Zee Bridge, slip through the Pennsylvania countryside where Katherine would point out a hex symbol on the side of a barn. When they reached the Shenandoah Valley, the ancient rolling green hills of southwest Virginia would offer comfort, and the blue sky fading to orange on the horizon would paint their faces with a russet-hued melancholy. When it became dark, they would turn off Interstate 81 onto 581 and pass underneath Mill Mountain, illuminated on the top with a giant neon star.

"Do you see that star?" I would ask Olivia when she was a little girl. From her bedroom window, her eyes would follow the length of my arm to the finger that was pointing at the tiny light on the mountain.

"It's watching over you while you sleep at night," I'd say, and then she'd recite her ritual evening parting.

"Night, night, sweet dreams. Stay home, Daddy."

"Always."

That night, I slept in the silent house while Maggie walked from room to room, searching for Olivia and Claire. After all of the boxes were packed up and the movers cleared the house, I would do a final check for the missing keys but would not find them.

Months later, I returned to the gym to close out my membership. "I think these are yours," the woman behind the desk said. "They were found in a locker." She dropped a set of keys into my hand. Like some time machine, they unlocked a door to the past that I was not prepared to enter.

"Is everything OK?" she asked.

"Everything is fine," I said, and wiped my eyes. "It's just that I thought they were lost forever."

CHAPTER SIXTEEN
THE OTHER BILL

WE ARE TWO MIDDLE-AGED LESBIANS WITH TWO SMALL NON-SHEDDING DOGS.

This was how the advertisement for the apartment began. I was halfway out, halfway in, and this would be my halfway house, a place where I could transition from a fraction of a person to a whole.

When I began the search for a new home, I was looking for less of a spot to live and more of a place to begin a new life. Fearful of discrimination, I ruled out a number of potential apartments because of many perceived defects. The owners lived next door and would question why men stayed overnight, or the landlord was homophobic because he spoke of nothing but sports, or the neighbors were so close they might hear me with someone. I must have anticipated a much more active and promising sex life than what would come to fruition. In the end, I was discriminating against myself. If I didn't accept me, how could I expect others to?

The first acceptable apartment I found, a duplex, was half a mile from Enzo's house.

"We could commute to work together!" I told him.

"Oh," Enzo muttered.

I could see it in his blanched expression. I was one boiled pet rabbit away from becoming Glenn Close in the movie *Fatal Attraction*. *I will not be ignored, Enzo!*

"I mean, I have others to look at before I make a decision," I replied.

Then I saw the craigslist advertisement for a basement apartment posted by two middle-aged lesbians. It was close to the city, a stone's throw away from my therapist, and the price was well within my range. If this was not an accepting environment, what would be? I crafted a reply that summarized my life in four sentences. I was married with children. I was now separated. I was gay. I was homeless. These were not the exact words, but it all came down to the same.

The house was a gray colonial with a purple door at the end of a cul-de-sac in a quiet suburb west of Boston. When I walked up the slate walk to the front door, two small, white fluff balls, barking and falling over one another on the other side of the screen door, greeted me.

"Rusty, Lucas!" I heard someone yell.

This did nothing to stop the dogs from barking and in fact further incited them, so that within seconds they were attacking each other. A full-figured woman with short, tight, curly brown hair approached the door, walking with the assistance of a cane.

"You must be Bill. I'm Linda." She smiled.

When I reached for the door, she yelled, "Stop it!"

I flinched, and then she said, "Oh, not you, the boys." She pushed the dogs back with her cane.

She opened the door, corralling the dogs with one foot, and then led me to the living room. The boys were stumbling and running in between my legs and barking. When I sat down, they both jumped up on the sofa. One of them stared at me vacantly, and the other licked my arm nervously as if it were a juicy bone. He would do this for the better part of an hour.

"Rusty is the one licking you," Linda said. "And the other is Lucas. Poor thing was deprived of oxygen when he was a pup. Do you like dogs?"

"I love them," I said as I looked down at Rusty's pink tongue darting in and out of his mouth. He never took his eyes off my face. "I lost custody of our dog."

"Apparently they love you. We think Rusty is gay," Linda said, and let out a laugh.

The basement apartment had been intended for a friend of theirs who had breast cancer, but its construction outlived her. When Linda developed a chronic illness and had to stop working, she and her partner, Debra, a social worker, decided to rent it out to Audrey, a young woman who would now be moving to New York, she explained.

"Do you have a partner or a boyfriend?" she asked.

The look on my face must have resembled that of the doe-eyed, oxygen-deprived Lucas, because she quickly added, "Oh, if so, we'll need to make another key, that's all."

My face flushed, and I stumbled over my words. "I'm actually still married but separated. The divorce isn't final. I never cheated. I think I just need to work on some things before I start a relationship," I blathered. I thought all women would hate me when they heard my story.

"Everyone has their internal clock," she replied. "You weren't ready until you were ready."

I wanted to hug her.

"I'm seeing a therapist who specializes in coming out," I confessed. "He lives near here."

"David?" she asked.

"Yes, do you know him?"

"We're friends. Debra was his first boss."

Later, I would ask David about Linda and Debra, and he would say, "They're good people," as he shifted a little in his seat, angling his body away from me while clearing his throat, like Enzo's reaction to my initial search near his home. It was too close as if there were some personal wall that he needed to keep from being breached.

"Go on down and take a look," Linda said, pointing toward a door in the kitchen.

I walked down the purple-carpeted steps and said, "Hello?"

A young woman with beautiful onyx skin greeted me. She could have been a model with her high cheekbones. She looked to be in her twenties. I wondered what she must have thought of me, this middle-aged man looking at a basement apartment, which was little more than a dorm room. She was holding a Tupperware container and eating the contents with a fork.

"I don't want to interrupt your dinner," I said.

"Mama Linda makes the best food in the world," she said, pointing to the container. "Please, take a look around."

There was a living room, a bedroom that could only be reached through the bathroom, a kitchenette comprising a sink, two burners, a microwave, a few cabinets, and a slice of laminate for the counter. The refrigerator was in a separate room with the washer and dryer.

"Do you cook?" Audrey asked as we both glanced at the after-thought of a kitchen.

"Not if I decide to live here," I replied.

"They'll take care of you," Audrey said.

The square footage could not have been any more than our family room in Franklin. I took one more loop around the apartment and stopped to glance through the French doors, which overlooked a slate patio. Rusty and Lucas were running along the length of the picket fence in the backyard, chasing some phantom intruder. They ran up to the door and stared at me as if I were another rescue.

"What do you think?" Linda asked after I returned upstairs.

I thought it was too small. It didn't make any sense. Where would the girls stay when they visited me? I thought that I would hear every creak of the floor and every conversation above me. I thought that I would miss Olivia's and Claire's laughter, tears, and even the sound of slamming doors. I thought that at night, when I came home from work and the silence was too heavy to bear, when my hand reached for the empty spot where Maggie's head used to be, and when there would be no one to shout, "Daddy's home!" I might walk up the basement steps, knock on the door, and Linda would be there to pat my arm and say, "There, there, boy, everything's going to be all right."

"I think I'm home," I replied.

Within a month, I moved in the few remnants of Katherine's unwanted belongings, a few cast-offs from Enzo, an old nightstand and a dresser and a few items bought at a yard sale. I painted the walls in exchange for the first month's rent. Somehow, it all worked.

Many nights I would come home from work and find a plate of food wrapped in plastic, sitting on the top step with a yellow note from Linda: *Chili Verde, nuke in the microwave for two minutes*. I would devour the food, lightly knock on the door at the top of the steps to return the plate, and then spend the better part of the evening sharing beers and stories with Linda and Debra.

Just as I devoured the food, I devoured their lives and their experiences. They were my link to the history I had ignored and the future that I would come to embrace. They shared personal recollections of significant events—the Stonewall riots, the AIDS epidemic, the assassination of Harvey Milk, the marches, and political figures I was too embarrassed to admit I did not know.

They had been together for twenty-five years; Linda moved from Buffalo and Debra from a potato farm in Maine. Linda was an accomplished cook, and Debra was a social worker who passed up a degree at MIT, after she was accepted but could not afford to attend. They consoled me when life became too heavy and celebrated my milestones, no matter how trivial, on the path to recovery. Their love for each other and me was unconditional.

One evening in their home, I found myself beginning to read a handwritten letter that was framed with a faded photograph of a handsome man with blond hair and a mustache. He appeared to be in his midthirties. He was sitting on a tree stump, and the photo had been taken while he was laughing. As I continued to read, I became self-conscious and turned away. It seemed too personal, like I had breached one of their personal walls.

"That was Bill," Linda said. "When you moved in, all of my friends told me not to fall in love with another Bill." She winked at me. "But I guess I have."

I blushed and wondered about the caution from her friends.

"He wrote that letter to us on the day he died. He had AIDS."

"I'm so sorry," I said. I wasn't sure if I was apologizing for being named Bill or for bringing up painful memories from the other Bill or for avoiding the entire AIDS epidemic by hiding in the back of the closet.

Linda and Debra shared stories of their friendship with him, his humor, and his love for life. As the disease progressed, they stayed by his side, while most of his other friends vanished, unable to face the specter of his illness. The day he wrote the letter to them was also the day he chose his exit. I listened to the story and couldn't help but wonder if that Bill could have been me if my life had taken a different turn. If I had stayed in Colorado with my aunt when I was a teenager, would my farewell letter and faded photograph be gathering dust on someone's wall? It was called the *gay cancer* in 1981. Sheila warned me not to do poppers, the inhalant that was used by many gay men to enhance sex and was initially thought to be a cause of the disease. So little was known about HIV and AIDS then that Sheila's warning would have done nothing to protect me. It was the portrayal of AIDS and the specter of death, televised nightly on the evening news, that was another hand of fear that clutched me and held me tight in the closet.

"You were such a sad sack that first night when you showed up here," Linda said, "and now, just a few months later, look at you."

"There's still a long way to go," I replied.

"It takes time," Debra said. "When David came out to me, he was incredibly insecure."

"What?"

"Well, he wasn't born a therapist, you know." Debra smiled. "I was the first person he came out to. He was very serious about it, and when I said, 'Well, of course, you're gay,' he became angry at my response."

I laughed and had to put my hand up to my mouth to keep the beer from spraying, because I understood his response, but also because the image of my self-composed therapist as a regular human was somehow absurd.

"Well, I—uh—I mean." Debra continued her recollection, holding her hands out, palms up. "I mean it's obvious," she had told David, and he had become angrier.

Linda and I were both laughing at this point, and then I stopped and asked, "Wait, is it obvious that *I'm* gay?"

In unison, they both said, "Take it as a compliment!"

One day in the distant future, I would see David on a chilly early morning, walking toward me on a sidewalk in Boston. His eyes would be bloodshot, his clothes wrinkled, and his hair amiss. He would be returning home from a late night out, and I would learn that he had just broken up with his long-term companion. I would hesitate and then say hello. We would hug, and then he would continue on his way.

That was what Linda and Debra were teaching me, how to be human again, and it would take a long time, but someday I would find not the confidence I had lost, but a truer one. On a snowy day in the future, I would gather up my ragtag collection of belongings and move on. Linda would cry and say, "It's time for you to stop saying goodbye and start saying hello." Debra would console her, and they would recognize the completeness. Without sadness, happiness cannot exist. On that day, Linda and Debra would cry for the Bill they could not rescue and for the one that they did.

CHAPTER SEVENTEEN

MATCHMAKER

David took a deep breath and asked, "Can you describe what you are looking for physically in a man?"

He was granting me permission to fantasize and therefore normalize it verbally. I could have replied, *Someone who looks like you.* It would have been truthful, though awkward.

"Tall, black hair, green eyes, athletic build, maybe he plays soccer."

"That's fairly specific," David remarked, one eyebrow raised. "And it sounds like someone you have described to me before."

"Also, he probably has an Italian accent," I added.

"You know we've discussed this many times before," David sighed. "Enzo is a safe target, and once you begin to meet other men, *available men*, your feelings for him will subside."

"Can you describe someone other than Enzo?"

I narrowed my eyes, attempting to create the ideal man. After forty-four years in the closet, I found that the physical details regarding my ideal man were basic: someone over twenty and under fifty. Even then, I was willing to grant some leeway. It was the UPS man, the bag boy at the grocery store, the shirtless jogger, the soccer dad, and the guy at the gym. In my fantasies, I was an indiscriminate slut. In real life, I was a gay virgin. I had never been with a man other than a single kiss. There were times when I wondered if I was truly gay, as if sex with another man were the only determining factor. Could fantasies alone confirm my sexuality? If I had a devil and an angel on either shoulder, one was a gyrating go-go boy in a tiny G-string and the other was a gay Pat Boone.

"How do you think you'll meet someone other than Enzo?"

In my daydreams, these men simply appeared. The guy at the gym might compliment me on my upper-body development and then ask me to spot him. The UPS guy would ring my doorbell and deliver a package, and the shirtless jogger would ask me to spray him down with my hose. But reality required some planning.

"I was thinking of creating an online dating profile?" I offered.

"You're a good person, you'll attract a good man, but it's important that you understand what you're looking for," he replied.

There was a warning of sorts, couched in that compliment, but as most people would do, I focused on the praise and ignored the warning.

"I *am* a good person," I said, and that night, while sitting on the blue-and-white-striped sofa in my tiny basement apartment, I sucked down a glass of red wine and created my first electronic dating profile on Yahoo Personals.

Initially, I filled in the personal description fields with gibberish so that I could get to the good part quicker—looking at the profile pictures. Now that I was granted the permission to ogle, it seemed like my civic duty to do so.

There was something deceptive about the thumbnail photographs. From a distance, many men looked really attractive, but when I expanded them, I saw all of their flaws. The eyes were too close, or the teeth required work, or there was something just not quite right about the way all of the parts were put together. And then there were the photographs that looked too good. The lighting was soft and reminiscent of a Parisian sunset in autumn, the skin flawless, and the features chiseled like Roman gods. These men were too beautiful to be in love with anyone other than themselves, I thought, or else they had become extremely proficient in Photoshop, in which case they were still in love with the *image* of themselves. A profile with no photograph was the kiss of death. These men must have been either so hideous that no amount of good lighting would compensate, or they were married (which I still was, though officially separated).

I chose a photograph of myself that was truthful and the only one I thought flattering. It was one that Claire had taken of me. In it, I was standing in a church parking lot, wearing a white shirt with the sleeves rolled up and a pensive look on my face. It was taken six months previously, before a family photograph at my mother's church in North Carolina. In the background, you could see the steeple in a slice of blue sky, surrounded by thunderhead clouds. But the photograph was less about what was behind me and more about what was in front of me. Claire, from her angle, captured someone who appeared stable, tall, and ready to move forward.

As I searched through the list of potential profile matches, a mixture of feelings bubbled up in me: excitement, fear, satisfaction, and finally confusion. The text of the profiles read like those legal-document templates that one could buy on the internet: standard terms that could be selected from a list to create a custom contract. A set of phrases and acronyms appeared over and over again, like secret passwords. I was learning a new language.

Comfortable in my own skin: I understood what this meant, though it still creeped me out because it made me think about the fraction of men who might desire to wear someone else's skin. *When you love someone, in a way, you want to become them.*

Able to laugh at myself: This one seemed to be vital because it appeared in just about every profile. After decades of being the brunt of someone else's joke, it was time to take matters into their own hands. "Look at me; see how funny I am? I laugh at myself all of the time, dammit, I really do. I'm probably laughing right now, LOL!"

Straight-Acting or *Masculine Man*: "Even though I laugh at myself, it's not a girly laugh." It seemed to be at odds when combined with the *Comfortable in my own skin* comment.

Not into the gay scene: No one was into the gay scene. Not a one. Did gay scenes even exist anymore? They must have been replaced with straight-acting extras.

Well Adjusted and *No Drama*: No further fine-tuning was needed. These men would not put up with any drama bullshit, unless it was a Broadway show, in which case, "OMG, I love *Wicked!*"

DDF, LTR, VGL, GWM, BDSM, Hung, Top, and *Bottom*—and the list went on. Drop a fork on the keyboard and whatever letters appeared were probably a valid acronym or term.

After I finished my crash course in online dating terms, I completed my profile, careful to drop in a few of the learned phrases and describe myself in a way that was normal and not tinged with the train wreck that was my life. I needed to manage the crazy. My online self was the friend you could call in the middle of the night, the guy next door. In gay-dating terms, I would learn that I was a *breeder* and a *Daddy*. These were solid and desirable classifications, to a certain subset of men. My tagline was "a Southern Gentleman."

Within a few hours, I received numerous "electronic winks" and a few emails. I was trending. The next day, I received an email from "Balanced Laid-Back Masculine Guy," a.k.a. Sam.

Hey, handsome,

I consider myself a confident, secure guy, always been pretty comfortable in my own skin . . .

He called me handsome.

His profile said all of what I thought were the right things: *Work out a lot, Red Sox fan, masculine man here*. Many of the profiles used sentence structure like this, adding *here* to the end to make it breezy and casual, not at all desperate. Verbs were too heavy to lift and place into a sentence, after all of that working out. It sounded like caveman speak, *sexy* caveman speak, though. *Masculine man here*: even the act of crafting a proper sentence appeared to be too gay. He was a man's man, in every sense of the phrase.

Sam's profile indicated that he had children, which I considered a plus, though they did not live with him. He was someone who could understand me and who had taken care of somebody other than himself. While there were three or four pictures of his good-looking face— strong jaw with just the right amount of scruff, dimples, shaved head, and blinding white, perfect teeth—there was one *shirtless* picture of him. It was probably just a photo that one of his friends casually took while he was standing on the beach. I imagined that he hemmed and hawed about whether to include the picture. "Go ahead. You have a nice body. Why not show it off?" perhaps a friend had said to convince him. In my mind, he was modest. I zoomed in on his abs and counted. It was a four-pack. A six-pack would have been showing off, but a four-pack said, "I *care* about the way I look, but I'm not *obsessed* with it."

In one day I had found *the one*, and I immediately shared the news with Hans, my gay father email pen pal. By the time we eventually met, we had shared our life stories with one another, and I felt as if I knew Hans and his partner, Gavin, intimately before I even laid eyes on them.

They had been together for three years. Hans was tall with a slender build, wore a manicured goatee, and let his dark brown hair grow to shoulder length. He would often tuck it behind one pierced ear, an act of freedom after living his entire life as a Jehovah's Witness from South Dakota. He was married to a woman for twenty-five years and had three sons before he came out. When I met him the first time, I recognized myself in his eyes—irises ringed with a certain vulnerability, but in the pupils burned a steady flame of hope.

Gavin often gave Hans grief about having three children.

"One child I could understand, two maybe, but three? And then he didn't just open the closet door, he busted through it singing show tunes!" Gavin would say this with outstretched hands, à la Liza Minnelli to illustrate the point.

Gavin was originally from Ohio, with impossibly thick blond hair and a wiry frame; his only experience inside of the closet was to color coordinate his clothes. He was a Harvard librarian by day and an artist by night. They seemed like an odd couple, but it worked. As Gavin put it, like fashion, you never wanted to be too "matchy-matchy."

They lived together in a small condo on the top floor of a 1920s building in Harvard Square. I would visit them often and dream of living in the city with the man I loved. They decorated eclectically with acrylic side chairs and a down-filled sofa in the living room anchored by a marble fireplace, colorful wool dhurrie rugs, a bright blue farmhouse table in the kitchen, and casement windows that opened out onto a leafy green courtyard. It was like a photograph from the pages of *House Beautiful*. Although in *House Beautiful*, I doubt there was a charcoal drawing of a winged penis on the refrigerator.

Hans worked for a kitchen remodeling company run by the Jehovah's Witnesses. Gavin had hired the company to remodel his kitchen, but when the crew spied a photograph of Hans and Gavin in what could not have been mistaken as a platonic embrace, Hans was ex-communicated. "Oops," Gavin said. Hans kept his job, but the employees were forbidden to speak to him. There were so many risks to living an openly gay life. I had worried about AIDS, but through education and awareness, I could protect myself. When it comes to emotional harm, queer people take risks every day just living their lives. What protection is there for that? Hans was trapped in an emotionally violent work atmosphere in the liberal bastion of Massachusetts. This weighed heavily on him and left bruises that could not be seen. I too worried that if my manager found out I was gay, I might too lose my job. Even though I was no one's husband anymore, I still had a family to support. We both needed someone to talk to during our workday, and so the emails flowed. But tonight, we met for drinks at their condo, and the topic was my list of potential Mr. Rights. Sam was at the top.

"Look at that Semitic nose," Gavin purred while regarding Sam's profile picture, and then continued. "There's just something about a strong-nosed man."

"I don't think he's Jewish," I replied.

"You'll find out, honey," Gavin said, raising an eyebrow, without removing the straw from his lips while he sipped on a cocktail.

"Let's read his profile," Hans said politely as he angled the laptop away from Gavin.

"He's a gay father," Hans said, nodded approvingly, and then added, "He's a handsome guy."

"Thank you," I replied. I felt the ability to attract someone handsome somehow reflected positively on me.

"Let's see some more pictures," Gavin said, pulling the laptop back as he began to scroll through the other profiles.

"There's one next to an Italian flag." I pointed. Hans and Gavin exchanged a look.

"Honey, the man you end up with will probably only have a remnant of what you find attractive in Enzo, like green eyes, or drive an Italian sports car. Open yourself up to that opportunity, but don't limit yourself to it," Gavin said.

"Oh my God, so many of these men are the same ones who were on here before I met Hans. These poor men—not you, honey—you're fresh meat," he said, patting me on the shoulder.

How long would it be before my meat began to spoil?

"Oh! Oh! This guy is a little person," Gavin said, pointing to a picture and using two fingers on each hand to make air quotes. "But I didn't mind. I thought it might be fun, you know, to have a little pocket gay I could swing around and put on my lap." He gesticulated wildly with his arms to demonstrate how this would be accomplished. "I met him at a bar for a drink. I was sitting there, in this hot little number," he said, pinching the collars of his shirt. "The bar was packed, and then the sea of people parted, but I couldn't see anyone." Gavin said this in a hushed tone like it was a great mystery.

Hans looked at me, smiled, and then rolled his eyes toward the ceiling.

Gavin continued. "The crowd stood silently watching. This little man appeared below me. He tilted his head to show me his scalp. He asked me if I thought the red bumps on it were a rash! That was a fine how-do-you-do, don't you think?"

Hans and I looked at each other.

"So, 'Small in Stature, Big in Heart' is a no," I said, referring to the person's profile tagline.

"Oh, honey, let's go through them all. I'll tell you which ones to avoid with a ten-foot pole," Gavin said, then raised one eyebrow and added, "Or the ones with a ten-inch pole."

Hans rolled his eyes again.

It felt incestuous knowing that I could potentially date some man that Hans or Gavin might have had a relationship with. While I appreciated their insight, I didn't want to end up with sloppy seconds. This would be the first man I was going to have an open relationship with. I was glad they didn't know Sam.

"Think about it—if we haven't had sex with Sam, we probably have had sex with one of his partners or a partner's partner," Hans said, looking at me like he was reading my thoughts.

Sloppy seconds by proxy, I thought. I waited for Gavin to chime in, but when I looked up, he was dancing by himself in the living room. There was no music playing.

"What does DDF mean?" I asked Hans.

"Disease- and drug-free," Gavin shouted from the living room, and then continued. "Honey, did I tell you about the time I did LSD with my friend Angie from high school? Her mother opened the door to her bedroom, and Angie shouted, 'Shit, it's my mother!' I said, 'That's not your mother; it's a big crow!' We started screaming and throwing pillows at her, trying to shoo her away."

Hans gave me another upside-down smile, pushed himself up from the table, walked over to Gavin, and kissed him. They put their arms around each other and started swaying back and forth, laughing. I watched them dance to music that only the two of them could hear.

They were madly in love with each other. When I looked at them, I could almost hear the music playing, and if I narrowed my eyes just a bit?

I could see my future.

CHAPTER EIGHTEEN
264 HAIRCUTS

Katherine pulled out the black cloth cape as I placed a dining-room chair in the middle of the small kitchen and centered it beneath the single overhead light. I unbuttoned my shirt, removed it, and draped it over a chair. A tender breeze drifted through the open window above the sink and wandered across the room. The heady scent of freshly cut grass sailed on the back of the wind, teasing with it the squeals of neighborhood children who were playing tag or chasing fireflies. I sat down on the wooden chair with the woven seat as she lifted the cape and let it billow in front of me like a sheet blossoming on a clothesline. It fell in languorous folds against my chest and legs. She moved behind me, fastened the buttons around my neck, then placed her hands on either side of my head and whispered, "I can't do this anymore."

"Do what?" I asked.

"This," she said, holding her hands out, referencing the ether about us, and then continued. "You can't stay in this house when you come to visit the girls. It's too hard on me, pretending to be a family."

"But we'll always be the girls' parents," I said.

"We're getting divorced, Bill. I have to accept that, and I can't be excited to see you when you come into town. I have to let you go."

She reached into the old black briefcase and pulled out scissors and a comb. The camel-colored interior smelled of rich leather, and the brass latches made a double-popping sound when the buttons on either side were pressed to release them. Three tiny numbers on a dial next to the latches ensured the contents' security. Katherine and the girls had given it to me as a gift, early in my career when I shuttled papers back and forth to work, instead of a laptop computer. When it was replaced by a more practical backpack, I returned it to her, to house her haircutting equipment. When I needed a trim, no words were exchanged; I carried the briefcase into the kitchen. Earlier this evening, I brought the briefcase in and placed it on the dining-room table, and she nodded.

She held up the scissors for a moment, paused, and then lowered them.

"Promise me something," she said.

"What?"

"That you won't get married again."

I struggled to make sense of her words, and then it dawned on me. I could marry a man, even if it would only be legal in Massachusetts. The concept of two people of the same sex marrying each other did not naturally occur to me. It was like the riddle about the patient's being brought to the hospital and the doctor's stating, "I cannot operate on this boy. He is my son." The twist: the doctor was not his father. Many years ago, people would have been stumped if asked what relation the doctor was to the patient, as if a woman could never become a physician. I wondered if I could ever completely erase my own learning and think of another man as my husband.

"I don't think I could," I said, and she exhaled.

"Who will cut your hair?" she asked.

For more than twenty-two years, we played out this scene, roughly 264 haircuts. She would run her fingers through my hair and hold my head in her hands, guiding it forward and sideways. For all of these years, her fingers were inches away from the thoughts swirling inside of my skull, but she could never fully get a purchase on them.

When we first met in the 1980s, I wore my hair parted neatly on the side, the preppy, closeted-Republican look. I would watch clumps of black hair slide down the cape and pool in small piles on the kitchen floor. Over the years, the side part vanished, and flecks of gray mingled with the black hair. Now, the hair that fell was mostly gray, peppered with a few black strands.

Who would cut my hair? I shrugged my shoulders.

She rubbed her hands through my locks, picked up the scissors and the comb, and then began to snip.

"Let's try something different," I said, and then asked, "Do you have the clippers?"

She reached back into the briefcase, pulled out the heavy Wahl clippers, and plugged them into an outlet. When she turned them on with a snap, they emitted a low electronic-buzzing sound.

"Cut it all," I said.

"What?"

"I want you to buzz it all off," I replied.

Who would cut my hair? If I didn't have any, then it did not matter.

"I'll start with the number-three blade first," she said as she fitted it with a plastic guard and then pushed the clippers up the sides of my head. She paused at the top of my forehead.

"Go on. Do it," I said.

I watched the hair tumble down my face and fall on the cape. I could feel her breasts pressing against my shoulder and her hand brushing the hair from the top of my head. And then I felt something wet fall on my cheek. I heard a sound, like a hiccup over the buzz of the clippers, and then I heard it again, but it was more like a sucking noise, like someone attempting to catch a breath. Her tears began to fall like clumps of hair.

"Shh, shh, it's OK," I whispered.

"It's just that you look so different now," she said, standing back, her face screwed up with red blotches around her eyes. She looked tired, and when she used her forearms to adjust her braless breasts beneath the old T-shirt, the intimacy of the act filled me with an unutterable sadness.

I stood up and walked into the bathroom. I turned on the light and looked in the mirror. *Oh shit,* I thought, looked away, and then glanced back again. There was something honest and bold about the face staring back at me, a goatee with a shaved head. *Dammit, Sam,* I thought. This was the visage he fitted me with on our first date, *shaved head, goatee, tight T-shirt, tattered jeans.* He wanted me to look gay. I looked *très* gay.

"My handsome Southern man." This was the last thing I heard him say to me when I kissed him good night. He was standing in the foyer in his boxer-brief underwear. That was more than two weeks ago when I told him I was coming here to Virginia to visit the girls, and then finally, yesterday, a single mistyped text message: Ben busy. *Buy a fucking vowel,* I thought. He was too busy to type a second *e?*

When I returned to the kitchen, Katherine was dabbing her eyes with a paper towel. I sat back down in the chair.

"Go ahead and make it shorter," I told her.

"But you'll look like a cancer patient," she protested.

"It's just hair," I replied.

After she clipped the rest of the hair off, she rubbed lotion on the back of my neck and pulled out the straight razor; I felt the cool metal against the nape of my neck as she nudged my head forward with her fingertips.

As if my thoughts were laid bare now too, she said, "You know, I'm strong now. I can make it on my own."

"I know that," I said, still looking down.

I closed my eyes. I could hear Claire chattering on the telephone in the living room, the indistinguishable sound of words and music coming from the television set, and Maggie's nails clicking on the hardwood floors.

"I never cheated on you," I said without moving, keeping my head down and my eyes closed.

The blade stood still for a moment, and then she carefully skimmed the razor down, slicing the tiny hairs from the back of my neck.

"I had to get that HIV test," she replied, and then added, "Everything you did seemed so out of character." I was offended when she first told me this. Of course, the test was negative. How many times did we make love? Was it a number greater or less than the haircuts? I could count on one hand the number of people I had been intimate with before her. And yet, had I ever been truly intimate with anyone?

The first was my childhood neighbor in Greensboro, North Carolina. He and I were too young to understand our dark fumbling during sleepovers. In college, I lost my virginity to Marie, in a rite of passage that I simply wanted to get over. In Colorado, there was a single kiss with Don that confirmed the man I was, and who I later vowed to never reveal.

When I was twenty-one, before Katherine and I made love, I told her about Marie, but not about Don. That part of my life was supposed to have been erased by my mother's personal conversion therapy program. The first time Katherine and I made love was on a pull-out sofa in my brother's off-campus apartment in Raleigh, North Carolina. Neither one of us virgins, there was no awkward fumbling, just as there was no passionate taboo. I recognized it for what it was. This was as good as it would get.

For more than twenty-two years, as my hair became grayer and Katherine's body became softer and rounder, I kept it locked away.

And then finally, at age forty-four, after our marriage was over, there was Sam.

After we finished, Sam held up his pants and examined the broken zipper and popped button. "Those were my favorite pants," he said. I laughed. He did not.

"We're done," Katherine said.

She brushed the hair from my shoulders and face and removed the cape. I stood up, put on my shirt, buttoned it, and pulled the broom from the kitchen closet. I swept up the hair—all of my hair—and placed it in the garbage can. I turned off the kitchen light as Katherine opened the refrigerator door and stooped down to inspect its contents. For a moment, her face became illuminated by the dim light, and then as the door closed, it vanished.

When I walked into the living room, Claire, sitting on the sofa and talking on the phone, glanced up at me and cringed. Olivia bounded down the steps, paused, and said, "Oh my God, Dad, your hair!"

"Go ahead and try to mess it up," I said.

She let her palm skim the bristles.

"Freaky," she said.

I turned to look at Katherine, who offered a wan smile, and for a moment, as if buoyed by a fresh breeze entering the room, we all sailed on.

When the girls went to bed, I wandered the house, taking stock of things that were no longer mine. There on the dining-room table was the blue metal pitcher we found in an antiques shop in New Hampshire. This painting, above the brick mantel, was my gift to her on our twentieth wedding anniversary. That was my old black briefcase. Here was an oversized damask-upholstered sofa where Katherine and I used to lie, side by side with a black-and-tan snoring dog at our feet. The refinished wooden floors creaked as I passed.

When I reached the top of the stairs, Katherine stood motionless in the dark hall.

"Can I sleep, *just sleep*, with you this one last night?" I asked.

"Don't wake me in the morning," she replied.

She removed her nightgown. I took off my shirt.

That was her side of the bed, and this used to be mine. Here was the blue comforter in which we cradled our newborn babies. These were the flattened pillows stained with perspiration, with age.

I lay awake on my back. She rested her hand on my neck. I turned to my right side and she to her left as we twisted through the night in our bittersweet ballet of goodbye.

After more than twenty years in this bed together, there were just a few hours left to sift through it all. How we wept when Katherine gave life to our children, how one night after dinner, Katherine made me scream at the top of my lungs to show emotion, the school recitals that I secretly hated attending, and the gut-wrenching pain at the thought of never attending another one. Would my daughters look out into the crowd for me and then remember, *Oh, he's gone?* And for everything I would miss, there were the things we both needed that our marriage could never give, a love without innocence, a youth devoid of passion.

From her side of the bed, what did Katherine see? She found this house on her own. After more than two decades of making big decisions together, she had to walk through houses that were not hers and imagine a life in those rooms for three people, not four. She would be the single parent that the girls would come home to, the one to make sure they made it to school, the one who would have to console her daughters when they cried and said, "I feel like my father has died." Would the old wound of her father's death throb with pain every time her daughters glanced at the empty dining-room chair?

She held this family close, because it was her first and last hope, a family of her own that she chose and was not chosen for her, and one that she thought her husband and the father of her children would never intentionally leave. Katherine lost the story that she believed was her life. What would she do with all of those memories, the wedding photos, the home videos, the moments of intimacy and lovemaking? She had been making love to a ghost. And when the pain of loss could not get any worse, I asked her to spend one last night in bed next to the man who destroyed her, the one she was trying so desperately not to love. Even to this day, I think of that night and how there was a strength to Katherine I had underestimated, a resilience I had failed to understand.

"Will you be OK?" I asked.

"Bill, just make sure you will always be there when the girls need you," she replied.

In the grainy morning light, I closed the bedroom door and tiptoed to their rooms. This was Olivia's bedroom. Those were the boxes filled with her dolls. I tucked her dark hair behind her ear and kissed her warm cheek.

Here was Claire's bedroom. These were her glasses. I picked them up and cleaned them with the tail of my shirt.

"I'm just going to work now," I muttered, a half-truth in the half-light.

CHAPTER NINETEEN
JAGGED LITTLE PILL

Linda held up a clear-plastic lunch bag in front of my face that contained pills in various shapes and hues.

"This is a Percocet, in case you end up at some bar where they hate gays, and you get beat up," she said.

She then fingered a large, round white pill through the plastic, like Karen Silkwood handling plutonium with rubber gloves. "This is Ritalin, which works opposite for adults to how it does for children. Take it when your plane lands, and you won't have any jet lag."

"Linda Jean, I'm raising my objection to your dispensing these," Debra said.

Debra tilted her head down and glared over the frames of her glasses as she lowered and shook a wrinkle out of the *New York Times*. We were lounging in their living room. The November sun traveled low in the sky, throwing bright midmorning rectangles of light on the wooden floor.

In the evening, I would board a plane for a business trip to Singapore and Thailand. Linda cobbled together this small travel pharmacy from her medicine cabinet, much the way I filled a flask in high school with varying amounts of alcohol from my mother's liquor cabinet. A sip of this or a nip of that would produce little effect, but combining them all could be deadly.

"They cane people just for spitting out chewing gum on the sidewalks. If Bill gets hurt, I want him to at least be able to medicate himself," Linda said.

"Well, what do you think the penalty is for illegally obtained drugs?" Debra asked.

"They're prescription," Linda said, waving away the objection with one hand, and went back to describing the small cache. "Now this—*this* is Valium."

Instead of a steaming bowl of chicken soup, she mixed this chemical concoction. It felt good to have someone worry about and miss me when I departed. I was slingshotting halfway around the world, and it seemed as if their thoughts might keep me tethered to Earth somehow.

Katherine and the girls used to drop me off at the airport when I left for business trips. Claire confided to me that she would comfort her mother, who would be in tears, hunched over in the driver's seat of the minivan in the airport parking lot. She was unable to face the empty spot in our bed for even a few nights. There was no one on the other side of that bed to miss me now.

Linda sat back in her velvet purple chaise lounge and squinted, taking me in. Rusty and Lucas were wedged into either side of her, balled up like furry white throw pillows, their heads meeting their tails. They jerked when she moved and lifted their heads to regard me with a sleepy expression.

"You're looking so"—she searched for the word—"gay." Linda made a circular gesture with her outstretched hand as she spoke.

We had a discussion before about how various people reacted when I came out to them. Some seemed shocked. "Not in a bad way, mind you," they quickly added, "just that I had no idea." Others said that they loved me no matter who or "what" I was, and still others told me, "It doesn't surprise me."

Initially, I took offense to this last reaction.

"What do you mean, you're not surprised?" I would query them, indignation rising.

"Take it as a compliment," Debra had told me. "Being gay is not a negative thing."

When I looked back at my life in the closet, I began to understand. While not all of the men I knew checked out the ass of every woman who crossed their paths, I *never* did, but I might have stealthily glanced at the good-looking guys. Maybe my tentative peeks at the boyfriends and husbands of the women Katherine thought I was checking out were not as ninjalike as I had imagined. In any case, the stereotypes most of my friends had about gay men were positive, as in "Why are all the good ones gay?"

"Thank you," I replied to Linda's compliment.

Ill-fitting clothes had been the hallmark of my masculinity. Men did not *shop*. Their wives did that for them. Katherine would have me try on a pair of pants and then stick two fingers in the waistband, tugging at them. "These are too tight," she would say, frowning as she pulled at the fabric. I would have been too embarrassed to wear what I had on now in the before, just as I would never have had the guts to shave my head and grow facial hair. My whole purpose in life had been to fit in, not to call attention to myself. Now that I was a minority, I was beginning to embrace it. I took the time to look for clothes that hugged my body, instead of covering it. Out with the pleated khakis and blue button-down shirts (the man suit) and in with the slim-fit jeans and tight V-neck sweaters.

One of the people I had not yet revealed myself to was my manager, Drew, who acted like a teenager on spring break when we traveled to conferences together. He was always the first to buy a round of drinks, follow it with shots, and then suggest we go to a strip club. His head was big and round, like the thick roll of cash he always carried in his pocket. He was a child in a large thirty-something-year-old body. A caricature, with bulging blue eyes and spiky brown hair, he was always searching for mischief, behavior that was equally endearing and grating.

On my most recent business trip with him, before I came out, we spent a night in New Orleans after a conference. We stumbled down Bourbon Street. The night air was heavy with humidity, and young women were standing on balconies, behind ornately scrolled iron railings, lifting their tops for anyone who would toss up a strand of cheap, colorful plastic beads. I looked up, weaving back and forth a little, and squinted, attempting to merge the alcohol-induced phantom third and fourth breasts on one woman's body into two. Drew pushed me through the door of a "gentleman's club," and when I tried to object, he asked, "Would you prefer the strip club next door with male dancers?"

Yes, absolutely, I would have preferred the male strippers, but I felt compelled to prove my straightness by sitting at a table with Drew as he peeled off dollar bills from an endless roll of cash and placed them in a girl's G-string or between her breasts.

I glanced over at the table to my right and saw two couples, young men and their girlfriends, clink shot glasses and knock them back. One man wore a fedora, and when the stripper onstage playfully grabbed his hat and placed it on her head, he pulled out some cash and waved it in the air. She got down on all fours, with her ass facing him. He placed the bills in her G-string and then smacked her rear end as all four clapped and hollered. I envied them. I hated that they could indulge in their desires, while I sat stifling mine. What was it like not to feel guilty about what turned you on?

A topless dancer, who smelled of fresh soap, sat on my lap as Drew handed her a wad of cash to give me a lap dance. When I tried to object, Drew said, "I already paid her." She took my hand, stood up, and pulled me to a back room.

There was a man sitting in what looked like a reclining chair. Another stripper with long blonde hair and small breasts sat on his lap, straddling his legs. His eyes were closed, and his head rested on the back of the chair, as he thrust his crotch against hers. I could tell by the rhythm and intensity that he would soon be done.

My dancer was petite with shoulder-length dark hair. She wore high heels and black, lacy thong panties. She sat me down in a chair and then picked up a small step stool and placed it in front of me, climbing onto my lap. Was it some OSHA safety requirement?

Two men stood by us, sipping their beers, and watched, laughing and pointing, as if they were at the zoo and caught a couple of monkeys in a mating ritual. The stripper ran her fingers through my hair, messing it up, and I stifled the urge to fix it. She moved around on my lap, trying to find a position that would turn me on. At one point she was on all fours, with her rear end facing me, and then she stood up and bent forward from her waist, looking between her legs back at me. I was trying to focus my gaze anywhere other than on her ass, and then she snapped her fingers and waved her tiny hand, like *Yoo-hoo, I'm working here!*

When she finished, I handed her a ten-dollar bill. She looked surprised and said, "Oh, you want to tip me?" I suppose most men attempted to find a place, other than her hand, to leave a tip. We walked back to the table, and Drew regarded my messed-up hair and disheveled clothing.

"Yeah, baby, now that's what I'm talking about," he said.

The two topless lap dancers sat down next to us. They looked tired as they put a leg up on the table and ran a hand through their hair. When I turned to look at them, the blonde stripper playfully stuck her tongue out at me. It was pierced and studded. She began to talk to me, asking where I was from, why I was in New Orleans, small talk that turned into other questions and then to an admission.

"Most of us have asshole boyfriends," she said. "Some of them hit us."

As far as I could tell, this was not foreplay. Drew had checked out of the conversation and was watching a stripper on the stage spin around a pole upside down, her legs spread wide apart. Fantasy was much more entertaining than reality.

"I'm sorry," I said to the stripper.

"Ain't nothing you can do," she said. "You want another lap dance or anything?" She said this like she was asking if I wanted a side of fries.

"No, thanks, I'm all set," I replied.

I was more comfortable with women when they were real, and Drew was more comfortable when they were sex toys. They must have known there was something different about me, but they didn't say a word. Perhaps they might have been the ones to say, "I'm not surprised; all the good ones are gay."

I was living in that liminal space now, not entirely out to everyone and finding it increasingly difficult to pretend anymore. I knew there would be many nights on the town and an entire weekend in Bangkok when I would have to act straight. As much as Drew behaved like a child, he was still my boss. How would he react if he knew I was gay? Would he find a way to fire me? I was supporting two homes now and barely making ends meet. That worry bubbled up and settled in the furrows on my forehead.

"Is everything OK between you and Enzo?" Linda asked.

Just as Linda wanted to provide me with a chemical shield of pills, she desired to place a protective layer around my heart. I had confessed to her my love for Enzo and the difficulty he experienced when I came out.

"We're fine," I assured her. "It's Drew that I'm worried about."

Linda and Debra rolled their eyes, having heard one or more of my stories about his lewd behavior on company trips.

"This is Tylenol with codeine." Linda resumed the chemical tour.

CHAPTER TWENTY
ONE NIGHT IN SINGAPORE

When the gods want to punish you, they answer your prayers. I sat on the chair next to my bed and watched the sunlight filter through the blinds. It crept up the bed, over his feet, and then fell across his face. His eyes fluttered. He lifted his head and with one eye open, he peeked at the unfamiliar room, slowly looking around, and when he saw me, shook his head a little like maybe he had seen a ghost. He blinked his eyes wide open.

"What did we do last night?" Enzo asked.

We had returned to Singapore from Bangkok, and this morning, we would board a flight for Boston, but last night began when Enzo said, "One more for the road now, huh, Billy?"

My gut recoiled at the thought of more alcohol, but it was our last night in Asia, and the glimmering green lawn next to the white Gothic church beckoned us, a final summer night in the midst of winter.

Enzo and I skimmed the perimeter of the courtyard of the church complex where nuns used to pray, and Singaporean girls learned of the sins of their bodies. The buildings were constructed of white stucco with red tile roofs. In the middle was a sunken courtyard floored with stone tiles and surrounded by thick adobe walls and graceful arches. Strings of light bulbs hung from the low branches of the surrounding rain trees, and the whole complex glowed as if a light emanated from the buildings themselves, as if sunlight had sunk into the thick white walls during the day and seeped out at night. In the courtyard, people sat at outdoor tables, and a peal of laughter rose up into the air. The chapel, once part of the Convent of the Holy Infant Jesus, had been reborn as Chijmes, a cloister of restaurants and bars.

"How about this one?" I asked as we walked in front of a noisy club.

Enzo waved his hand and said, "Nah, too many people."

We found a bar on the edge of the complex with a couple of green-felted pool tables illuminated beneath low brass lights, and accordion glass doors pushed wide open. We walked in, and a cluster of young Asian women sitting at a table glanced up from their drinks at us. One, wearing a thin-strapped pink tank top and with long, silky black hair falling over her shoulders, leaned in and cupped her hand to another girl's ear, whispering something without taking her eyes off us. Enzo and I stood at the bar, and I could feel the edgy tension rising up from his hunched shoulders as his eyes darted around like a caged animal looking for an exit.

"Let's get our drinks and sit there," I said, pointing to an iron table outside of the bar, beneath a rain tree on the lawn.

We ordered the special, a pitcher of Long Island Iced Tea, so we wouldn't have to go back for more, and grabbed the glasses. We walked to the table and sunk down into our chairs, letting out heavy sighs, like the journey was a thousand miles. We rested our heads on the back of the chairs and stared up through the leafy green branches framing the nighttime sky.

"Too many people, Billy. Too many people," Enzo said, leaning forward and pouring the drinks. "I was feeling jittery back there, but this is better."

I lifted my glass and said, "To Bangkok."

Before we returned to Singapore, our weekend in Bangkok began as most do, with a visit to a strip club, forced upon us by my manager, Drew. We escaped when Drew tossed a basket of Ping-Pong balls into the air and the dozen or so topless women dancing on the stage came charging at him. We jumped into a cab that a slender, young Thai prostitute already occupied. "Billy, where do you want to go?" Enzo asked. I looked over at the young woman and introduced myself. "I'm Meow," she said. I asked her where the gay clubs were, and her eyes widened. We ended up in the gay neighborhood of Silom. Enzo left his comfort zone in the straight world for mine at a bar called Guys on Display. When Enzo went to the restroom, Meow shocked me by asking point-blank if I loved him. How quickly she could see what I tried for years to hide. "Yes," I whispered. When we parted, she bowed in the traditional Thai farewell, hands in the prayer position. She looked up at me and said, "You are not God. You can't change who you are." I looked down at the stamp on my hand from the bar. The stamp was "GOD," an abbreviation of the bar name. I handed her a few hundred baht, smiled, and wondered as she stepped into a cab and disappeared into the night if she believed the same about herself.

Enzo clinked his glass against mine, and we both took a sip. I looked around and saw a young man with his back to us, sitting alone at another table, perhaps fifty feet away, and staring at a laptop-computer screen that glowed in the darkness. In the distance, music from the bar was punctuated with laughter and the crack of pool balls.

"Can I ask you a question?" Enzo asked.

"You already have," I replied, and he gave me a weary look. I smiled.

"Why did you not sleep with the man you met in that bar in Thailand? The gardener?"

I laughed at his description of James, the landscape designer I met at the bar. He was rugged, charming, and handsome, and toward the end of the evening, he asked me to join him in the bathroom of the nightclub for a little party, just the two of us. Why did I not sleep with my gardener? I wasn't entirely sure, but I knew that if I was going to sleep with a man, love was part of the answer. I looked down at my hand and laughed, the faded stamp, still on my hand. *You are not God. You can't change who you are.*

A subtle breeze turned the leaves above us, and I looked back up at the sky. In Indonesia, across the South China Sea, a forest fire smoldered, lending the air a nutty, lingering scent of incense. Here we were on the tail end of a business trip, an Italian from the North End and a gay man from North Carolina, sitting on the lawn of a nineteenth-century chapel in Singapore and gazing up at the stars.

"I mean, it must have been so fucking difficult to hold it all in for so many years," Enzo expanded.

"Enzo, it's not all about the sex," I replied.

"I knew that about you."

We both took another sip of our drinks.

"Can I ask you a question?" I said, and he smiled. "Do you believe in fate?"

"You and your fate, Billy," he sighed.

"I wouldn't be where I am today if we hadn't met," I said.

"Are you telling me you're drunk because you met an Italian? Ya' fuckin' racist," he said, smiling and wagging his finger at me.

"I just wanted to say thank you."

"Ah, Billy, you shouldn't be thanking me," he said, looking down at his drink, and when he looked up, I could see that his eyes were watery. "I've made things difficult."

He knew. How long had he known? How do you tell someone that because you fell in love with him, your life had changed profoundly, that up until that point, you were just sleepwalking?

"I love you, Billy. I do," he said.

"I love you too," I replied.

He wiped his cheek.

"It's one thing to think you're all liberal and accepting and quite another to be so when a friend tells ya' he's gay. It did my head in at first. I saw you as one thing, and then you became another."

"Enzo, I'm the same person I've always been. The only difference is now you know who I am."

"No, Billy, you're not the same." He paused and then looked me dead in the eye. "You're better."

I looked back up at the sky, inhaling deeply through my nose and stemming the tide of tears.

Perhaps this would be the only romance I would ever have. I could have questioned every step and misstep I took. In the crushing weight of the inky blackness at night when I lay alone in bed and felt small, I often did. What if my mother accepted me when I was nineteen? In the early 1980s when I knew nothing about safe sex, surely I would be dead—an AIDS victim. What if I had not married Katherine? Well then, there would not have been Olivia and Claire. What if we never moved to New England? I would not have met Enzo. Every step a necessary one on the journey to this very night at a table in a former chapel on the other side of the world. When I looked back, I would recognize its importance even more than I could see now.

We emptied our glasses, and I poured two more. I glanced over at the young man with the laptop, alone in a sea of people. The thought bothered me, like a tiny pebble in my shoe rubbing against my foot. Enzo followed my gaze.

"Strange, huh, Billy? To be out here all alone in the dark," he said.

"No, not really," I replied.

We drained the pitcher, and when I stood up, the world tilted. "We need food," I said as I helped Enzo stand up. His head was pointed in one direction to the left, but his legs had another idea, and they veered to the right. I grabbed his arm and reoriented him. We crossed the street, and in the sickly fluorescent lights of a twenty-four-hour convenience market, I could see how bloodshot his eyes were. He grabbed a bag of chips and held it up so that it touched my nose. I pushed it back until I could make out the wording. "Shrimp chips," I told him. He walked up to the counter where a young Asian woman regarded him warily while I searched for something salty without fish as the main ingredient. When I joined him with a package of barbecue corn chips, Enzo was engaged in conversation with the clerk.

We stumbled back to the hotel and made our way to my room. I cracked the seal on two small liquor bottles from the mini bar and poured them into two glasses. Enzo was propped up on my bed, with his back against the headboard and eating chips. "This shit tastes like shrimp," he said. Handing him the bag of corn chips and a glass of gin, I sat down on the end of the bed next to him and removed his shoes.

"I'm moving back to Italy. That's my fuckin' fate," he said, staring at the glow from the TV in front of us.

"What, when?" I asked.

"My parents are getting older, and I'm the oldest child," he said.

"But you have siblings who are already there," I said. I couldn't lose him now.

He winced as he took a sip of his drink.

We looked back at the TV and watched some Japanese game show that didn't make any sense, the animated host speaking too quickly while making exaggerated Kabuki-like faces.

When I turned to look at Enzo in the reflected light of the TV, his eyelids had grown heavy, dark hair spilling over his forehead, and the cup in his limp hand was in jeopardy of toppling over. I took the glass and set it on the nightstand. I stood up, turned off the TV and the lights, and sat down in a chair next to the bed, waiting in the dark for him to stir. When he didn't, I lay down on the bed and pulled the blanket over us, the heat from our bodies pulsating beneath the landscape of the covers. *I mean, it must have been so fuckin' difficult to hold it all in for so many years.* I lifted my hand to his head and combed my fingers through his dark hair. It felt sacred. He twisted his body, his legs brushing mine. I moved my hand toward his waist, holding it in the air, hovering for a moment. *Come on, Billy. There's no place you'd rather be.*

"Shit," I whispered as I stared up at the ceiling. There were no stars to guide me.

Can I sleep with you this one last night?

I pulled my arm back and then rested it on his shoulder.

It would be the first time I slept, I mean *really slept* with a man I loved.

CHAPTER TWENTY-ONE

GROUP THERAPY

Group therapy is like online dating, becoming intimate with strangers to avoid suffering alone. I began both of them after the girls left, one to fill the void where my daughters used to be and the other to seal the fracture in my heart.

The "Coming Out Later in Life" support group met on the second floor of a Brookline Victorian townhome. On a crisp autumn evening, five other emotionally wrecked men and I gathered in a circle of chairs for the beginning of a twelve-week journey from one side of the closet door to the other. David, our leader, often gave us homework: come out to X number of people this week, make a list of things that are positive about being gay, watch a gay-themed movie—something other than porn, please. It was like conversion therapy but in reverse. After a lifetime of straight conditioning, we needed to work out what it meant to be authentic.

"The group is always full, even after fifteen years," David told us at the first meeting, and then added, "There is one rule—no dating each other."

There was a married limo driver who frequently had sex with his boyfriend in the back seat of his car. A single, good-looking guy in love with a Latino married minister; a Jewish man whose parents were Holocaust survivors, but he didn't think they could survive the knowledge that their son was gay; a recovering alcoholic who could have sex with a man only when he was drunk; and a Boston-Irish PR executive struggling to accept his sexuality, though he had no problems expressing it, especially with Asian men. And then there was me, a gay father whose small family moved seven hundred miles away and who had never had a boyfriend.

"You didn't even fool around?" the men asked in astonishment when I divulged my virginal past.

"I have—I mean I had a crush on this guy."

I felt inadequate.

If the group was representative of what I might encounter in the dating world, I ignored that fact and hurtled headlong by creating the online profile on Yahoo Personals.

The first spin of the bottle landed on Sam, who was even better looking in person than his numerous profile pictures, one of them in which he was shirtless. As a fellow gay father, I imagined he would be grounded, stable, and humble, as if all of the crazy had been corralled and cordoned off into the circle of our little support group.

On our first date at a Mexican restaurant in Cambridge, he wondered aloud if I might be more appealing if I looked gayer.

"Shaved head, tattered jeans, tight T-shirt, goatee." He listed these items as if selecting them from a straight-to-gay made-to-order catalog. "We'll have you looking gay in no time."

"I don't do drama," he said, and then spent the first twenty minutes of our date telling me about his previous boyfriend from New Hampshire who left him at 2:00 a.m., peeling out of his parking spot and destroying the wall in front of his parking space.

I should have used that time to question why his boyfriend fled in the middle of the night, literally busting through a brick wall. But instead, I let my eyes wander over the way his tan biceps strained against the fabric of his shirt as he gesticulated, and how his white teeth resembled a row of Chiclets gum inside a strikingly strong jaw while his mouth never stopped moving. It was the first time in my life that I felt the freedom to objectify another man in public. The support group would have been proud.

When he finally said, "Tell me about yourself," I lapsed into group-therapy mode and recounted my failed marriage and lamented the difficulty of maintaining a long-distance relationship with my daughters.

"And isn't it funny," I said, "the way we think we raise our children with the same parenting style, but then they turn out to have completely different personalities?"

He should have spent this time searching for the nearest exit, but instead, he let his eyes wander above my head to the TV at the bar and objectified Jason Varitek, the hunky catcher for the Boston Red Sox.

After that first date, the silence from Sam was surpassed only by that from my daughters. When I repeatedly called Olivia's and Claire's phones, there was no answer and then finally days later, a text message, Sorry, Dad, busy, and then one from Sam, I think the cilantro made me sick.

While the group was hoping for a more tantalizing conclusion to my first gay date, they were encouraged that he texted me, even if it was only to describe the status of his intestinal discomfort.

"He blew me off," I confided.

"It's a start," the good-looking guy said, and then Boston-Irish chimed in, pushing the glasses up on his nose, "It's where I like to staht."

"That's not what I meant," I replied, but then I realized the group was laughing, and then I was too.

While my daughters refused to talk to me, Sam eventually agreed to a second date. After dinner, he kissed me without warning. "I was just curious what it would feel like," he said, and then we were in his bed. I felt this great sense of accomplishment that was surpassed only by a feeling of *What the fuck have I been missing all these years?*

"I think this might be the one," I told the group, mistaking the powerful release of repression for love. They humored me by being supportive, and David said while picking at an errant thread on his sleeve, "It's unusual that the first turns out to be the one, but it happens."

But my newly shaved head, tight T-shirts, and goatee lasted longer than Sam's curiosity, which peaked after four dates.

Each one of us in the group had a "Let me tell you about my mother" story. Some moms were covert in their quest to make us straight. There was the mother who knitted a sea of baby blankets one after the other and said, with a heavy sigh, "Well, I guess I'll just store this one away too," and the mom who said, "Oh, you might be interested in this," while pushing the church's gay-abstinence group leaflets into her son's hand. Others were more overt: the mother who told her only son that if he didn't marry a nice Jewish girl, the family heritage they clung to in Auschwitz would be extinguished forever, and then, there was mine.

Instinctively, we knew our parents loved us, but when you're a self-loathing, middle-aged man in group therapy who can't maintain a healthy relationship, you're not there because you were blessed with the unconditional love and support of your parents. If your mother would have happily performed a do-it-yourself lobotomy to chisel out the gay feelings you were now coming to terms with, conflicted emotions were bound to surface.

And when my mother phoned me shortly after learning of my impending divorce, it was time to face the confrontation I had long been avoiding.

"Hello?"

"Bill, don't hang up," my mother said.

The hollowness in my gut was the same feeling I used to experience when my mother would walk up the stairs to our bedrooms when my brothers and I were kids, the ring on her finger clanking on the banister, *clank, step, clank, step, clank.* We'd jump to pick up the mess, throwing clothes into the closet, closing dresser drawers, swiping the cat off the bed, and later, if I was alone, jerking up my pants.

"I'm at work, Mom."

"I know. I called your work number. Bill, I just spoke with Katherine, and she told me you're getting a divorce."

"And what else did she say?"

"Well, she was not very pleasant. I've always thought—"

"Mom, what did she say?"

"She said that if anyone knew why you were getting a divorce, I would, and I do."

"Oh, you do now, do you?"

I amassed the troops. I stood outside of myself, remaining cool, watching the scene play out. I'd deliver the fatal assault when the timing was just right.

"I made a mistake, years ago. I said and did the wrong things," my mother said.

My mouth hung open.

"I wanted to tell you, but you were married. You had Olivia and Claire, and I didn't think it was my place."

"Your place? Where exactly do you think your place is?"

"I know you're angry. I was wrong. Being gay is normal, a part of your genetic legacy. Bill, can you ever forgive me?"

Could I forgive her? That was a good one! For years, the thought of the damage my mother had inflicted on me and, by proxy, on my family had fueled my anger, and now—now, and now? And now, she was disarming me. I was angry because she was making it difficult for me to be angry. Damn her.

"It's going to take some time," I replied, but by then, something inside of me had already decided that I was going to forgive her. I was starting to lose it in my office because finally, my mother accepted me.

After all of these years, I never knew how much it mattered. Why did it matter?

"Mom." That was all I could say before the troops retreated, running in the other direction.

"You were always special," she replied. "When you were a child, you were filled with so much joy, you used to laugh in your sleep."

"Oh shit, Mom." I surrendered. "What have I done to my girls?"

The girls were seven hundred miles away from me, and at the end of each month, my bank account was nearing the single digits. Katherine would no longer allow me to sleep at her house.

"Mom, if you are truly sorry, you can help me," I said.

If I thought beginning a relationship with a man in a ten-mile radius of my zip code was difficult, it paled in comparison to maintaining the long-distance one with my daughters and resuming the one with my mother. Once or twice a month, I would fly to my mother's house in North Carolina on a Friday afternoon, borrow her car, and then drive halfway to Roanoke, Virginia, to meet Katherine at the official halfway mark, a McDonald's in Bassett, Virginia, to pick up the girls. We'd return to my mother's on Friday, and then I'd repeat the journey back to Boston on Sunday.

I tried to cram hundreds of hours into a precious forty-eight-hour window. The lapse of time and the miles that stretched between us made each visit feel like we were on a first date. I wanted the time with Olivia and Claire to be perfect—dinner, movies, laughter and long walks while discussing deep and meaningful topics. But how could I expect teenagers to agree on a movie without arguing, or answer the question "How is school?" with anything other than "I dunno. I guess it's OK?" And often the condensed time we spent in my mother's small house ended up exploding, like a pressure cooker boiling over with too many ingredients.

"You're not my father," Olivia once screamed, and Claire added, "You don't even look or dress like my dad anymore."

They ran upstairs to a room that was not theirs, slamming the door behind them, and called their mother. I waited for my phone to start ringing.

"Bill, what in the hell is going on there?" Katherine asked, and when I told her I didn't know what just happened, she told me Claire walked into her classroom that week and discovered someone had scrawled *Claire's dad is a faggot* on the blackboard. "She made me promise not to tell you," Katherine said, her voice softening. My heart broke into bits in a way it never had before, and I wondered if I would ever be able to reassemble the pieces.

If my relationship with the girls was on rocky ground, the one with my mother was improving.

"I just realized," my mother said one morning shortly after the girls had moved back to Virginia, "that you'll never have the same amount of time with them ever again." The realization seized me. How could I expect to salvage our relationship when the time was so scarce, and if I didn't know what was happening to them the majority of the time, how could I protect them?

My mother woke up early each morning and made Belgian waffles and a cheesy grit casserole and bought a particular brand of orange juice for the girls because she had asked a teenager in the grocery store what type she preferred. She'd take us to her art studio located in a former school building, and we'd walk the halls, Mom acting as curator; the almondlike scent of old textbooks baked into the walls mingling with the wet smell of oil paint. She wanted to make everything perfect too, knowing that it never would be, but it was an island of calm in a sea of turmoil. It was her penance.

She opened up her home to the circle of crazy that was me, Olivia, and Claire, often acting as peacemaker and counselor. "Bill, they just want their father back. You don't even look the same anymore. Give them time."

When I returned to Boston, I'd wander through my basement apartment and pick up the mail and a plate of food covered in plastic that Linda left on the top step. Eating my reheated dinner alone, I'd rummage through the memories of the weekend, weeding out the bad ones and clinging to the good ones. And when the bad memories outnumbered the good, I went to another support group.

In the basement of a Unitarian Universalist church, a group of gay fathers gathered to share their "God knows I tried" stories. It was a larger support group than the "Coming Out" group, and most of the men were sad dads. But Greg, a beefy guy who sold cardboard boxes for a living, stood out from the crowd, mostly because he was not, in fact, a father, but was looking for a Daddy, and also he was a good six inches taller than everyone else in attendance.

After the meeting, he flirted with me at the bar and asked for my number. When he asked if I liked mountain biking, I replied, "I love it," and later that week when he asked me to join him for a ride in Western Massachusetts near his house, I bought a bicycle.

After our ride, he offered to show me his vintage washing-machine collection in the basement of his small home, and I decided to find it cute and quirky. When he told me that he had recently ended a relationship with a guy because he was "too nice," I nodded my head in agreement. "People can be so needy." And when he told me it was difficult just sitting there talking to me with a raging hard-on in his pants, I offered to take them off.

Afterward, he stripped the sheets from his bed, walked down the cellar steps, and tossed the laundry into a washing machine.

"I'll call you later," he yelled up the steps, but he never did.

I should have been concerned that Greg was at a gay fathers' support group but did not have any children, just as I should have second-guessed walking down the basement steps with a man I barely knew and feigning interest in his washing machine collection. What really should have alarmed me was that I was so willing to become someone else, without fully understanding who I was, to prove that I was worthy of being loved.

"I'd date you," each of the men in my support group said when I broke down over my languishing relationship with the girls and the nonexistent one with a boyfriend. "I mean if it were allowed," they added, referring to the number-one prohibition against dating each other.

They consoled me after a disastrous date with a guy who called himself a bitch and who proved it by sending me a nasty email when I told him he wasn't my type. I have a full head of hair, and you don't, dammit! he had written. They sent text messages of encouragement when I went back to North Carolina for Thanksgiving. Their support extended beyond the circle, and soon we were spending time with each other outside of the group at a local bar in Boston called Club Café. Boston-Irish looked around the bar and laughed. "It looks like a fucking set from a soap opera. 'Welcome to the Port Charles café.'"

"How did you guys become friends?" strangers would often ask.

"Group therapy," I replied.

Boston-Irish would narrow his eyes while adjusting his glasses and say, "Dameron, you don't need to be so fucking honest."

They were my first real male friends.

I was more than halfway through the twelve-week mark of the support group when I met Paul, a father of three, at a Cheesecake Factory restaurant in the Burlington Mall. I had grown weary of the same faces on Yahoo Personals and the all-too-familiar *Masculine man here* and homophobic *straight-acting* profile lines. On a whim, I widened the radius of my online search of available men from ten miles to sixty, which expanded into New Hampshire. That was when I saw his pictures, with the tagline "Attitude Is Everything." He looked normal, good normal, like he could have been the dad next door in a barn coat and button-down shirt who didn't know how attractive he was. There were no shirtless pictures of him, but it was the triangle of skin peeking through the top of his Brooks Brothers shirt that strangely did more for me than Sam's blatantly displayed four-pack abs.

And I? I looked nothing like my one profile photo anymore.

"I sent an updated picture to you. Didn't you get it?" I asked.

I forwarded it an hour before our date so that I could say I sent it and so that he would be unable to call off the date.

"I didn't get it, but I recognize that smile," he replied.

When he pulled out three crisp photographs of his children, two girls and a boy, and laid them on the table, I peeled through the paper receipts and detritus of my wallet and placed a tattered photo of Olivia and Claire down next to his. All of our children were with us on our first date.

When you first look at a photograph, it's easy to miss the finer details, those shapes that fade into the background, but without them, the picture is incomplete. Here were the things that came into focus that night: the way Paul placed his hand on the small of my back and allowed me to go first as the waiter showed us to our table; how he didn't comment on my altered looks, but recognized my smile; and the surprise that he was a part of the story before I knew he was a part of *my* story. He was the man from New Hampshire who had fled from Sam in the middle of the night and was also the guy whom Greg had labeled "too nice."

In this strange new gay world, I would come to learn that the chance of dating an ex-boyfriend of an ex-boyfriend was highly likely. How many spins of the bottle would it take before I was kissing myself?

When I hugged him good night beneath the haze of the parking lot light, he turned his head, and our lips brushed. Like the triangle of skin at the top of his button-down shirt, it was just the right amount of flesh. The next morning, instead of silence, I received a text message from him: Good Morning. Good conversation. Good Looking. Good first date. It's all good!

I would reveal all of this to the men in my group, and they would listen with rapt attention. I had learned to corral my secrets and shield them from a first date—not to be so fucking honest. But with them, I could share everything. We were all flawed in some way, and a piece of us had been lost, but we did not run away from each other, and that was when the picture became more detailed because they were a part of it too. I had fallen in love, and yes, maybe a part of it was from the powerful release of repression, but it wasn't because I had sex with anyone. I had been searching for validation from random strangers, but it was there all along, and it would be there for many years to come from those five emotionally wrecked men. I had fallen in love with them and perhaps, with Paul too.

CHAPTER TWENTY-TWO

WHAT ABOUT BOB?

I was setting up the artificial Christmas tree Linda had given to me, humming Christmas carols and telling her about my growing feelings for Paul. She handed me a rainbow-colored ornament printed with the words "My First Out Christmas," then asked me if his dating profile was still active. I sat down on the sofa and stared into the middle distance. Rusty jumped up, sniffed the ornament, and then gave my hand a tongue bath.

"Well, I'm sure if it is, he just hasn't gotten around to taking it down yet," she said.

Lucas hopped onto the sofa, causing Rusty to bark and growl, and then there was a blur of white hair, snapping mouths, and scratching paws. I shoved them off the sofa with a thud, and they whirled about the room like a kicked-up white fur storm.

I didn't know the answer to Linda's question, nor had I considered it, until now. I had suspended my profile because I couldn't imagine dating another man. It had not occurred to me that Paul still might.

"We don't have an agreement," I said.

It sounded too professional, like we were business partners, and so I rephrased it. "I mean, we're not going steady or anything."

I was a sixteen-year-old girl.

We had officially been on four dates, but we spoke daily, often multiple times throughout the day. I would call him on my drive home from work, and he would send me cute text messages in the morning and again before he went to bed. All of this and we had sex too, which was a bonus, as my limited experience with guys had taught me that sex was a parting shot, so to speak.

"You could ask him if he is still seeing anyone?" Linda said, her inflection crafting it more as a question.

Could I ask him? Were four dates too early? Or would it scare him off? I stood up, walked over to the tree, and finished decorating, but my mind wasn't in it. I was placing the ornaments on the tree as if each one were a pro or a con for and against asking him, like picking petals from a daisy. He loves me. He loves me not. I turned on the tree lights, stood back, and surveyed the completed job. The ornaments were clumped together, which made the top of the tree lopsided.

"So pretty," Linda said, making a little golf clap while tilting her head to the side. "This is going to be the best Christmas ever."

She stood up and kissed me on the forehead. Rusty and Lucas started barking for affection, and then Rusty sniffed the tree and hiked his leg.

"Rusty! No!" Linda shouted. Rusty's ears shot back, and his small body crouched down.

Linda walked toward the steps, the dogs trailing her like baby ducks following their mama.

"You're a catch," she said, walking up the steps, and then added, "I'll leave a plate of food on the top step," and closed the door behind her.

I glanced at the borrowed, lopsided tree, the afterthought of a kitchen, and then at the dirty snow through the tiny rectangle of light coming from the basement apartment window that highlighted a silvery cobweb. The door opened at the top of the steps, and a flurry of letters and magazines spilled down. "Mail!" Linda shouted. I was a catch, all right. The only thing separating me from the dogs was my use of an indoor toilet.

Maybe I couldn't ask Paul if he was still active, but I could certainly check whether his profile was viewable. I sat down, turned on the laptop computer, and then logged onto Yahoo Personals. Funny how you become conditioned to respond to those indications of activity on your profile. It's a tiny thrill. But I had no winks, views, or emails. I was let down, even though I knew there wouldn't be any. My profile was disabled, but like Pavlov's dog, I was hoping for a treat. I searched for Paul's profile. Mr. "Attitude Is Everything" was still active. I closed the lid of the laptop.

I wanted to believe that he had forgotten about his profile. He told me that he rarely checked it. He had been on Yahoo for years, and after dating "about a hundred guys," he had just about given up.

"A hundred?" I asked. I did not mask my horror.

"Lunch and learns," he replied. "We'd have lunch, and most of the time, I'd tell them there wasn't a romantic connection, but I'd love to have a new friend."

"And that worked?" I asked.

"Sometimes."

"How many new friends did you make?" I asked.

"One, maybe two." His eyes darted to the side, and he cocked his head. "Well, one," he replied.

He looked at me with a crooked smile and asked, "And what did you tell those poor boys who didn't make the cut?"

I didn't want to answer because A) there was only one, maybe two, and B) I was always the one who was cut.

"I lied," I replied.

I was vague because for some reason, Paul made it sound like he thought I was a catch, and I didn't want to hurt his feelings by letting him know that I wasn't. Maybe he didn't think I was "all that." Perhaps he was just biding his time.

For the next several days, my thoughts ran wild. Paul was a successful, handsome, emotionally stable man who lived in a beautiful home, and I was a troll who lived under the bridge, or at least underneath two lesbians and their non-shedding dogs. I couldn't get over this feeling that he was just being nice. I was so new to everything. How could I possibly compete against one hundred experienced men?

After letting this thought marinate, one night while I was driving home and talking to him on the phone, I told him that I was the type of person who didn't sleep around.

"I only have sex with one person at a time," I said.

"So, a threesome is out of the question?" he joked.

"You know what I mean. I'm old-fashioned."

"I know that about you."

He said it in a way that made it seem like he knew who I was, but he didn't say that he wasn't dating anyone else, and I couldn't bring myself to ask him. If I mentioned it, I was afraid that it would tempt him, like offering someone a dessert. Like maybe the person hadn't thought about it, but now that you brought it up, sure, they'd have another slice or two.

That thought rubbed and rubbed a groove in my brain, until there was nothing left to do with it but turn it into an action. One night after work, I logged onto Yahoo Personals, checked his profile, and then I created a new profile with a fake name. I sent Paul an email from my new alias, Bob Anderson who was a transplant to Boston from Michigan. I invented an entire backstory. Bob was a divorced dad and just beginning to dip his toes into the dating pool.

It took a couple of days before I heard back from Paul, and the little indication that Bob Anderson's profile received did not thrill me. It made my hands tremble and my hollow heart turn over in my chest.

> You can put some sentences together, and you
> sound normal. While I have had some good expe-
> riences, I still haven't found Mr. Right.

He gave me (Bob Anderson) his phone number, as he did in his first email back to me. In fact, the email was boilerplate, except for a few references to Michigan (Go Tigers!) and the fact that I (Bill) was not Mr. Right. It was a cut-and-paste job, which sliced me in two.

I walked into the bedroom, turned on the light, and reached up to the shelf in the closet. My hand searched for and found a brown paper bag, sandwiched between some sweaters and a pair of jeans. There were a cluster of syringes with needles inside and a package of five-sided pink pills, D-Bol. They were a reshipment from my steroid supplier after the order was seized by US Customs and Border Protection for "unauthorized importation of a controlled substance." That was what the letter from them stated. When I emailed the supplier with my concerns of going to federal prison, he replied, I don't think they have any way of tracking this, and six months after Katherine and my daughters had confronted me, to my surprise, another shipment showed up.

I'd like to say that I took the package and threw it away, but I didn't. I shoved it back in between my clothes. I held on to it all of this time because it was my safety net, my worry stone—better living through chemistry. If Paul ended up deserting me, I could bulk up again, literally physically catfishing, and attract someone else. I most certainly would not become his friend.

The next time I saw Paul, he came to Waltham to attend a holiday get-together with my office colleagues and me. I worked from home that day so that we would be closer to the city, where the event was taking place. I was on a work call when he knocked on the back door. It was cold and gray outside, and tiny flakes of snow were clinging to his hair. He waved and smiled, and I motioned for him to come in the door. I was still holding the crime of responding to my fake profile against him. If I had said that aloud, I might have realized how ridiculous it sounded.

He opened the door and glanced around my apartment and then stood next to me while I remained seated at the dining-room table with the phone wedged between my shoulder and ear. I could feel the heat radiating from his body. I typed some commands into the laptop and glanced up at him. He was too damn handsome. How could anyone always be in such a good mood? Look at that grin. He leaned down and nibbled on my earlobe as I swatted at him and put my finger to my lips. *Shh.* When I hung up the phone, he kissed me, and, like the snow melting in his hair, I turned into a puddle on the dining-room chair.

"Your apartment is cute," he said, looking around.

"Are you ready for the lengthy tour?" I asked. "You might want to pack a lunch."

We took five steps, and when we arrived in the bedroom, I said, "It's just a queen-sized bed."

"Nice," he replied.

"You don't mind sleeping here tonight? I mean you don't have any other plans?" I asked.

"The only plan I have is to be with you," he replied.

"OK, just checking," I said.

He cocked his head to the side and looked at me, *What's going on here?* I wanted to be angry with him for responding to my fake profile, but my body wanted to throw him onto the bed and rip off his clothes.

"Is someone still in work mode?" he said, smiling, and took my hand.

The touch of his hand sent an electronic signal through me that trumped the obsessive neurons firing in my head, and so I listened to my body and ignored my brain. Afterward, as I stood on my toes and washed his back in the shower, taking in his square shoulders and looking down at his tan line, I put one leg against his, turning mine back and forth, comparing them.

"Jesus, you've got massive legs," I said.

He flexed his thigh muscle, which made it bulge out, easily twice the size of mine.

"I like your sexy little hairy legs," he said.

He thought my legs were tiny, something new to obsess over. Leg day at the gym was never my strong suit. *Maybe if I had injected directly into my thighs,* I thought as I looked down and flexed a calf muscle.

"But look at your breastesses. Being so top heavy, do you have trouble toppling over?" he said.

This lassoed my thoughts in their tracks and kept them from running away again.

I was excited to show him off, to be the one with the good-looking guy on my arm, but when we exited from the shower, and I saw the snow falling and piling up at the back door, I knew that the work event would be canceled, which the message on my phone confirmed.

"Do you still want to stay?" I asked.

"Haven't we been through this?" Paul replied.

I needed to prove to someone that he existed and, if only for a brief moment in time, that I could attract someone who was so out of my league. When I knocked on the upstairs door and opened it, the dogs began barking. "Hello?" I said, and Linda replied from the living room to come in. I held Paul's hand and led him through the kitchen. Linda stood up from her chaise lounge and extended her hand, but Paul held his arms out and kissed her on the cheek. I kept blinking my eyes.

"I got soap in my eyes. I haven't been crying," I said.

Linda glanced at me quizzically while Rusty licked Paul's shoe.

"Please sit down," Linda said.

"I'll get us some beers. Do you want one, Linda?" I asked.

"I don't drink, but Deb has some in the fridge," Linda replied, and I thought, *Oh shit, I knew that.* What was wrong with me?

After exchanging pleasantries, we talked about how we met, which Linda had heard from me, perhaps a dozen times. She matter-of-factly asked, "So, Paul, are you still on Match or Yahoo or whatever?"

I choked a little on my beer and looked at her, unblinking, willing her to shut up, but she fixed her gaze on Paul.

"No," he replied.

Liar!

"I mean I'm enjoying concentrating my time on Bill," he said, turning his face toward mine. He patted my hand. His eyebrows were raised, and he had an upside-down smile, which I found adorable. But what was his answer? I didn't say anything. I just held on to his hand.

Rusty jumped up onto the sofa, and Paul was petting him with his other hand. When Paul became involved in the conversation, the frequency of the pats would slow down or stop entirely, and Rusty would start licking Paul's hand, *Love me.* He could never thoroughly enjoy the attention because he was always too concerned it might end.

After our visit with Linda, we drove to downtown Waltham and ate dinner at a tapas restaurant on Moody Street. We sat at a table by the window, and under the yellow light cast from a streetlight, snowflakes glittered and danced. The branches of a small pine tree in a planter by the door collected snow in its boughs. Inside, soft jazz mingled with intimate conversations and a sprinkling of laughter. We shared small plates of Spanish meatballs, croquettes, and artichoke, mushroom, and goat cheese crostini. He offered me the last bite and then reached his hand around the pitcher of sangria and took mine.

"I wanted to meet your work friends, but being here alone with you is perfection," he said.

"I think so too," I said, squeezing his hand.

I loosened my hand, but he didn't let go. He was unafraid to show his affection in public, and I could feel a warmth spreading through my cheeks. It was a combination of wine, embarrassment, and a feeling I was not ready to admit. It would have been perfection if only two of us were sitting at that table, but there was a third, and he kept nudging me and vying for attention, like Rusty licking Paul's hand. I wanted to enjoy my time with Paul, but my alter ego kept poking me and asking, *What about me? Do you think you deserve to feel this happiness when your children are alone? He doesn't want you. He wants me.* And so, the next day, I logged onto Yahoo Personals and put Bob Anderson down.

CHAPTER TWENTY-THREE
A TERMINAL CONDITION

We were eating breakfast at Andy's Diner on Mass Ave, just outside of Porter Square in Cambridge, when I asked Hans how long he had been dating Gavin before his kids met him.

"Is it getting that serious?" Hans asked.

"Sweetie, don't make it sound like a terminal disease," Gavin said while stirring honey into his chai tea.

I told them Paul had invited me to see *A Christmas Carol* at the Palace Theater in Manchester with him and his three children. He was going to make dinner beforehand, and then I would be sleeping over. It seemed like a big step, and the thought both thrilled and frightened me. What if the children didn't like me?

"But you're not married. Are you sleeping in the same bed with him?" Gavin asked. He placed his hand over his mouth in mock alarm.

I put my fork down and stared at Gavin and said, "Actually, I am married. The divorce isn't final yet."

Hans told me that his sons were older than Paul's kids, and because they were Jehovah's Witnesses, it was more complicated. He didn't introduce his children to Gavin for at least a year after he met him. By church law, they weren't even supposed to speak with their father after he came out. When his oldest son met Gavin, it was unplanned.

"There I was, sitting on the edge of our bed in my robe and curlers, smoking a cigarette," Gavin said. "It was all very Bette Davis." He held his hand above his shoulder, two fingers up, holding a phantom cigarette.

I looked at Hans, and he mouthed the word "No."

"Maybe you could buy them a little gift, like some candy?" Hans said.

"I'm not certain that giving his diabetic daughter a handful of sugar would go over well," I replied.

"Oh, right," Hans said, looking up, and then added, "Just be yourself. You're a father."

Paul had told me that when he was driving his children back to his ex-wife's house, after they spent a weekend with him, his older daughter, Sarah, asked, "So, Dad, what's going on with your dating life?" He responded that he was seeing me.

"Did you tell them my name?" I asked.

"Uh, yeah," he responded slowly, like *Why wouldn't I?*

I was still searching for clues that I was the only one he was dating. It would be easy to lie to someone you had just started dating. I knew that all too well. But lying to your children was entirely different, which, unfortunately, I also knew too well. He reasoned that if they were asking about me, then they were ready to meet me. I supposed that if he was prepared for me to meet his children, I must have become the main attraction.

I had not told my daughters about Paul. It was difficult enough just getting their attention on the phone. I didn't want to give them another reason to be angry with me. I would be flying to Greensboro, North Carolina, in a week and then driving up to Roanoke to pick up the girls. We would spend the holidays at my mother's house. We were all forging new relationships with one another, each of us in a new position.

It was a precarious arrangement, stacked up like a house of cards. I was not confident the foundation was sound enough to hold another card.

I don't know what I expected when I walked through the door into Paul's kitchen that evening. Perhaps that the children would be standing there gawking at me like a zoo animal, or the atmosphere might be tense with me thrown into the mix, but when I entered, Paul greeted me with a kiss, swatted me on the rear, and said, "Pour yourself a glass of wine." His older daughter, Sarah, was at the dining-room table, typing on a laptop computer, and glanced up briefly. Two men kissing did not seem to faze her, though it still made me uncomfortable to show affection in front of anyone. I heard laughter and the patter of feet upstairs.

"Sarah, this is Bill," Paul said.

"Hello," Sarah chirped. It was a polite and unassuming voice. She had her father's distinctive nose, shoulder-length dark hair, and kind eyes.

Paul walked to the end of the hall and yelled up the steps, "Nasty little children who live at the top of the stairs, come down and say hello!"

I laughed. Sarah smiled and rolled her eyes.

Paul walked back into the kitchen, with a dish towel thrown over his shoulder. He was wearing jeans and a gray sweatshirt, and his feet were bare. He was the kind of guy who could look handsome wearing anything or nothing.

"The bottle of red is over there," he said, pointing across the kitchen to a sliver of counter next to the refrigerator. He remembered my preference in wine. The kitchen's tiled floor stretched the length of the house, and next to the bay window overlooking the backyard and a grove of pine trees was the dining-room table where Sarah sat.

I opened the bottle and poured a glass of wine as Paul bent down to check the oven, and then he turned up the volume on a speaker. Mariah Carey was singing easy runs, turning a classic Christmas carol into something new. The smell of chicken parmesan wafted through the kitchen, and my mouth began to salivate.

"Dad listens to Christmas music nonstop from Thanksgiving until New Year's," Sarah said. "He puts up the tree the day after Thanksgiving. He's OCD. All of the gifts are color coded," she said with a sigh.

Paul cleared his throat and said, "Excuse me, child, who color coordinates the wrapping paper?"

"Oh, sorry, parental unit, that fat man who breaks into our house while we are sleeping does," Sarah said.

"That's right, Santa does," Paul said, and kissed Sarah on her forehead while wiping his hands on the dish towel. She pretended to bite his nose.

The other two children ran into the kitchen. They all had thick dark hair, flawless ivory skin, and eyes the color of dark chocolate. The youngest could have been Claire at nine years old and Sarah, Olivia three years ago.

"This is Gigi," Paul said, placing his hand on top of her hair, and she jokingly screwed up her face as if he were crushing her head. "And this handsome young man is Nick," he said. Eleven-year-old Nick made an *aw shucks* face, pointed both index fingers at himself, and said, "Who, me?"

"They're both deranged," he said, staring at them as they made faces.

They said hello, and I replied, "Nice to meet you," and shook their hands. They stood there in silence.

"OK, strange children, you may leave now," Paul said, knitting his brow and laughing. "Gigi," he said, "check your blood sugar. Dinner is up soon."

They ran into the family room, and I stood there for a moment motionless. Mariah Carey was singing "All I Want for Christmas Is You." The smell of garlic bread was joining the chorus of flavors lingering in the air. Children were running and laughing, and this good-looking, barefoot father was flirting with me.

I remembered waking up that morning, and there was this sense of promise like anything could happen. It's that same feeling you get when you're a kid, and the air is crisp and cold, and the sky is filled with pregnant clouds. There is this electricity, and then the snow starts falling, and the world becomes silent and rearranges itself. Here I was. It was happening, but I didn't want to blink because I was afraid the world would melt when my eyes focused.

"Hello?" I heard Paul's voice reach across the gulf.

I shuddered and said, "Your children are great."

"They'll do," Paul said, and kissed me again.

There was a rhythm between Paul and his children, and I was afraid I would change the beat, but throughout dinner and when we went to the theater, I became swept up in the playful banter. Paul and I sat side by side in the dark balcony as three ghosts visited Ebenezer Scrooge. Paul reached down and took my hand. I looked at him. His face was glowing from the reflected lights of the stage, and then I looked at the profiles of the three kids. When the first act ended, I took my hand back to clap, and when I placed my hand back down on my lap, he clasped it and put it on his thigh and patted it. There was that electricity. I could feel him looking at me. What was he thinking? Was he looking at my ghosts, and which ones did he see, the past, present, or future?

When we returned to his home and the children went to bed, we made love. There was a new dimension to our lovemaking that night. It was tender and humorous and unrushed. "What are you doing, crawling around like a little monkey?" Paul asked as I climbed over him, and I could not stop laughing. What he said was not that funny, but there was this joy inside of me that needed to be released. Though I was three years his senior, there was an energy that he exuded. I saw it between him and his children. He was the rock, the caretaker. I would have to surrender some control, to become the one in the passenger seat. I was ready to surrender, to give it all.

In the dark, while Paul was sleeping, I lay awake, staring through the blinds at the crescent moon cradled in the arms of a pine tree. I felt a tear roll down the side of my cheek, and then I was attempting to muffle the sounds of my galloping sobs. The world transformed, and I was dropped into this sliver of life, a puzzle piece that had been in the wrong box and was now home. I cried for all of the years that were lost and for the ache of loneliness in my heart stirred up by the laughter of children not my own. I cried because there was just too much, too much pain in the past and too much hope for the future, and as he lay next to me, his long limbs stretched across the bed, there was too much that I needed to say to him. I didn't want to keep secrets anymore, the steroids, the catfishing, my hidden but waning infatuation with Enzo. After all these years of pretending, how could I be sure of the truth?

Paul dropped me off at the airport the following Friday, and for the first time, I kissed a man publicly in broad daylight. When I arrived in Greensboro, I saw my mother smiling at the end of the long hall of the terminal, standing with her purse held in front of her. Always fashionable and now in her late sixties, she had a regal look to her, the shock of white hair swept back from her forehead. She wore purple linen pants with a matching, loosely constructed linen jacket. The years did not diminish her stature but seemed to accentuate it. She appeared taller and her posture more erect. She watched me approach, and after we hugged, she stood back while holding on to both of my shoulders, and said, "My goodness, you look so handsome, even with that shaved head."

She had seen the change in my physical appearance before, over the Thanksgiving holiday. She was shocked then. "I can't get over that tough exterior and this," she said, poking my chest with her index finger. "But when you speak, it's my same soft-voiced son."

"It's advertising," I said, cupping my chest with my hands.

"I don't want to talk about that," she said, flicking her hand and dismissing the thought of me with another man. While she could accept who I was now, she still could not wrap her mind around what that meant, the physicality of it. But now, standing at arm's length, she saw something that could not be wiped away with the wave of a hand. She saw happiness.

"I've met someone," I told her, "and he makes me very happy."

"That's wonderful," she said. "Tell me about him."

We drove to my mother's home through the streets of my youth, past Saint Pius X, the parochial school of my childhood, the ancient elms that I used to climb, and Buffalo Creek, where I escaped to catch crayfish on summer days. I described this man to my mother in a way that a young boy lying in the grassy fields of Latham Park and staring up at the passing clouds could never have imagined.

"I want you to meet him," I said.

"I'm not quite ready for that," my mother replied.

"You can accept my being gay, just as long as I never bring anyone home?" I exploded.

There was that rage bubbling up like lava cracking through the crust with hubris and indignation.

"Bill, just give me some time to get used to it," she replied, holding her hands out, palms up.

"You wouldn't have any problem meeting Alex's girlfriend," I said, referring to my older brother's girlfriend of the month, and when my brother Christopher got divorced, Mom had no reservations meeting his new girlfriend.

"I don't want to meet Alex's girlfriend either," she said.

I took a deep breath and decided to let it go for the moment. It was Christmas, and she accepted me. For now, that would have to be enough. We were all learning to walk the long, rocky road of forgiveness.

My mother sold our childhood home on Latham Road years ago, but the house she bought was still in the same neighborhood. It was smaller, a Cape Cod with a sunny front porch, a picket fence in front, a half circle of green awning over the door on the side, and in the backyard, her garden. When I walked through the side door into the kitchen, the fresh scent of home was the same. It was the smell of sweet tea and roses. It was as if she packed up all of the air, along with the belongings, the upholstered living-room furniture, the oil paintings, and in the sunny, terra-cotta-tiled dining room, the blond-colored table upon which all of our meals were served. Scattered about the house were the memories, pictures of my brothers and me at various ages, resting on an end table or hanging in the hall, and next to them, the paintings my mother had created.

"Mom, you are getting so good," I said.

I was standing in front of a painting of Buddhist monks in yellow flowing robes, walking beneath a canopy of broad green rubber trees. She painted it after a trip to Cambodia.

"I see things now that I didn't see before," she said, and placed her arm around my shoulder. "I went to this shrine, and it had this sense of peace, you know?"

She looked at me and laughed like she might have been a little embarrassed.

"I told one of the monks that I was Christian, but this place, it felt so spiritual to me. Do you know what he said?"

I shook my head.

"'Same God, different name.'"

She hugged me while patting my back and said, "I'm so glad you're here, Willy."

"Me too, Mom, me too. I'm happy that we're both here."

My older brother, Alex, who was now divorced, joined us, and we spent Christmas Day together, drinking mimosas and talking about our love lives. The day after, I climbed into my mother's car and started driving north to Virginia to pick up the girls. Katherine and I had agreed to meet at the McDonald's restaurant in Bassett, Virginia, our halfway point. As I drove north on Route 220, outside of the city limits of Greensboro, the landscape flattened out, and the occasional simple brick ranch, tobacco barn, or single farmhouse flickered by the window. A billboard proclaimed that "Jesus Saves," and a trio of crosses was planted in a field of red clay to remind you that someone died in a horrific way for your sins.

At the Virginia line, the road snaked and climbed the foothills, and on the horizon, the shape of the undulating Blue Ridge Mountains filled me with an aching loneliness. When I pulled into the McDonald's parking lot, the girls were already there, and I regretted that the handoff would take place in some godforsaken location on the edge of nowhere.

I parked the car and walked over to the gold-colored Chrysler minivan. Katherine rolled down the window.

"Hello," I said.

"Merry Christmas, Bill," Katherine replied. The smile was forced, and when she looked at me, it was only for a brief moment before turning around and telling the girls to have a wonderful time.

Claire was the first one out of the van, and when we hugged, I lifted her up and planted my nose in her hair, breathing in the scent. Olivia walked over and said, "Merry Christmas, Daddy," and my eyes became wet as I hugged her.

We picked up French fries from the drive-through window and began the trip south, reaching my mother's home just as the sun was dipping below the horizon and the sky became purple.

My mother hugged the girls. Told them how tall they had gotten and how beautiful they had become.

"I'm going to put my luggage upstairs, Bill," Claire said, and Olivia followed.

When they were upstairs, my mother turned to me and said, "She calls you Bill?"

"That's something new," I replied.

"It's a form of disrespect," Mom said. "I think you should—" She shook her head like there was an internal battle over what she thought and what came out of her mouth. "Well, I'm not going to tell you what to do anymore. You're a good father."

When the girls came back downstairs, we sat in the living room, and in front of them I placed two large stacks of gift-wrapped boxes, which I had shipped to Mom's house.

"My goodness, they just keep on coming," my mother said with eyebrows raised as the girls unwrapped one package after another. I refrained from responding to the comment.

When my brothers and their children showed up, in clusters of three or four, the girls clung to me as if they were still toddlers holding on to my pant leg. For many years, we rarely interacted with them. Their aunts, uncles, and cousins were strangers to them, and in many ways, I was a stranger to them.

"I don't think I've ever seen you so buff," my sister-in-law remarked when she first saw me while squeezing my arm.

"Oh yeah, what's this?" Olivia said, poking my belly.

Glasses of wine were passed around as laughter and stories of our childhood were recycled. My brothers and I reverted to some internal age whenever we came together, frozen in time like one of the photographs collecting dust on a shelf. Alex, always the Eagle Scout leading the pack at fifteen; Christopher, the one who bore the brunt of our jokes at eleven; and Damian, the baby with eyelashes as thick as a girl's. Then there was me, at twelve. Who was I?

"Can I have a glass of wine, Bill?" Claire asked.

"It's Dad," I replied, "and no, of course not."

"You're not my father," she said under her breath.

"Excuse me?"

"Never mind," she said, and walked away.

When I walked into the living room following her, I found Olivia curled up on the sofa, her face buried in the cushions.

"Olivia?" I said, sitting down and placing my hand on her shoulder. "Are you OK?"

"This isn't right," she said, and a sob escaped.

"I know it's hard," I said, pulling her toward me.

"Mom should be here."

I wrapped my arms around her, and she put her head on my shoulder. I rocked back and forth slightly, the way I did when they were babies. I felt self-conscious as the others looked on as if they were judging me, the man who broke up a family.

"Why couldn't she come here?" Olivia asked.

There were red splotches around her eyes, and she dragged the back of her hand across her nose.

"Sweetie," I said as I struggled to find an answer.

"Do you miss your mama?" Rebecca, my youngest brother's wife, asked.

Olivia nodded, and then Rebecca was sitting next to her, telling her that they should all come down and visit her, that they would have a girls' weekend. They would sit together and paint their nails and watch romantic movies. Olivia smiled. I looked up at Rebecca and mouthed, "Thank you."

That night I lay on the mattress in the upstairs bedroom, staring at the ceiling. I opened the window to let some fresh air in, and the lone bark of a dog drifted into the room on the scent of pines. Downstairs, I could hear the clink of dishes being washed in the sink. I was the uncertain teenager in my mother's house again. I opened my phone and called Paul.

"The first Christmas is tough," he said. "It takes time, but keep on being the rock, and they'll figure it out, Daddy-O."

He could say anything, and I would believe it. There was a strength and honesty in his voice that reached across time and spoke to me.

"What are you wearing?" he asked.

"Pajamas and a T-shirt," I replied.

"Lose the shirt."

"OK," I replied, and peeled off my shirt, but then I heard a knock on the door.

"Dad?" I heard Claire's voice.

"Yes? I'm just getting dressed," I said too loudly, and Paul said, "She's calling you Dad again. Take care of your girls, Daddy-O, and call me later."

As a young girl, Claire never could sleep through the night. She would come into our room and gently tap me on the shoulder. I would move over. I often joked that she would be sixteen years old and still sleep with me, and now here she was, doing just that.

We spent the following days filling up the time together going to the movies, shopping at the mall, and then we drove to our first home on Dellwood Drive. It was a twelve-hundred-square-foot postwar box in a neighborhood riddled with patriotic street names (Independence Road, Liberty Drive, and Colonial Avenue among them). On the Fourth of July, a makeshift parade, led by the *stroller patrol*, would materialize like pillared clouds on a hot summer day. Young parents would affix red, white, and blue crepe paper and balloons onto wagons, tricycles, and baby carriages and march through the blocked-off streets—cold beer in one hand, baby bottle in the other.

"We even tried cloth diapers for about two weeks," I told the girls. But our love of convenience trumped our love of the environment.

The house seemed smaller, as they always do, but the memories seemed so much more significant.

"Were we happy here?" Olivia asked, and I replied, "Very."

I wanted the girls to smell the grass, see the sidewalk, and touch the trees in the yard. These memories and this love were as solid and real as the tiny brick house they first lived in. None of that was ever a lie.

I drove the girls back to Virginia and kissed their faces over and over until they said, "Dad, stop!" On the ride to the airport, I thought about what I needed to say to my mother, some version of "I love you," or "I forgive you," but when I looked over at her, she said, "You know, I did the best I could with you."

"I know, Mom."

Through the plane window, I watched the shape of Cape Cod come into view, like a flexed arm with the gnarled-up fist of Provincetown jutting out into the Atlantic Ocean. When we landed, I let out a sigh, and as I walked down the hall of the terminal, I held my hand up like a visor to block the reflected light of the afternoon winter sun. Between me and the light, a throng of bodies flickered, but at the end of the hall, Paul stood motionless, his smile as bright as landing lights. I felt a heart palpitation like I never had before, and for an instant, a flash, I wondered if I had some terminal condition.

CHAPTER TWENTY-FOUR
DON'T SAY IT

He was stirring steamed green beans and butter in a red plastic bowl when I realized I could watch the way Paul's long fingers gripped that fork for the rest of my life. He scooped the beans out onto two plates, turned, and handed me one while raising an eyebrow.

"What?" he asked.

"Looks good," I replied.

They were frozen green beans, nothing special. Eat them, and you would grow strong. But there was a feeling growing inside of me, and I could sense the tendrils squeezing my lungs.

"Don't be the first one to say it," my brother Alex told me. "You'll look silly if he doesn't say it back."

When we drove along the rocky coast of Maine and watched the green ocean swell like it was a living being larger than eternity, I did not say it. When the snow danced and clung to the branches of the pine trees, I did not say it. When the full moon kissed his sleeping face, I did not say it.

Night after night, I watched him cook buttered green beans, turkey meat loaf Florentine, and buffalo chicken and listened to him pour the gurgling red wine. I told him that I was not dating anyone else. I told him that he made me laugh. I told him that I had never been so happy before, but I did not scare him away because I did not tell him those three words.

"I have to say it," I told Alex.

"Are you sure?" he asked.

"Positive."

"What if he doesn't feel the same way?"

His question seized me with doubt. I was a fool. It was too soon. I packed up the words and stored them away. The ocean was a body of water. The cold snow was something to shovel, and the moon was just a moon.

On a Monday morning, the alarm clock failed me, and I was running late for work.

"Have you seen my striped shirt?" I yelled.

"It's hanging up in the closet. It's ironed," he shouted up the stairs.

"I don't have time for breakfast," I said, running down the steps. "Where are my shoes?"

"They're by the door," he replied.

I slipped on my shoes. He stood in his pajamas by the cellar door, smiling and clutching a brown paper lunch bag, the top creased beneath those long, perfect fingers.

"It's breakfast," he said.

My lips grazed his lips.

"I love you." It slipped.

"I love you too," he replied. "Now, get your ass to work."

The tendrils of the vine clutched my heart and squeezed the air out of my lungs as I ran down the cellar steps and into the garage. When I reached the highway, I called Alex.

"What did he say?" he asked.

"I am such a fool," I replied.

He had told me through his actions long before I ever told him.

CHAPTER TWENTY-FIVE

MY ADULT WALK

Olivia was fourteen years old when I realized she had settled into her adult walk. It was no longer the carefree skip of a child, but not yet the determined gait of someone who had lost sight of magic in the world. I can't remember what triggered the recognition; perhaps it was the day itself. Brilliant sunlight danced on the tender leaves of spring.

It struck me, strolling behind her then, the unhurried, graceful walk she would carry into adulthood was the essence of that day. Sadness followed pride as I realized the little girl I had carried on my shoulders would from now on carry herself.

I remember too, following in my father's footsteps. I would take great strides as I placed my feet in the imprints of his on the sandy shores of North Carolina's Outer Banks during summer vacations, stepping into them before the water could wash them away. I held my arms out as if balancing on a tightrope. Growing older, I began to notice how his feet turned outward, which seemed awkward and ducklike to me. I started to modify my walk, choosing to make his style my own.

In college, none of us could afford a car. We'd walk to the local pub in groups and drink "quarter" drafts served in plastic cups. As I headed home from the bar one night, a female classmate following behind me shouted, "I wish I had a porch swing like that!" implying that my walk had more of a swish to it than a man's should. I corrected my walk again, keeping in mind that my feet should not turn out like my father's and that my ass should not have more of a swing than my mother's.

It's hard to walk naturally when you're consumed with how not to walk. But, for all of my life, that was what I had been doing. When I began dating Paul, I felt again like the little boy stepping into his father's footprints on the beach. As Paul walked ahead of me, I noticed the confidence in his posture, the square shoulders, arms straight by his sides, palms always facing back, head held high, and the giant stride of his long, muscular legs.

On the night after I confessed my love for him, he walked into my apartment, kissed me, continued to the refrigerator, with garbage bag in hand, and started pulling out items. He squinted as he held them up to his face and then tossed a container of cottage cheese and a six-pack of yogurt into the bag.

"Hey, that's still good!" I yelled.

"Sweetie, these have been in here since our first date," he replied.

"They're sentimental."

"They have all separated into their original ingredients," he said while lifting the lid on a container of sour cream and tentatively sniffing. "Sheez." He turned up his nose and tossed it into the bag while waving away the stench in front of his face.

I watched him pull out some items from a grocery bag and put them into the refrigerator, a bag of lettuce, turkey burgers, unexpired yogurt. I followed him as he walked into the bathroom. He pulled out a small black pouch from a tote bag and placed it in the drawer of the vanity. He turned around, smiled, gave me an eyebrow flash, and nodded toward the bedroom, *Follow me.* He pulled out a set of clothes from the bag, opened the drawer of the dresser, frowned, rearranged my clothes, and placed his pajamas next to mine.

"I guess this means you're sticking around?" I asked.

"Well, now that I know you love me," he replied.

I felt my face flush.

"About that, it just came out. I don't want you to feel backed into a corner or anything. I mean, it was out of habit, something I used to say to Katherine every morning."

"Now it feels even more special," Paul replied.

"Shit, that's not what I meant to say."

I worried all day that Paul told me that he loved me because he was a nice guy who couldn't think of another way to respond. "I love you too," sounded better than "OK." I was a forty-four-year-old man in romantic love for the first time in my life. Where there had always been a no, there was a yes, and my heart might burst from the possibility.

"I'm sorry," I said.

"There's no need to apologize. I've found Mr. Right," he said.

But I wasn't Mr. Right. I was wrong in many ways, and the evidence snaked up my back and hid in the dark on the shelf of my closet and lingered as a fake profile on the internet. Would he love me if he knew I was a liar and a cheat?

"I know I'm not much now, but I've got potential," I said as I looked around the tiny basement apartment.

"You mean there's more than this?" he asked, his hands outstretched and his face filled with exaggerated surprise. "Look, I've dated guys with money, remember? I'd rather be in love with a handsome poor man living in a lesbian lodge than a rich banker who cheats on me."

Often, I would come home from work and find Paul upstairs, laughing and sharing a beer with Debra and Linda. We all fell in love with him at the same time.

When Linda and Debra escaped the cold New England winter to watch the Red Sox at spring training in Florida, we promised to take care of "the boys."

"It's called a belly band," Linda said, holding up a rectangular piece of fabric.

She placed a pad on the inside of the fabric, and as Rusty squirmed, she fitted it around his waist, wrapping it over his tiny penis, and then secured it with the Velcro stitched on either end. She put the same apparatus on Lucas, and we watched them waddle about the room, like Slinky Dogs wearing pants for the first time.

When I demonstrated this to Paul, he gave me a blank look and then asked, "We're putting tampons on dogs?"

"This way, we can leave them for a while, and they won't pee all over the house," I said. "And technically they're feminine napkins or pads or whatever. They're not tampons."

"Oh dear God," Paul said while grabbing Rusty's squirming body, and wrapped a belly band around him. "We'll use this time to do a little training."

Paul worked from my apartment that week and issued daily dispatches in the form of email report cards regarding the dogs' progress while I was at work. On Monday night, when I arrived home, Rusty was sitting on the sofa as Paul was typing on his laptop. When Rusty attempted to stealthily lick Paul's hand by sticking his pink tongue out to the side, Paul made a quick "Ah" sound and held his finger up. The tongue retreated. *Good boy.* Lucas hiked up his leg at the corner of a door and attempted to mark it, but because the belly band absorbed it, it was a urinary dry heave.

"Yeah, that one is dumb as a chicken. I can't do anything with him," Paul replied.

On Tuesday night when I came home, there was no barking, but I heard the shower running. I leaned my ear against the bathroom door and heard Paul talking to someone. When I opened the door, I could see through the frosted shower door the shape of Paul's body and at his feet, two white objects. "Hello," I said as the water stopped and Paul asked me to hand him a towel. I tossed it over the door, and then I could see him bend down and dry off what I now recognized as Rusty and Lucas. When he opened the door, the dogs went charging into the living room, ears back as they rubbed their wet, wriggling bodies against the sofa and the carpet.

"OK, dirty boy, it's your turn," Paul said, holding his hand out for me.

"But—" I started to reply, and before I could finish, Paul lifted up his finger and said, "Ah."

As he scrubbed my back, I thought about a statement his mother had made regarding his previous boyfriends: *No more wounded animals.* That phrase had become wedged in my brain. Was I just another stray dog that he couldn't resist? How long would it be before he tired of me weeping on Sunday nights when the house became still after the children left? When I tapped his garage wall with the front of my car, he hung marine bumpers from chains and placed a motion sensor that indicated the visual proximity of my car to the wall: *green, yellow, red, stop!* He cleared out my refrigerator and restocked it at every visit. When he first gave me a set of keys to his home, I left the front door unlocked and the garage door wide open. His patience seemed infinite, but I worried that my affection for him would not be enough and eventually he would grow tired of reengineering his life and would return me to the pound with all of the other broken animals.

When I discussed this at group therapy, all of the men said with a personal urgency, "You're not a wounded animal!" but in reality, we all were. Perhaps they wanted to be reassured that whatever was broken could be fixed, that we could somehow reclaim our natural walk, but even they did not know my entire past. After the first closet door, there was another and after that another.

"It sounds like Paul brings a lot to the relationship," Boston-Irish said. "What do you think you bring?"

He said this in a way that was meant to be reassuring, but when I sat there speechless, mouth open and eyes darting while trying to come up with something, anything, he said, "Dude, don't worry, clearly the guy loves you."

That night after group, I drove home feeling more confident. Maybe it was the sense of fun or the unexpected that I brought that kept our relationship exciting. When I called Paul at a stoplight on Harvard Avenue to let him know I was on the way home, he said, "I'm standing shirtless in your apartment."

"Well now, that's an image," I replied.

"I'm rearranging the apartment, and it got a little hot," he replied.

My mind began to race like the frenzied dogs running around the apartment, and then it went back to that night a lifetime ago when Katherine called me and told me to come home. *Just get here.*

How dare he go through my stuff, I thought. There was that old anger, just below the surface, ready to lash out at anyone who peeled back a layer. Why didn't I just throw the shit away? What if he thought it was something more? Would he believe me when I told him it wasn't heroin or some other narcotic? He could be packing up and leaving now. When I pulled into the driveway, I half expected his car to be gone, but there it was. I walked around the back of the house and up the path to the slate patio. The palms of my hands became sweaty, and my heart ran wild. I paused for a moment in the yellow lights spilling from the French doors and peered in like a voyeur watching his life from afar.

There was Paul, standing in a pair of jeans, shirtless with his back to me, square shoulders and arms outstretched, attaching a wine rack to the wall. How well I knew the back of that head, the shape of it, and the way his short salt-and-pepper hair swirled. On our first night together, I lay behind him, and when he turned his head to the side, the handsome shape of his profile, each feature in perfect proportion, the slope of his nose, and the glow of his smile made me ache, my heart expanding to take it all in.

The clean glass of the French doors sparkled as I placed my hand on the doorknob and pulled it open. Paul turned around and walked toward me. I looked around the room. There were new cushions on the worn-out sofa, a new lamp, and in the sunroom a new rug and book-shelves. "Welcome home," he said, and kissed me. I waited.

"I've just rearranged a few things and bought some items to make it more workable," he said, looking around.

I walked around the apartment, taking in the change, and then I walked into the bedroom, leaving Paul in the living room. "It's beauti-ful," I said. He raised his voice so that I could hear him. "If there was something I was unsure of, I just left it where it was." I closed my eyes and took in a deep breath. He knew. I opened the closet door in the bedroom and reached up to the shelf. I couldn't tell if it had been moved, but it was still there. *Wounded animal, drug addict, Mr. Wrong.*

I could have confessed right then and there. He gave me the opening—*If there was something I was unsure of*—but I didn't say any-thing, because how do you convince someone that you're not injured when there are hypodermic needles in a brown paper bag sitting on the shelf of your closet? I was taking a low dose of dermatologist-prescribed antibiotics that would soon erase the acne, and when that disappeared, I could forget that part of my life. Why bring it up now when it would soon be behind me?

Though we might try to forget the past, it does not forget us, and like the tide, it returns, sometimes with great force. My past caught up with me after thirty days of antibiotics ravaged the good bacteria in my gut, leaving the bad to flourish. When this happens, you find yourself alone in the bathroom with a lot of time on your hands to think about the decisions you have made. Those thoughts can center on distant choices like the ones you made on a dark night months ago or recent ones, such as what you ate for your last meal. Paul stood by me, or rather by the bathroom door, as I struggled with a nasty case of diarrhea, caused by bacteria aptly named *C. difficile*. When someone does not leave you when you are living in a basement as a closeted drug addict, pimply, smelly, your head shaved bald, you owe him something—gratitude indeed, but more than that, the truth. Maybe I didn't have much to offer, but there was something I could give to Paul that I had never given to anyone, even if that very thing might spell the end of our relationship.

I spoke with David first. When I told him I had taken steroids, I felt like I should have been bigger, more buff. Did he believe me? I shared with him my fears that A) my body was a big part of what attracted Paul to me, and B) that Paul might leave me. Would he still love me if he knew that I was chemically enhanced?

"Why do you think he might leave you?" David asked.

"Because he'll think I'm a fraud," I replied, because I was a fraud, had been for my entire life.

"Then be real. Tell him the truth."

For all of my life, I had been an impostor, lying about who I was, changing the way I looked, modifying the way I walked, shape-shifting. After so many years of adjusting my walk, what was the truth? Was I prepared to let him go?

That night after Paul made dinner and cleaned the dishes, I sat down with him on the sofa and said, "I met with David again for a one-on-one session."

"Oh, I thought you were done with those," he replied.

"I know you found the needles in my closet."

Paul looked at me without saying anything. He stood up and then walked toward the door.

My heart sank. *This is when he leaves me.*

When my father left my mother, he moved into the Yester Oaks apartment complex on the other side of town. In the late 1970s, it was known as a place for swinging singles and key parties. Women in macramé bikinis with long red fingernails would sun themselves by the pool, casting sidelong glances at my father.

He stopped by "the house" one day—that was the year language changed, "our house" becoming "the house." Possessive adjectives were too heavy to place in a sentence. He asked my brothers and me if we used the barbell set. I was too embarrassed to say that I did. He carted it off and set it up in his new apartment. He would sit on the bench, shirtless, cigarette perched in the side of his mouth, and curl weights. I thought that he, at his age, ancient in my mind, but younger than I was now, was so foolish. Here I was, falling into Dad's footsteps again.

Paul leaned against the door and then turned to look at me, raising one eyebrow in the way he did when he reprimanded one of the dogs.

"I wasn't happy with who I was on the inside, so I changed myself on the outside, and I did that by using steroids," I blurted out.

He wagged one finger at me and said, "Shamey boy." He tried to maintain a serious expression, but his eyes were twinkling. He then sat back down on the sofa.

"Is that how you got these big breastesses?" he asked while cupping one of my pecs and making it bounce.

"I stopped using them long before we met. I just didn't know how to throw the paraphernalia away," I said, swatting his hand and attempting to maintain the appropriate amount of seriousness, but Paul was having none of that.

"Do you have any left? Can you pump these up a little more?" He poked my chest with his index finger, *boing, boing*.

"This doesn't bother you, does it?"

"I'm dramatized," he said, lying down on the sofa, placing the back of his hand to his forehead, and closing his eyes. Then he opened one eye to peek at me, smiled, and pulled me down so that I was lying next to him.

"Sweetie, you would be sexy if you were one hundred pounds or four hundred pounds. If you were bald or not, and I love you even though you are an intravenous drug user," he said.

"They were intramuscular, not intravenous," I said, slightly offended as if this made a world of difference. "And I'm not using them anymore."

"Whatever, Chemical Ali. Give me the syringes, and I'll dispose of them properly with Gigi's insulin needles. Are these little 'mus-cel-lies' just for show?" he asked, squeezing my biceps.

I was waiting for a blowup, a scene, a fight, drama, but this was not Paul's way. It would take time to understand this, to retrain myself. After decades of a relationship fraught with turmoil and the weight of secrets, I would have to learn how to accept one that was not, to stop waiting for the other shoe to drop.

We would take strolls around Walden Pond, and I would struggle to keep up with Paul's pace. He would turn around and look at me, smile and say, "I'm sorry, I forgot you were from the South." He would then take long, exaggerated, slow steps. Laughing and in love, I forgot to think about the way I walked.

Once, Paul filmed me with his video camera when he was uncharacteristically trailing behind, and then he showed it to me. Some people might cringe to look at themselves walking, but I was surprised to find I rather liked what I saw—a blending of both my father's stride and Olivia's unhurried pace.

When Dad became ill, there was a sense deep down in my marrow that I needed to say something to him. The old "if you need to say anything, you'd better say it now" feeling. We'd be sitting in the afternoon sun on the brick patio, just the two of us, and I'd rack my brain, trying to fish up something worthy to say. I'd look over at his chemo-withered frame and hairless head, but the words I was trying to push out would be sucked back in by a tide of embarrassment too strong to ford.

On a chilly October evening, my father's footprints were washed away for good. My brothers and I sat by his bed and counted the seconds between his final breaths, and then I said, "It's OK, Dad. You can go now."

I wish Dad could have known who I became and met the man who would help me become the father he never was. But I can still hear Dad's footsteps in the click of my shoes on these streets laid out by ghosts. I walk comfortably along the avenues I have come to know so well. After so many years, I finally settled into my adult walk.

CHAPTER TWENTY-SIX

WHERE HAVE YOU BEEN?

Maggie was our first and last dog.

As a family, we had our share of unfortunate pets. A rabbit that kicked up shavings in great plumes as it scurried away from our daughter's hands. A cat that sulked behind the kitchen cabinets, and a desiccated goldfish that we scraped off the dresser, discovered a weekend after its tragic leap for freedom. However, Katherine never gave up hope that somewhere, out there, was a pet that suited our family.

After reading an advertisement for a sweetly tempered rescue dog, Katherine traveled up a winding mountain road in the verdant hills of western Virginia to fetch her. Unfortunately, that sweet dog had a temperamental stomach. When she traveled back down the winding mountain road, she vomited the entire way.

Katherine would often surprise me with an impulsive adoption. Maggie was no exception.

"She didn't cost anything, Bill," Katherine said.

"A pet is an investment," I countered. "Nothing is free."

To say that Maggie was sweet-tempered may have been a marketing ploy. When I met her, she cowered, and her black-and-tan body shivered, while her tail retreated between her legs. She stood eye level with our daughters, whom she would run from, scared silly by a pair of girls, ages six and four.

We fretted over another poor pet choice. It was clear that Maggie had been mistreated by her previous owners, and we worried that she might never recover. We decided to give her a week.

In the cool of the morning, I would sip my coffee, watching Maggie dart to the far corner of the yard and tremble beneath the girls' trampoline. I'd crawl underneath and tug on her collar, and she'd crouch down as if she could somehow disappear into the dirt. "Come on, girl." She would peer into the den, where the girls were playing, and when they looked at her, she'd scurry, nails clawing to get a purchase on the hardwood floors.

As the end of her probation week approached, Maggie must have sensed that her fate would soon be sealed. She placed a paw next to me on the sofa. I looked at her timid, brown eyes and patted the cushion. "It's OK, girl. Come on." Slowly, cautiously, she inched a paw forward and then another. It was a Herculean effort, as she wiggled her body, her legs shaking, one leg up, one leg down. Then, she placed her head on my lap.

"There you are," I said while rubbing her soft head, and looked over at Katherine who was wiping her eyes.

From that point on, her metamorphosis was astonishing. When sunset's glow painted the walls orange, she waited by the front door for my workday return, and when the girls placed a homemade newspaper hat on her head and draped a scarf around her neck, she sat still, looking quite miserable. Other times, she would playfully chase the girls around in a circle, crouching down on her front legs with her rump high in the air, her tail curled up into a C—Miss Maggie the Courageous. When she caught them, she would lick their faces while they laughed uncontrollably.

"Maggie, stop!"

We were shocked the first time we heard her bark, a deep woof that echoed. When the girls were playing softball in the front yard with a group of neighborhood kids, Maggie situated herself in front of our elder child, acting as a canine speed bump to trip the boy who was running toward her.

On our annual trips to the beach, I'd take curves gingerly to keep from upsetting her tender stomach, but invariably, she'd start puking. Each of us was so in love with her that we stomached the stench of vomit so that she would never again smell the inside of a kennel.

When we moved to Massachusetts, I often wondered what Maggie must have thought, jumping into the car just before we left and ending up in some foreign yard in another part of the country. Her adjustment was far easier than ours; while we struggled with all of the changes, Maggie's love was unwavering, a constant. Wherever we were, that was her home. When I lived apart from the girls for that year in Marlboro, Maggie took my place in the marriage bed, her head resting on my pillow, her paws on Katherine's shoulders, spooning her.

When our marriage ended, and the girls moved back to Virginia, I was heartbroken. Many nights, I would come home to my basement apartment and shout, "Maggie, I'm home," before reality struck me. The empty spot by my outstretched hand yielded not a soft head to rub, but a hollow emptiness.

Still, a piece of me was in Virginia with the girls. Maggie acted as my surrogate, the one who let their heartbroken tears roll onto her warm hide and nuzzled their sweet faces; the one who listened without judgment or reproach. When I visited, Katherine would stand motionless in the doorway, holding on to Maggie's collar, until she wiggled free and bolted toward me. I'd crouch down, letting her lick my face, and she'd whimper, as if to ask, *Where have you been?*

As with grief, there are stages of a divorce: denial, anger, hate, bitterness, indifference, and acceptance. We experienced them, much in the way we had collected ill-fitting pets with their nasty yellow teeth and a bite that induced pain and regret.

We fought over the mundane and argued about money. We were petty with our insults and name-calling. I became cold and distant with her. When my phone rang and Katherine's number appeared, I braced for another round of bitterness, another nasty bite.

"Bill, Maggie's sick."

That was what it took to shift us into the acceptance stage. I wrote a check for Maggie's final care.

Shortly after that call, I returned to Virginia, traveling up and down those winding mountain roads to fetch my daughters for Christmas. When Katherine opened the door, I crouched down before I remembered, and as I glanced up, in the gloaming winter light I noticed the empty spot next to Katherine's waist. I rose and then slowly, cautiously, placed my head on her shoulder.

"There you are," Katherine wept. "Where have you been?"

Our investment in Maggie matured, and so had we.

CHAPTER TWENTY-SEVEN
THE FACE OF DECEPTION

As the IT director for a global economic consulting firm, I am responsible for teaching employees about the threat of cyberattacks and how they can do us harm. I lie awake at night fretting over how we'll be hacked and what items of valuable data will be stolen.

Every year, we hire approximately fifty kids who have just graduated from the best colleges and universities, their résumés already brimming with more achievements, awards, and travel to remote African villages and sun-dappled southern European countrysides in their twenty-odd years than I have experienced in my fifty-five. On their first day, we gather them for a two-week training period, and by the time they meet with me, they're restless and bored, none of them looking forward to a dry presentation about data security. That's when I perform my "party trick."

I ask them to raise their hands if they own a smartphone. Every hand goes up (except for those who are too distracted while using their smartphones). I ask them to Google "forty-year-old white man." Some laugh nervously, and then I watch them type it into their smartphones. I wait for it, the gasp. They look up at me, narrow their eyes, look back at their phones, and then at me again.

"'Your face has meant a lot to me,'" I say. "'And now I've found out it's a lie.'"

It's a line from the first email that I received from the woman who was deceived by my picture.

I tell the kids that this is how we'll be hacked. A person will pretend to be someone they are not, they'll gain your trust, and then you'll give them something you should not. It's easy to secure machines; they don't have emotions—yet—but humans do. We're malleable. We're riddled with holes.

My face—the Face of Deception—sticks with them. They'll think twice about the emails they receive, imploring them to click on a link, or before replying with private information. Maybe in their personal lives, they'll run a Google image search on a picture of a cute boy or girl before swiping right.

My party trick is something fun to share until you consider the emotional damage and the risk of ruination that social engineering can produce. It's one of the most prevalent forms of cyberattacks.

The first woman to contact me about being catfished with my photo, we'll call her Eve, had a four-year online relationship with someone she came to love, and the data taken from her included hope, love, fear, and compassion. These emotions and others are the valuable currency—the bitcoins—of relationships.

Eve began her online friendship with Renée, someone she believed was a Texas pastor's wife. They connected on a social media website. They became close friends and confidantes, sharing things with each other that they could not share with anyone else. Eve loved Renée, and wondered at times if she wasn't *in* love with her.

Four years into their relationship, Renée messaged Eve and told her she had just been diagnosed with breast cancer. The prognosis didn't look good. For three weeks, Eve heard nothing from Renée, until one day, she received a simple "Hello" from Renée's Kik account. The greeting came from a man claiming to be Renée's husband, Rico. He was grieving and told Eve that his wife had died. Eve was heartbroken. Rico then sent Eve my picture, stating that it was a photo of him.

Their relationship progressed, both of them consoling one another until Eve began searching for the digital remnants of Renée—her obituary and the Facebook and Instagram accounts of Renée's husband and their children. Eve came up empty-handed and began to question Rico. That was when Rico told Eve the truth. Rico, Renée, and their children never existed. They were all the invention of a forty-four-year-old husband and father who was unsatisfied in his marriage, and so he became someone else. Eve's heart was shattered. She had grieved to the depths of her soul over a piece of fiction. What do you do with all of the pain and loss when the truth is revealed? That was when Eve searched for and found me.

People are skeptical when I tell them this story—that a person could have a long-term relationship with someone who never existed. Have you ever fallen in love with a character in a novel? Have you wept at the movies? The holes in our psyche want so desperately to be filled, and it's the charged emotions, the relationship currency, that provide the stuffing.

I have searched for the question, "Why do people catfish?" on the internet, and one of the answers stares me down: people don't feel confident in who they are, so they pretend they're someone else. But what happens when the impostor begins to truly believe he is someone else? What happens when everyone, religion, society, your friends, and your family, lies to you? What happens when you are riddled with holes of insecurity and the key to your survival is to become somebody else?

You catfish yourself.

By the time I met my wife, I had already been buried beneath an avalanche of homophobia and self-hatred. North Carolina, my home state, was one of the most notoriously antigay states in the union and, when I was growing up there, led the nation in the number of reported violent incidents against gay people. I believed all of the lies and thought that at age twenty-three, I could be another person for the rest of my life, but I was wrong. How do we take responsibility for the things we did when there was a gun to our head? I am still trying to figure that out.

Every now and then, I still get another message from a woman who believes in a love affair that is wrapped in the mask of my face, like Ellen, who was married to her virtual husband, Robert, in a make-believe world called *Second Life*. Or Sandra, who was electronically swept away by a marketing executive, Tyler, in Savannah. "Do you know me?" they ask. The lie has traveled the globe. I get messages from women in the US, Canada, Sweden, Brazil, and these are just the ones who have sought me out. Their messages are tinged with pain and dismay. They feel ashamed and angry. As one woman put it, "Southern girls don't play nice when deceived." Often, they still want to believe that there has been some type of mix-up.

Why do they contact me? Because the cure is the truth. They are holding on to the belief that there is still some truth to their story. The door has been left cracked open, but my responsibility is to close it and to take away the hope. To live in the space of *perhaps* would be an untenable situation.

"Do you know me?"

"Are you gay?"

These were the questions I needed to answer unequivocally.

Every time I am contacted by a woman who asks, "Do you know me?" I must face my own history of lies, the ones I told and the ones that were told to me. It is a karmic checkup.

It took me more than nine years to tell Paul about the fake profile I used to catfish him, which was early on in our relationship when I was still riddled with holes. For years, I had not considered it anything of significance, until I confided to a friend. My friend asked me, "How do you think you would feel if Paul had done the same thing to you?" It seized me with panic and provided new insight into how Katherine must have felt.

"I was still so insecure then. I just needed to know if you loved me," I told Paul. It was the final lie revealed. In typical Paul fashion, he responded with, "You're so cute. Were you worried about telling me?" Paul has taught me a lot about forgiveness.

The women who have been catfished by my photo have fallen in love with an emotional connection attached to the image of my face. They contact me because they want to know who the man behind the face of deception is, in order to bury the imaginary one. The irony is that these men are using the picture of a gay man to catfish straight women. I often wonder how this revelation would affect their masculinity. It was something I struggled with for too many years. Recently, a man contacted me to say that he was catfished with my photo. In a strange way, it was satisfying to have my photo stolen by someone of the same sexual orientation. But make no mistake about it—gay men struggle with masculinity too. Consider the insipid phrase many gay men employ in their dating profile, *straight-acting*. We are all catfishing the world in some small way.

Katherine once asked me, implored me, to tell her I was bisexual, and though the cure is the truth, it can be the most painful therapy. I was begging to ask for the truth, *Do you know me?*

When I look back, I can see now that my relationship with Katherine followed the classic example of a catfishing/social-engineering attack. Except in this case, I had been catfishing both Katherine and myself. It was not what I planned, and it pains me to illustrate the points, those that make me look both like the villain and the fool, but when a breach has been detected, one of the most important steps is gathering all artifacts and details in order to analyze the origin and impact of the attack.

- First, I gained Katherine's trust. I had few friends, and those I did had no idea who I really was. We both felt lonely in our own worlds, and this formed a connection. I told myself this connection was enough to build a life on.

- Our vulnerabilities exposed each other's. Katherine's trauma around the idea of family was perhaps her greatest vulnerability. She wanted desperately a family of her own.
- The face I shared was not mine. Outwardly, my face expressed ambition, certainty, and that of a straight man. For years, I told myself I could be straight.
- I gaslighted her. I pretended not to understand the undercurrent of doubt that she felt in our relationship.
- My stories were vague. When you live in the closet, you become superorganized so that you know where everything is at all times, so that you can alter your stories if needed. To maintain this lie, I had to tell myself many different versions of my own story.
- I took what was not mine. Katherine's love, trust, and hope were her most valuable assets, and I squandered them.

The path that Katherine and I shared unmistakably split into two in this final point. I took from her what was not mine to take. While I too had motivations for committing the crime, it is important to give Katherine the unadulterated truth without diluting it with protestations of "But look what happened to me!" I need to name my crime fully as part of my process of making amends, though understanding the pain does not make it any less ugly.

But despite all of this, in the end, Katherine was the only one daring enough to ask the question that unmasked me, to bury the imaginary man, so that the real one could survive. She did this, understanding that everything she held of value might be hacked into and taken from her. Often, I stay up late at night marveling at how brave Katherine was, and how she taught me more about honesty than anyone I know.

CHAPTER TWENTY-EIGHT
GIVING UP COMPLETELY

Forgive is derived from the Latin word *perdonare*, a word constructed of two smaller ones that belie the enormity and complexity of its power. *Per*, the first of the two, means "for" in the sense of "completely." The second is *donare*, meaning "to give." *To forgive* is to give up completely, a concept that is foreign to our society, one that is taught to win at all costs. And so, the act of forgiveness first requires an unlearning—an undoing. Katherine's and my undoing was the beginning of our story of forgiveness. In order to begin the process of healing, we had to first shatter everything we thought we knew.

What must be given up completely in order to forgive? If it is a smaller offense, let's say someone accidently tripped you and they ask you to forgive them, the offering is small. There was no malice or deception, and so giving up a sense of pride, of feeling hurt for momentarily looking foolish, is all that is required. You both move on rather easily. As the size of the offense grows, and the length of its duration expands, so too does the act of forgiveness.

When I look back, it is a wonder that either of us survived, considering all of the forgiveness that needed to take place. At times, it seemed necessary to give up everything. Before the pain, anger, hatred, and feelings of betrayal could be vanquished, Katherine had to give up completely the idea that the past could be any different, a past that almost destroyed her. She deserved a different and better life, one that did not include an accumulation of devastation. When the crime is this immense, forgiveness is a maze in which there are dead ends, false leads, and painful discoveries that can take years to navigate in order to make your way through.

I once stood in the liminal space before I came out to Katherine, where the lies were behind me and the truth was ahead, and this held me in a heart-stopping grip of terror. Going in either direction was an act of betrayal toward Katherine. I chose truth, but this did not mean that Katherine then joined me on my journey from that point forward. She was transported back to the very beginning of the maze where it all started, and she had to revisit every memory to examine its veracity.

I too often find myself retracing the steps. In my dreams, I keep waking up in my old marriage, in a decrepit house where the rooms don't make any sense. I walk across the warped wooden floors, disturbing the dust and causing it to spill through the cracks between the boards. The yellowed wallpaper is peeling, and rust-colored water stains pockmark the ceilings. What were we thinking when we bought this broken-down house? I fear we'll never be able to leave. I lie down on the edge of the bed and try to remember something. *Think, Bill. What have you forgotten?* And then it comes to me. I didn't tuck in the girls. They'll be terrified on their first night in this haunted old house.

We've done it again—purchased an old home without any understanding of the costs involved. I look up at the cracked windowpanes in the bedroom, and then it begins to rain. I know the crumbling roof won't hold back the storm.

Why did we move here? The girls hate moving, and now they'll have to start a new school again and make new friends, and we don't have the funds or the energy to make the repairs. We're stuck.

And then it hits me like a punch to the gut. Where is Paul?

My heart is racing, and I'm searching through my memories, trying to remember the turn of events that brought me back. We were married. We are married, Paul and I. But I left him. How can I be husband to both Katherine and Paul at the same time? Does Paul wonder where I am? I feel such pity for him and regret for putting Katherine through this again. I can't leave her. I can't abandon the girls, but I have to get back to Paul. The air becomes too heavy, and I can't breathe. My chest is pounding, and then silence. At first, there is a buzzing, and then I hear the whirring of a fan, and the hum of familiar sounds. When I open my eyes, my heart is still racing. Moonlight splits between the blinds, casting horizontal shadows on the walls. When I look around the room, the windows are not cracked; the floors are not warped. The girls are grown up now—Olivia is engaged to be married; Claire is in medical school—and Katherine has found a new love. We are all in good places. I reach over and place a hand on Paul, fearful that he may turn to mist. When my hand rests solidly on his shoulder, a wave of relief passes through me. But this old ache thumps in my heart.

More than a decade has passed since the divorce, and my mind is still trying to make sense of it, trying to make amends for the pain I caused and the pain I endured.

I can see the series of events that destroyed me as a child in North Carolina before I ever met Katherine. While many crimes were committed against queer people in my youth, most people thought victims of "gay bashings" "had it coming." Many still do. In 1981, the year I graduated from high school, murder befell Ronald "Sonny" Antonevitch because he was gay. In Durham, North Carolina, at a swimming hole on the Little River, a group of four men and two women approached four male sunbathers and shouted, "We're going to beat some faggots." They beat the men with clubs the size of fence posts and threw tree trunks at their backs as they fled. Ronald Antonevitch was handicapped, sitting on a rock in the river, and could not flee. One of the men hit him in the skull with a club, grabbed his own crotch, and then said, "You want to suck my cock, faggot?" When Antonevitch replied in the negative, two of the men from the group hit him again in the head with a club, punched him with their fists, and held his head under water. Ten bystanders watched and did nothing to prevent the attack. When one of the injured men called the police, the dispatcher replied, "You know it's illegal to sunbathe nude."

Thirty years after I graduated from high school, I returned to a school reunion in my hometown of Greensboro, North Carolina, with my husband, certain that enough time had passed to heal the trauma of my youth. I was proud to return with Paul. When we went into the restroom, we heard the door fly open, and then one of my former classmates shouted, "Are there any faggots in here? There better not be any faggots in here." I felt the shock of those words hit me as sharply as the club hit Sonny Antonevitch in the head. It took my breath away. I was embarrassed and ashamed, not because of who I was, but because Paul witnessed my undoing. How do I forgive the world for the yoke of pain it has placed upon me, which in turn I bestowed upon Katherine and my daughters? How do I help my daughters understand that not every man they become romantically involved with is going to lie to them?

It can be helpful to know and understand the motivation of the person who hurt you in order to forgive them, but it is not necessary, because forgiveness is a solitary act that requires only one participant. I am certain there were times when Katherine wanted me to feel pain, unhappiness, and remorse, and those emotions I have felt deep in my marrow. They have at times threatened to destroy me. I know from firsthand experience with my mother that the remorse she felt helped me to move forward, just as I have also come to learn that if I had wished her continued pain (and there were days that I did), it would have trapped me in the maze of anger for an eternity. Forgiveness is not given to help the one who hurt you, but to navigate through the pain in order to free yourself.

Cruelly, I sometimes still lie, to strangers, acquaintances, and people I've just met, because the world is a brutal place for queer people. There are times when safety trumps honesty. The little daily lies like brittle, stinging snowflakes accumulate until they are several feet deep, and I have to trudge my way through. I dig my hands deeper into my pockets when I want to hold my husband's hand in public. When the taxi driver with the crucifix proudly displayed on his dashboard asks about my wife, I don't correct him. I tell myself it doesn't matter when family members say they don't believe in same-sex marriage, as if not believing in something will make it go away. And so I live in the space between the lie and the truth, between the heterosexual life I lived and the gay community I shunned. But in reality, my waking life is the dream I never dared dream, and Katherine's nightmare became her reality. How do I reconcile this?

For years, the lie supported my work, my life, and my family. It was necessary to keep telling the lie in order not to lose everything, but eventually, it began to sag, like a roof filling with too much water, until it broke. Objects are better at holding the weight of emotions, and so my writer's brain presents this house to me in my dreams, a broken house to represent my broken marriage.

In order to make amends, you must first see the world from the viewpoint of the one you hurt. I wake up at night in my old marriage, picking through the rubble, rebuilding the house. It is old, and the rooms don't make any sense. Paul is missing. That's when it hits me like a punch to the gut; the broken house is not a symbol of our broken marriage. This is the house I put Katherine and my daughters in, and I am the one who is missing that returns as a ghost to haunt it. At night, I conjure it up and amble through the rooms, rearranging them so that my addled brain can attempt to put things in order, and then I settle in, so that I can see it play out through Katherine's eyes.

Look, there we are walking on the uneven sidewalk. Beneath the shade of oak trees, cicadas scream and brown, gnarled roots push up the cement rectangles of sidewalk at a glacial pace. Our dark-haired girls skip in front, and we trail behind. Katherine furtively glances at me. My brow is furrowed, and I look down at my feet. She reaches for my hand, and I hold her fingertips for a few moments before letting go.

And here is another scene: Mothers huddle together on the benches at the ice-skating rink in a small New England town. Katherine sits on the outer edge and tugs at her coat, pulling it closed to ward off the chill. She watches her daughters as they glide through their lessons.

"Katherine," says one of the mothers who has spent too much time in the tanning booth, "what do you think of Franklin?"

Katherine looks around the dim rink, through the windows and the piles of snow that are black with grime and gravel. She is searching for an answer that is truthful but not uncomplimentary. Katherine, unlike me, has not learned how to lie in order to keep up appearances.

"It's different," she replies.

The tanned woman laughs and looks at the other mothers. "'It's different,'" several of them titter. Katherine tugs her coat tighter. When she gets home, the girls run before her to the front door. Katherine looks up at the gray sky framed by twisted limbs as her breath turns to mist. Claire reaches into the mailbox and pulls out an envelope. "It's for Dad." She fingers the package. "It's lumpy," she shouts back to her mother. "What does *par avion* mean?"

Katherine's heart leaps. "Your father said he had more Christmas gifts that he ordered and not to ruin the surprise by opening the parcel, but I think we can make an exception."

A desk with a lamp, a sofa, a box of tissues slid across the table toward Katherine. The therapist takes off her glasses, pulls out a tissue, and hands one to Katherine.

"Don't you think a part of you always knew?" she asks.

Rooms are stacked with a lifetime's worth of objects packed into boxes; a dog's nails click across the hardwood floors. In the upstairs bathroom, Claire sobs beneath the stinging shower spray in a tub with no shower curtain.

Katherine walks down a darkened hall to search for Maggie, a companion to share this night with her. She hears footsteps and then my voice, "I can't sleep without you." In the morning, the sound of my footsteps walking away in the hall, a bedroom door creaks open slowly. It closes. Footsteps, and then another bedroom door opening and closing. Katherine listens to each and every creak of the stairs, the sound like gunfire as her closed eyes flinch. The crystal knob twists. The front door opens, birds chirping. She waits for it to close; her heart thumps.

She waits.

She waits.

She waits.

And just as she thinks I have left the front door ajar, she begins to rise. The bedroom door shudders as the front door shuts.

———

The day I started to look at my story as one that did not hinge on a lie, but one that told the story of forgiveness, was when I came a step closer to freedom, but with seven hundred miles between us, the process of healing was long and difficult. Katherine raised our daughters through her own pain and theirs. I have tried to imagine the devastation she felt, but I can't. Even as a writer who spends countless hours peering into people's brains, I can't fully fathom it. Before forgiveness could enter, anger needed to be extinguished, and like wildfire it would often jump paths and spring up in surprising and terrifying places. Resentment over lives unlived smoldered in both of us. Often, I wondered if I even deserved to be happy.

And yet, sometimes I wonder if it's even my place to forgive myself or what to do with a lie that begat truth—Katherine, the girls, times of immense wonder, beauty, and joy.

Making amends is not the same as forgiveness. It is undoing a wrong. I can't go back and unlie. I can't go back and change the past. The only way I know to make amends is to live in the truth and to be humble with those I've wronged—Katherine and my daughters—and through the sharing of my tale, to give those I'll never meet the chance to speak their truth as well. We are not the first generation of queer people who have found ourselves trapped in a straight marriage, but please God, let us be the last. In a world filled with hate and lies propagated by the Trump administration, living the truth is a form of resistance and persistence.

I am not an expert at forgiveness, but I know that when I started to understand what forgiveness meant, I realized it was not something I could ask for. That it is not mine for the taking, not mine to request, is something I have grappled with. The past is a spiderweb, and no amount of forgiveness will allow me to go back and unweave what I have done, and if I tried, I would become trapped in its stickiness, so this means I have to leave it there. I can't erase my lie, and so I live in that space between what I cannot fix and what I can. The lie is a part of all our truths.

CHAPTER TWENTY-NINE
LIGHTING DARK SPACES

Paul says that in every relationship, there is one person who holds up the light so the other can stand beneath it. To him, it's all about the lighting.

The night before our wedding, Paul stood by the kitchen sink, pointing at the window. My gaze drifted down the length of his arm, along his hand, and then fell to the yard below where a cluster of dark-haired children, all five of our children, formed a circle, talking and playing games. They sat by the little stone wall we created at the end of the garden, beneath the purple foxgloves nodding in the golden sunlight. A sepia-toned light washed Paul's face and illuminated specks of brown in his hazel eyes. He turned to look at me, put his hand to my face, and said, "Oh, this lighting is good." Then, looking out the window and pointing to the children, he said, "That lighting is even better. See? We had nothing to worry about."

The first time all of our children were together was in a row of photographs lined up on a table at the Cheesecake Factory, and then they were all there, together for the first time in person. When I called Katherine and told her that Paul and I were getting married, she said, "I can't deny that it hurts. But I can't wish the father of my children ill will." Before she put them on the plane, she took the girls shopping for new dresses for our wedding.

It was a Sunday afternoon in October, the sky so blue it made my heart ache, when I asked Paul to marry me. I didn't come right out and say it. I printed the words on a transparent sheet of plastic and placed it on a piece of circular glass art with spiral streaks of color, called an Energy Web. When Paul admired it at a shop we visited on the coast of Maine, I secretly purchased it. I did not know then that this would be my engagement ring to him, a ring of words. I positioned it on top of the piano, the one he had tuned for me, in the family room, and illuminated it with a small spotlight.

That morning, I told his children that I wanted to be a part of their family and for them to be a part of mine. We sat on the sofa as the cool autumn air, heavy with the scent of pitch and pine, played with us, darting in and out of the open windows. Paul was upstairs, packing for a business trip. When he walked down the steps and into the kitchen, bypassing the family room, I made a little face to Gigi. She stood up and said, "What's that?"

"What are you talking about, Gigi?" Paul shouted from the kitchen.

"That," she said, pointing toward the piano.

Paul walked into the family room, drying his hands with a dish-cloth, glanced at the Energy Web, and then at me.

"You bought that for me?"

"Look closer," I said.

He walked to the piano and then cocked his head. I watched his facial expression change as each word registered and tears welled in his eyes.

"You're asking me now?" he said, laughing and dabbing his eyes with the dish towel.

"I couldn't wait any longer," I replied.

We hugged as the kids came running into the family room, clapping and laughing, and then we wrapped our arms around them too.

I thought the day of our wedding would be the happiest day of my life, but then I realized I'd been living for a while in that happiness, and this was just another day of joy capped by a celebration. Both of our families and all of our friends gathered beneath a white tent in the backyard on a glowing green lawn in the warm, early-summer evening air. "We're family now," said Paul's sister Patty, the sister I never had, while hugging me.

Almost everyone I loved was there, though my youngest brother, Damian, did not respond to the invitation. He could not see through his veil of fear and ignorance. The ghosts of those I had come to love through stories but had never met made an appearance. The other Bill was there in the heart of June, his sister, who performed the wedding ceremony that would not have been possible during his short lifetime. Linda and Debra were in attendance, celebrating for the Bill they could not save and for the one that they did. My mother read a Bible story about the love that David felt for Jonathan. My brother Alex made the first toast, and Christopher seconded.

Enzo arrived on a pair of crutches. "Sorry I can't dance with you, Billy," he said, hobbling toward me. "Soccer injury."

"It's OK," I replied. "I've seen you dance."

"Can I ask you something?" I said to Enzo.

He smiled and replied, "You already have."

"You once said that when you love someone, in a way you want to become them. What did you mean?"

"Did I say that? That's brilliant."

He turned to look at the scene, at our five children running through the grass, playing tag and catching fireflies, at the table with Paul's parents, their faces lit up in the reflective glow of the candlelight, at Paul's handsome profile as he held court at the bar, looking so confident and happy as he laughed with a group of our friends. My heart thumped so loudly, I thought everyone might hear it.

Enzo held his hand up and pointed. "Is there any other place you'd rather be?"

And I understood. We are all of us an assimilation, a collection of bits and pieces of everything and everyone we love.

In the days leading up to the wedding, my mother fretted. I could see her becoming agitated, and I decided to query her.

"What is it, Mom?" I asked.

"Bill," she said, and I could see her starting to crumble over something left unsaid.

"Go ahead, Mom. Say what you need to say."

"Bill, no mother wants to see her son marry another man."

I drew in a breath of air as my heart dropped. I could feel it welling up, all those years of anger and shame. This was the final straw. I was ready to cut the cord and let her drift out to sea. But there was something else, something I had never noticed before. I saw it when I looked at her uncertain eyes, at her tilted gray head. I could finally see it in the bright light of honesty.

Her tears began to fall as she held up her empty hands.

"No, I don't accept that, Mom. That's not why you're upset."

"Bill, look around you. Everybody has somebody, even that woman there," she said, pointing to our perennially single friend Ann, who was deliriously drunk and dancing with all of our gay friends. "I'm all alone. I've never had a love of my life."

"So, you're upset because I found my true love?"

"No, because I never found mine!" she said, and started sobbing.

And here was the choice to be made. The ship was sinking fast, and I could hold on to only one. I took Mom's hand and watched as shame and anger slipped beneath the silvery surface.

Mom, like Katherine, deserved more than she got in life from a romantic partner. My father cheated on her many times and then left her. When I looked at Mom in that moment, I saw a person, like me—and like Katherine—who deserved love too. In a surprise twist, we were so much more alike than we were different. From an early age, my mother was taught to adhere to unforgiving religious mores and the suffocating and insidious structure of Southern society. The undercurrent of doubt had held Katherine captive for years, and when the truth was released, she gained power over it. We had all been in our own closets, and now together, we were going to leave them behind.

Before we were married, Paul toiled for days, stringing up hundreds of paper lanterns in just the right shade of pale blue from the ceiling of our wedding tent in the backyard of his sister's house. The June air smelled of freshly cut grass, and when we stood under the canopy after the sun melted into the horizon, it looked as if the Milky Way had been lassoed and tugged into place so that it could drift above our heads.

Sometimes, I wonder if Paul is attempting to make up for all the years I faltered in the closet. He lights up the dark spaces so that I will always be able to find my way home. But if I asked him, he would never own up to it. For someone who loves to hold up the light, he hates to stand beneath it.

"That was Willy's vision," Paul told our guests—and it was, though I'd done no more than tear a photo from a magazine.

There is a memory that I return to over and over again. Most of the wedding guests have departed, and I'm lying on my back in the cool grass, looking up. My head is resting on Paul's chest. I'm listening to his heartbeat as our five children lie on their backs scattered about us, a constellation of arms and legs touching. I look up, and just like that, the glow from the lanterns splinters into a million points of light, each one a memory that spans the chasm between who I was and who I have become. To Paul, it's all about the lighting. But for me, it's all about what he has enabled me to see.

When I told David, my therapist, that I had created a fake profile, his brow wrinkled with concern.

"Bill, that's not you," he said.

What he meant was that my actions were not me, that I was acting figuratively and quite literally out of character. But the imposter had been my character for so long.

People often ask why I waited so long to come out. What they're really asking is how I lied for so long. How I survived. The closet is not small. A world of make-believe fits within its walls. The walls are permeable, not solid. The outside world seeps in and reassembles itself, but becomes a dull facsimile—the longer I stayed in the closet, the more difficult it was to find my way out. The world inside became vast and confusing. I learned there was more than one door to open; there were five, ten, a hundred, and just when I thought I'd reached the last one, another appeared.

I used to think when I opened the first door, the lie would end there, but there was so much more work I had to do to convince that gay, broken boy inside me that he could be loved. Though the closet was a place to hide, pain hid with me. It was in the closet that I learned that there would never be enough room for both my growing pain and for my life. The real journey has been learning to love my authentic self, not the image I had created. It was the same hard work as forgiveness.

After twenty years of marriage, I discovered that at the heart of every lie is a seed that when watered and cultivated grows mighty, like a windswept tree. The source of my lies—the biggest lie of all—was the idea that a gay boy could not be loved. It was planted inside me as a child, and it was fruitful and multiplied. This was where the limb of lies that twisted throughout my marriage—and within myself—began. But finally, the gnarled roots were unearthed and exposed to the light. Here was where the lie withered, the roots upended, and truth bloomed.

ACKNOWLEDGMENTS

It was important for me to work with a publisher that believes diversity is a strength and one that is passionate about sharing underrepresented voices. The mighty and diverse team members at Little A put their hearts into this book and stand proudly behind my story. Hafizah Geter, poet, editor, and friend, you challenged me to dig deeper and open myself wider in order to unearth the truth. It was painfully and sweetly redemptive. My story sings because of you.

Just as passionate about this book was my agent, Christopher Schelling, who spent many, many hours guiding me through developmental edits, encouraged me, made me laugh, and managed my crazy.

I am so grateful to Elizabeth Cohen at Gotham Writer's Workshop, who became my writing mentor and friend. You always believed in me, offered sage writing advice, and encouraged me to publish this story. Hats off to GrubStreet in Boston for their wonderful writing courses and guidance. Some of the best writing advice came from the wonderful Ann Hood, who taught me how to use objects to carry the weight of emotions, and that every good story is comprised of two: the one on the surface, the one beneath—and when they collide? Push it just a bit more.

Angela Knight, we bonded over a braided essay, and many years later, our friendship and literary lives are still wonderfully entwined. Your faith in my ability to produce this book sustained me. Samantha

Shanley, your pointed question about what was at the heart of my writing kept me going.

To my children, you kept telling me you had no doubt that it would happen even when I doubted myself. Your belief in me is as strong as my belief in you. Patty, my sister, your optimism was my north star when I felt lost. "Welcome to my home."

Paul Connelly and Peter Silvia, our journey together, our SAC nights, and our friendship kept me sane during this process.

Al Perez and Diarmuid McGuinness, our talks and city walks motivated me every step of the way.

Mom, you taught me that it is possible for people to evolve and to become an advocate. I know how fiercely you love Paul, and me, and that love is returned.

My husband, Paul, at one of my lowest points, I told you I had potential. It took me all of these years to figure out what you knew in the beginning—that we already had it all. Thank you for allowing me the time and space to write this story in order to prove it to myself.

ABOUT THE AUTHOR

Author Photo © 2018 Sharona Jacobs

William Dameron is an award-winning blogger, memoirist, and essayist. His work has appeared in the *New York Times*, the *Boston Globe, Salon,* the *Huffington Post, Saranac Review, Hippocampus Magazine,* and in the book *Fashionably Late: Gay, Bi & Trans Men Who Came Out Later in Life.* He is an IT director for a global economics consulting firm, where he educates users on the perils of social engineering in cybersecurity. William, his husband, and their blended family of five children split their time between Boston and the coast of southern Maine. For more information, visit the author at www.williamdameron.com.